HOW TO BECOME
A FEDERAL CRIMINAL

HOW TO BECOME A
FEDERAL
CRIMINAL

An Illustrated Handbook for the Aspiring Offender

WRITTEN AND ILLUSTRATED BY

Mike Chase

ATRIA BOOKS

New York • London • Toronto • Sydney • New Delhi

ATRIA
BOOKS

An Imprint of Simon & Schuster, Inc.
1230 Avenue of the Americas
New York, NY 10020

First Atria Books hardcover edition June 2019

ATRIA B O O K S and colophon are trademarks of
Simon & Schuster, Inc.

For information about special discounts for bulk purchases, please
contact Simon & Schuster Special Sales at 1-866-506-1949 or
business@simonandschuster.com.

The Simon & Schuster Speakers Bureau can bring authors to your
live event. For more information or to book an event, contact the
Simon & Schuster Speakers Bureau at 1-866-248-3049 or visit our
website at www.simonspeakers.com.

Interior design by Dana Sloan

Manufactured in the United States of America

7 9 10 8 6

Library of Congress Cataloging-in-Publication Data is available.

ISBN 978-1-9821-1251-6
ISBN 978-1-9821-1253-0 (ebook)

This book is dedicated to the United States Congress.
You guys are hilarious.

CONTENTS

Introduction

GETTING STARTED

If you're like most Americans, your first experience with the heart-pounding thrill of committing a federal crime came from a little white tag on the end of your mattress.

"Cut me," it dared you. "Tear me off."

At first, you probably resisted. You left the tag affixed to your mattress, letting it threaten you day after day in your own bedroom. DO NOT REMOVE THIS TAG UNDER PENALTY OF LAW, it warned in bold letters. But that just made you want to do it even more, like the legal equivalent of hearing someone say, "You can't hit a guy with glasses."

Then, one night, you'd finally had enough. Maybe you'd had a few too many wine spritzers. You gave in, ripped the tag off, and have waited anxiously each day for the FBI to show up with a warrant.

Your fear isn't totally unfounded. There really is a federal statute that makes it a crime to remove a mattress tag. Violations are punishable by fines and up to a year in prison. But if you're a tag cutter who once thought of yourself as a hardened federal criminal, you may be in for a shock: the feds aren't coming for you and they couldn't care

1

less about what you did to that helpless little tag. The federal mattress tag law exempts "ultimate consumers" from criminal liability. It even says so right there on the tag, if you had just bothered to keep reading. The only real criminals are the mattress dealers who would dare remove a tag from bedding before it finds its forever home. That means all Americans are free to cut off their own mattress tags with impunity, just the way our Founding Fathers intended.

But just because the government doesn't care what you do with a mattress tag in the privacy of your own bedroom doesn't mean it's particularly difficult to commit a federal crime. Far from it, actually. Congress has passed thousands of federal criminal statutes and has allowed federal agencies like the IRS and the FDA to make thousands upon thousands more rules that carry criminal penalties. These criminally enforceable rules cover everything from how runny ketchup can be to what you're allowed to do if a bird of prey takes up residence in your house. Federal law even sets limits on just how friendly you can get with a pirate.

The tricky part for the average person is that there's no comprehensive list of all the things that are crimes today. In fact, no one even knows how many federal crimes there are. What's worse is that the law usually doesn't require that a person even know something is illegal before they can be criminally charged and convicted for it. And when you can't always know whether something is a crime, you can't always know if you're a criminal.

But how did we get here? How did we become a country where so many things are crimes? After all, it wasn't always this way. The Constitution mentions just three crimes of federal concern: piracy, counterfeiting, and treason. In 1790, Congress passed the Crimes Act, bringing the total number of federal crimes up to just around twenty. And even though the Crimes Act added a few new and exciting crimes to the federal repertoire—like the one making it a crime to steal an executed convict's dead body before it could be surgically dissected—federal criminal law was still mostly focused on pirate crimes, counterfeiting offenses, and acts of treason.

By the late 1800s, however, Congress started passing broad statutes giving executive branch officials the power to make rules with the force of law. Sure, Article I, Section 1, of the Constitution gave Congress, and Congress alone, the power to make law. But Congress was busy, and tired, and wanted to spend more time focusing on the partisan bickering and general lack of productivity it had become so good at. Plus, as long as Congress was going to be regulating things it didn't really understand, lawmakers figured it might be better to have subject matter experts do the regulating. So Congress began delegating its lawmaking authority to federal agencies. As a bonus, congressmen didn't have to face the political repercussions when agencies made unpopular rules the way they would by voting on controversial bills. And if there's one thing that's popular in Washington, it's lack of accountability.

That delegation of authority paved the way for a couple of margarine dealers getting indicted in the late 1800s for disobeying federal margarine rules. It's how a New England bakery could have been criminally charged for listing "love" as an ingredient in its granola in 2017. It's how it became a federal crime to subliminally advertise liquor without any real evidence that anyone was doing that in the first place. I mean, who really needs to be tricked into buying beer?

The truth is, many of these crimes were probably created largely by accident. Congress passed a bunch of statutes making it a crime to violate "any regulation" issued by certain agencies. Meanwhile, the agencies kept pumping out rules—tens of thousands of pages' worth each year—never intending to create new federal crimes and never expecting that prosecutors would actually charge people for violating them. For the most part, the regulators were right: convictions for margarine crimes and other, sillier-sounding offenses remain relatively rare. The problem with these accidentally created laws, however, is that lots of them can be committed by accident too.

Congress has also managed to pass plenty of vague and dumb criminal laws all by itself, without any help from regulators. To compound the problem, lawmakers have left outdated and obsolete laws on the books for decades—although who doesn't sleep a little better knowing that it's still a federal crime to board a ship a little too early or bathe in a long-defunct government bathhouse without a prescription?

Sure, you may not have mailed a mongoose and you probably haven't made a habit of misusing the Swiss coat of arms. But you may have ridden a bicycle drunk in a national park or dressed up like a mailman. Maybe you've put a note in your neighbor's mailbox without paying postage on it. Or maybe you've doodled a little too much on a dollar bill. This handbook will hopefully help you see the error of your ways and show you how the government can put any one of us in prison if that's what it takes to be sure we're warned against the dangers of putting jock itch cream in our eyes and that we respect the licensing rights of Smokey Bear.

Unfortunately, if you're hoping to learn *all* the ways that you could possibly become a federal criminal in America, this book can't help you. In fact, no book can. Lawyers with the Department of Justice once tried to count all of the federal crimes on the books and gave up. Since then, others have tried and failed. Hell, as a criminal defense lawyer who has spent years researching and cataloging federal crimes in a daily effort to do the same, I'm not even sure it's possible.

Still, the ever-growing number of federal crimes is only part of the problem. The law is also constantly changing. The government churns out thousands of regulations every year and you'd never know it if you don't sit down and read the *Federal Register* (a truly thrilling publication). The feds can also quietly change, move, suspend, and delete rules, making it difficult for aspiring offenders to stay current. Imagine investing the time and effort to commit one of the many crimes in this book, only to find out later that it's not a crime anymore. It's the mattress tag nightmare all over again. And this book doesn't even touch *state* crimes, which account for the overwhelming majority of convictions in America.

When it comes to becoming a federal criminal, however, this handbook is a good start. For one thing, it has pictures. It also focuses on some of the more unexpected and seemingly bizarre things that the government can quite literally "make a federal case out of." Most importantly, though, it will give you some of the best possible answers to the age-old question "What are you in for?" Misshapen pasta? Unsanctioned llama visitation? Whatever your heart desires.

If you're a non-lawyer and you've never read a statute, or if you *are* a lawyer and you've managed to never read a statute, all of the numbers, letters, and squiggly "§" symbols in this book might be confusing. To better understand the laws discussed, here is a quick primer on how to read these citations to federal statutes and regulations, and the basic steps on the path to becoming federal criminal.

Step One: Reading Criminal Statutes and Regulations

Throughout this handbook you will see frequent references to the two main sources of federal criminal law. The first is the United States Code (or "U.S.C."), which contains all of the statutes passed into law by Congress. The second is the Code of Federal Regulations (or "C.F.R."), which is a compendium of rules made by executive branch departments and agencies.

The several thousand federal crimes that Congress has passed into law are found in the U.S. Code. Those are the ones senators and representatives voted on and the president signed into law. Consider this federal crime that many people may have committed back in their glory days:

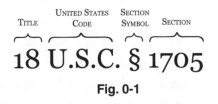

Fig. 0-1

Just looking at this citation may not tell you much at first. But if you turn to Title 18, Section 1705, of the U.S. Code, you'll see that it says, in part:

> *Whoever willfully or maliciously injures, tears down or destroys any letter box or other receptacle intended or used for the receipt or delivery of mail on any mail route, or breaks open the same ... shall be fined under this title or imprisoned not more than three years, or both.*

In other words, it's a federal crime to smash a mailbox.

So what's so hard about finding all the federal crimes? Can't you just go to Title 18 of the U.S. Code and start reading? Title 18 is, after all, the only one of the fifty-three statutory titles entitled "Crimes," and it contains a bunch of criminal statutes.

But Title 18 isn't the only place where federal crimes can be found. Criminal provisions are scattered throughout the more than fifty titles of the U.S. Code. Those titles address things like agriculture, railroads, and taxes. These are often the places where Congress has given agencies the ability to make criminally enforceable regulations.

As just one example, Title 7, Section 282, of the U.S. Code

makes it a crime to violate any regulation issued by the secretary of agriculture governing the importation of honeybees. Among those regulations is one that classifies dead bees as "restricted articles," and another that requires anyone mailing a package of restricted articles into the United States to "mark all sides of the outside of that package with the contents of the shipment and the name of the exporting region" and to do so in "black letters at least 1 inch in height on a white background."

Here's how all those citations become a federal crime:

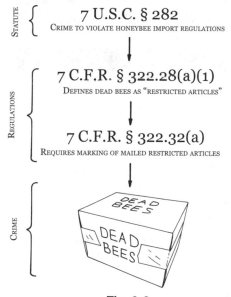

Fig. 0-2

Working together, 7 U.S.C. § 282, 7 C.F.R. § 322.28, and 7 C.F.R. § 322.32 make it a federal crime to mail a box of dead bees to the United States without "DEAD BEES" and the country of origin written on every side, in letters that are at least one inch tall. Because the package of dead bees shown in Fig. 0-2 lacks a country of origin and at least one side isn't marked at all, mailing it to the United States is a federal crime.

Other criminally enforceable honeybee rules restrict the transportation of live bees, bee semen, and even beekeepers' suits.

Step Two: **Committing a Federal Crime**

In order to be guilty of a federal crime, an offender doesn't necessarily need to know the law, but must commit a prohibited criminal act. Law students and other unlovable nerds refer to that as an "actus reus." Most of the time, the offender also needs to act with a particular mental state. That's called "mens rea."

Say a person decides to smash a mailbox:

Fig. 0-3. Mailbox Smashing

To be guilty of violating 18 U.S.C. § 1705, the offender must have injured, torn down, or destroyed the mailbox (the actus reus), and he must have done it willfully or maliciously (the mens rea). As shown in Fig. 0-3, the mailbox is clearly destroyed, so the actus reus is complete. Given the distance he put on that mailbox, he also seems to have acted maliciously.

Although it's not clear that this hypothetical offender acted "willfully"—a different mental state that requires proof he knew his conduct was unlawful—Section 1705 says he's guilty whether he acted willfully *or* maliciously. In fact, a huge number of federal crimes don't require an offender to have any idea that his conduct is illegal before he can be charged and convicted. Some crimes— like importing illegal bee semen—don't even require proof of criminal intent at all. Because of that, a person can often commit a federal crime by simply doing one of the countless things that federal law happens to make punishable by a criminal fine, imprisonment, or both.

Step Three: Getting Charged

For a person determined to become a federal criminal, it's not enough to simply *commit* a federal crime; they must be criminally *charged* to make it official. But with tens or even hundreds of thousands of federal crimes, this poses a problem. Prosecutors simply can't charge all of the federal crimes that occur in the United States. There isn't enough time. There aren't enough judges. They don't even know what all the crimes are.

Instead, prosecutors are expected to exercise something called "prosecutorial discretion." In theory, that means they should focus on the cases most deserving of prosecution. Statistically, it means they tend to prioritize drug crimes, gun crimes, and immigration crimes far above crimes of any other kind. As a result, the bird crimes, cheese crimes, and other lesser-known crimes discussed in this handbook may be closer to the bottom of the priority list.

That's not to say people can't or won't be charged for the kinds of crimes discussed in the chapters that follow. They absolutely can. People have been federally charged for possessing too much sugar, running a mail-order denture company, and, yes, boarding a ship before it arrived at shore. All you can do when the government comes knocking is hope your bee semen was properly imported, the letters you sent by FedEx were actually "extremely urgent," and you haven't brewed more than your annual allotment of tax-free beer.

Step Four: Getting Convicted

The last hurdle in becoming a federal criminal is getting convicted. This is the part where the government is supposed to do most of the work. In fact, you may have heard that prosecutors have to prove criminal charges "beyond a reasonable doubt." You may have heard that's the highest standard known in American law. You may have even heard that criminal defendants are presumed innocent.

And all of that is completely true. But in the United States, more than 97 percent of all people charged with federal crimes plead guilty and never even have a trial.[1] Taking guilty verdicts into account for those few who do go to trial, the overall conviction rate is nearly 100 percent. The odds that a person charged with a federal crime will walk away with a conviction are overwhelming. So, although you may think you'll skate free selling your illegal unpackaged margarine, if you do get charged, the odds are that there will be consequences.

The feds also have unbelievably powerful tools at their disposal. They can subpoena your bank records, listen to your phone calls, indict you in a secret proceeding called a grand jury, and, if they think you lied to them, they can charge you for that alone. Then, if they can get a jury to find you guilty on just one charge, the judge is allowed to sentence you up to the statutory maximum based on things you were never charged with, or even things a jury acquitted you of, so long as the judge decides you probably did them. It's seriously scary stuff.

But if there's one thing to take away from this book, it's that you should never, and I mean *never*, underestimate the government's power to put you in prison for something as simple as bringing a theatrical chicken—or any performing poultry—back from Mexico without an up-to-date health certificate.

Be careful out there.

⚠ WARNING

The crimes discussed in this book are real.

If you haven't caught on yet, this handbook is a work of humor and not legal advice.

Don't do anything discussed in this book.

Just stay home with the lights off and unplug your phone.

Chapter 1

HOW TO BECOME A FEDERAL CRIMINAL

BY MAIL

A s early as 1865, Congress passed a law providing that "no obscene book, pamphlet, picture, print, or other publication of a vulgar and indecent character, shall be admitted into the mails." In 1873, Congress passed the Comstock Act, which went even further by completely banning anything related to contraception or abortion from the mail. In 1920, the postmaster general supposedly had to tell postal workers not to accept human beings as mail after a few child-mailing incidents.[1]

CRIME BY MAIL

Even before the United States of America became a country, there was the Postal Service. It was established in 1775 and got its own clause in the Constitution a few years later. By 1792, Congress passed a statute giving postmen a monopoly on carrying letters. Since that time, anyone who has dared to compete with the Postal Service has risked federal prison.

The mail has always been serious business in America. In the late 1700s, Congress even made the death penalty available for anyone caught stealing mail. Believe it or not, the Postal Service used to deliver things even more exciting than credit card preapprovals and extended car warranty offers. People actually sent important things to one another, like love letters, which was basically sexting but slower.

Americans liked their mail and they didn't want to see it go missing. Sure enough, in 1830, two men were convicted of mail theft and sentenced to death by hanging. One of them, James Porter, was hanged right away. But his accomplice, George Wilson, had well-connected friends who were able to convince President Andrew Jackson to grant Wilson a presidential pardon. In an unexpected and unprecedented move, however, Wilson refused the pardon and chose instead to be hanged. It was probably the overwhelming guilt of having stolen mail.[2]

Aside from teaching us all that it's actually possible to refuse a presidential pardon and force the government to kill you, federal mail crimes have also served as a buzzkill in lots of other ways. For example, 18 U.S.C. § 3061(c)(4)(B) and a corresponding regulation, 39 C.F.R. § 232.1, make it a crime to go into the post office while drunk or high, or to smoke a pipe inside, climb onto the roof, or gamble while you're there.

Fig. 1-1. Abandoning Mail

AGREE TO DROP OFF SOMEONE'S MAIL

Okay. Someone has asked you to drop off some of their mail at the post office. "It's important," they say. No big deal. You're headed that way anyway. You can do this. Just agree, and they'll owe you a favor someday.

TAKE POSSESSION

Once you "take charge" of the mail, the statutory clock starts running. Deep breath. Just take the mail to the post office and it's over. You'll basically be a hero. In fact, you're already an awesome person for even agreeing to do this.

FU⬛K IT

You're no hero. And, honestly, who would trust you with their mail if it was really important? You abandon the mail. You're now a federal criminal.

In fact, even *not* going to the post office can be a federal crime under the right circumstances. Consider 18 U.S.C. § 1700, which provides:

> *Whoever, having taken charge of any mail, voluntarily quits or deserts the same before he has delivered it into the post office at the termination of the route, or to some known mail carrier, messenger, agent, or other employee in the Postal Service authorized to receive the same, shall be fined under this title or imprisoned not more than one year, or both.*

In other words, if you take someone's mail, agree to bring it to the post office, and don't follow through, you can be charged with a federal crime. And while the crime has mostly been used to prosecute fed-up letter carriers, there's no reason it can't be used to put a bad friend in prison. (See Fig. 1-1.)

Wear a Postal Uniform if You Aren't a Postal Worker

There are only a few clothing choices made criminal by federal statute. One of them is the federal ban on non–postal workers wearing the uniform of a United States letter carrier.

Specifically, 18 U.S.C. § 1730 provides that "whoever, not being connected with the letter-carrier branch of the Postal Service, wears the uniform or badge which may be prescribed by the Postal Service to be worn by letter carriers, shall be fined . . . or imprisoned not more than six months, or both." That means you can get up to six months in prison for stolen postal valor.

By its terms, the statute doesn't require that the uniform wearer do anything nefarious while playing dress-up. The crime is in the wearing. As one federal judge remarked: "The very act of

Fig. 1-2. Dressing Up as a Letter Carrier

(1)   **GET A UNIFORM**

Shirt: Available in long- or short-sleeve versions. Comes in postal blue or pinstripes for a little pizzazz.

Walking Shorts or Trousers: The letter carrier's pants must have a stripe down the side.

Socks: Available in three approved styles and lengths.

Shoes: One option: black leather.

Hat: The postal "sun helmet" (shown), baseball cap, visor, knit hat, and "winter fur trooper cap" are all approved headwear.

(2)   **PUT IT ON**

If followed in order, these steps will ensure that the offender puts on each essential element of the letter carrier's uniform.

NOTE: These steps can also be used in everyday, noncriminal dressing, so long as you don't mind wearing a safari hat.

impersonating a letter carrier is by nature an act of deceit."[3] When Americans see those little blue shorts and tube socks strutting down the sidewalk, we want to know we aren't getting duped. To be a crime, however, the offender must wear the officially prescribed uniform for letter carriers. That requires some attention to detail. (See Fig. 1-2.)

THE ACTOR EXCEPTION

From the time it was enacted in the 1880s until the late 1960s, the prohibition on civilians wearing postal uniforms was totally unforgiving. Any non–letter carrier wearing a postal uniform could be convicted no matter the circumstances. In 1967, however, the U.S. Post Office Department (the predecessor to the U.S. Postal Service) asked Congress to carve out a narrow exception that would allow screen and stage actors to portray like postal workers without risk of indictment.

According to the Post Office Department, actors had periodically requested permission to wear postal uniforms, but the department was forced to refuse because Congress wrote a law with no exceptions. When a House subcommittee held hearings on a proposed amendment to the law in August of 1967, the department's assistant general counsel testified:

> *In recent years we have had a number of inquiries and we felt this is a problem where people are probably disregarding the law. There is no public policy that we can see which would be served by continuing the prohibition against the wearing of the uniform in theatrical performances. Rather than have the law ignored, we think it would be better to have it amended.*[4]

Rather than be embarrassed by pretend postal workers thumbing their noses at the law, the department proposed an amendment that would allow actors to wear the uniform "if the portrayal [did] not tend to discredit that service." That is, actors could play letter carriers, but not bad letter carriers.

That led one lawmaker to ask what kind of portrayal might still be prohibited under the new law. The lawyer for the Post Office Department suggested:

> *I would suppose if the carrier were portrayed systematically opening people's mail or engaging in that type of activity we would certainly think that would be within this particular prohibition.*

Of course, that was before the internet, so the full range of unsavory things people in postal outfits might be shown doing on film hadn't been fully explored. The law was ultimately amended as proposed, allowing actors to play well-intentioned mail carriers.

Three years later, however, the Supreme Court struck down a similar provision in a statute concerning military uniforms. In that case, Daniel Jay Schacht was sentenced to prison for wearing an army uniform in a skit critical of the Vietnam War. When the case reached the Supreme Court, Justice Hugo Black wrote that "an actor, like everyone else in our country, enjoys a constitutional right to freedom of speech, including the right openly to criticize the Government during a dramatic performance." The court struck down the statute as an unconstitutional abridgement of freedom of speech, at least to the extent it required theatrical performances to be favorable to the military.

In 1990, about twenty years after the decision in *Schacht v. United States*, Congress finally got around to removing the same language from the postal uniform statute. Actors were now free to play even despicable postal workers. The following year, Newman made his first appearance on *Seinfeld*.

Fig. 1-3. Dressing Up as a Letter Carrier (cont'd)

CRIMINAL

This guy isn't a mailman. Don't be fooled by his great calves and regulation tube socks.

Maybe he's dressed as a mailman because he's a postal enthusiast. He may really like getting chased by dogs. Or maybe he's wearing the uniform at the request of his lover, who has a thing for mailmen.

Whatever the reason, he is a criminal.

LEGAL

This is the same guy, but now he has a film crew.

He's not a criminal.

Always bring a film crew.

Although performances are no longer required to cast the Postal Service in a positive light, the only non–mail carriers who are expressly permitted to wear the postal uniform with impunity are actors. There remains no Halloween costume exemption— even for "sexy" letter carriers.

Paint a Car to Look Like a Mail Vehicle if It Isn't One

Fig. 1-4. A 1980s El Camino (Arguably a Car).

It's not only a crime to *dress* like a postal worker, it's a crime to drive like one too. 18 U.S.C. § 1731 makes it a federal crime to paint, print, or otherwise put the words "United States Mail" on any vehicle that isn't actually used to carry the mail. Logos, abbreviations, and any other markings that falsely suggest a vehicle is a mail vehicle are also prohibited. Violators can be fined, imprisoned up to six months, or both.

But unlike impersonating a police officer, driving around in a fake mail truck doesn't have many perks. It won't let you do fun things like pull people over or run red lights. And forget high-speed chases. Actually, forget high-speed anything in a mail truck. At best, you might be able to get away with driving on the wrong side of the road at three miles per hour with your hazards flashing. Not bad, but plenty of people already do that every day in Florida with regular old Buicks.

The fake-mail-vehicle statute makes no distinction between offenders with sinister motives and those who just have a bizarre affinity for all things postal. In other words, driving around and delivering or picking up mail isn't required for a conviction, and other statutes prohibit those things already.

The law also doesn't require a fake mail vehicle to look even remotely convincing to be a crime. (See, for example, Fig. 1-4.) That makes it a little easier for postal imposters, because mimicking a real mail vehicle with a civilian automobile has been almost impossible since the 1980s. That is, unless you happen to get your hands on one of those boxy charmers known as the Grumman Long Life Vehicle, or "LLV" for short:

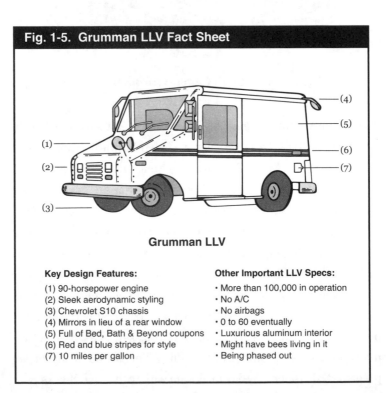

Fig. 1-5. Grumman LLV Fact Sheet

Grumman LLV

Key Design Features:
(1) 90-horsepower engine
(2) Sleek aerodynamic styling
(3) Chevrolet S10 chassis
(4) Mirrors in lieu of a rear window
(5) Full of Bed, Bath & Beyond coupons
(6) Red and blue stripes for style
(7) 10 miles per gallon

Other Important LLV Specs:
• More than 100,000 in operation
• No A/C
• No airbags
• 0 to 60 eventually
• Luxurious aluminum interior
• Might have bees living in it
• Being phased out

From 1986 to 1994, the Postal Service bought more than 140,000 LLVs, which have dutifully served as America's iconic mail truck ever since. In 2015, however, the Postal Service announced it would be putting the LLV out to pasture, replacing its fleet with newer, more efficient vehicles. And that makes sense, because at ten miles per gallon and around $500 million in annual maintenance costs for the fleet of LLVs, things can really add up.[5]

Still, just because a certain kind of mail vehicle has been retired from service doesn't mean it can't be used as an imposter vehicle. To this day, Section 1731 expressly prohibits falsely labeling stagecoaches and steamboats as postal vehicles, both of which were used as postal vehicles in their day. The retirement of the LLV may present new opportunities for aspiring postal imposters to acquire decommissioned mail trucks, a technique some offenders have reportedly already used to steal mail. But the law can also be violated with vehicles never before used by the Postal Service, like gyrocopters. In fact, it was under those exact circumstances that a gyrocopter once found its way in front of Congress.

No, literally—*in front of* Congress. Like, on the Capitol lawn.

THE MAILCOPTER INCIDENT

On April 15, 2015, an actual postman from Florida named Doug Hughes was completing the final leg of his solo gyrocopter flight to Washington, D.C. On board, he had two mail bins filled with copies of a letter he'd written to Congress urging lawmakers to take big money out of politics and implement campaign finance reform.

Rather than lick all those stamps, Hughes decided he'd just fly them straight to Congress.

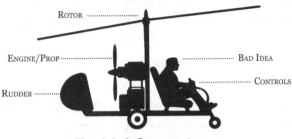

Fig. 1-6. A Gyrocopter.

Shockingly, Hughes wasn't blasted out of the sky by NORAD. He managed to fly under the government's radar. When he touched down just outside the Capitol Building, however, he was promptly arrested. His gyrocopter and its cargo were also seized, though not before a bomb squad had conducted a thorough sweep. At first, Hughes was charged with violating national defense airspace and released. But after taking a closer look at his gyrocopter, the feds realized his crime was even more serious: he had dared to affix the United States Postal Service's "sonic eagle" logo to the rudder of his gyrocopter.

A grand jury in the District of Columbia indicted Hughes on additional charges, including falsely labeling a vehicle as a postal carrier in violation of 18 U.S.C. § 1731.[6]

As count six of the indictment read:

> *On or about April 15, 2015, within the District of Columbia, DOUGLAS HUGHES, also known as Doug Hughes, knowingly and willfully operated and owned a vehicle and conveyance, and placed and attached words, letters, and characters on the vehicle and conveyance of like import to "United States Mail," to wit, the logo and emblem of the United States Postal Service, when the vehicle and conveyance was not used to carry United States Mail.*

Aside from having what might be the most innocuous alias to ever appear in a criminal indictment, Douglas (a.k.a. "Doug") Hughes was the first person to ever be charged with falsely identifying a gyrocopter as a mail vehicle. He will probably also be the last.

Hughes eventually pleaded guilty, but to a different count of the indictment. He was sentenced to 120 days in prison and agreed to forfeit his gyrocopter to the government, which the feds announced they would destroy. The government has yet to successfully convict anyone of falsely labeling a gyrocopter as a postal vehicle.

Reuse a Postage Stamp

Title 18, Section 1720, of the U.S. Code prohibits reusing postage stamps. The crime begins with a piece of already-sent mail and can be committed in just two steps:

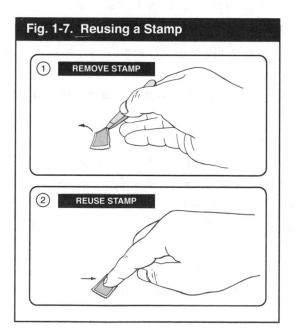

Fig. 1-7. Reusing a Stamp

① REMOVE STAMP

② REUSE STAMP

Understandably, these images may be hard to look at. They depict a serious federal crime punishable by up to a year in prison for civilian stamp reusers and up to three years for postal workers who traitorously reuse stamps. But that's what you get if you try to bilk the government out of a few cents at a time.

OTHER STAMP CRIMES

You may be surprised to learn that federal law allows people to perform philately in public. Some may be surprised that "philately" means stamp collecting and not whatever their sick mind thought it was. But for every good philatelist, there's someone out there misusing stamps, making these other federal stamp laws necessary:

Stealing Stamps and Using Them to Pay Debts

Under 18 U.S.C. § 1721, postal employees are prohibited from knowingly and willfully using postage stamps, stamped envelopes, or postal cards entrusted to them "in the payment of debts" or to buy other stuff. If they do, they face up to a year in prison.

Making Fake Stamps

Federal counterfeiting laws don't just prohibit making fake money; they also prohibit making fake postage stamps. Specifically, 18 U.S.C. § 503 makes forging or counterfeiting a postage stamp punishable by up to five years in federal prison.

Putting Unstamped Mail in a Mailbox

Even without a stamp, it's possible to become a federal criminal:

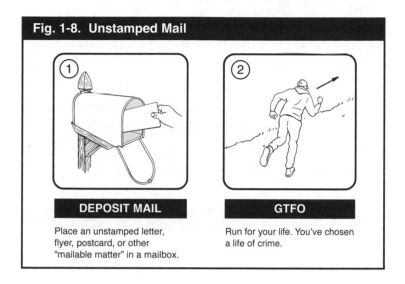

Fig. 1-8. Unstamped Mail

(1) **DEPOSIT MAIL**

Place an unstamped letter, flyer, postcard, or other "mailable matter" in a mailbox.

(2) **GTFO**

Run for your life. You've chosen a life of crime.

Mail a Gun

If you feel like nothing exciting ever comes in the mail, blame Congress. They've made it illegal to put all kinds of things in the U.S. mail. That includes guns.

More specifically, 18 U.S.C. § 1715 makes it a crime to mail "pistols, revolvers and other firearms capable of being concealed on the person." Giving it a quick read, the law wouldn't seem to apply to rifles, shotguns, or other "long guns" bigger than a pistol. When it comes to federal criminal law, however, things are never quite what they seem.

In *United States v. Josephine M. Powell*, the Supreme Court was asked to decide whether mailing a twenty-two-inch-long sawed-off shotgun violated the gun-mailing statute. Having been convicted for doing just that, Josephine Powell said no; after all, the statute spoke specifically of pistols and revolvers. Surely, she thought, firearms "capable of being concealed on the person" didn't include shotguns. They're too big to conceal on one's person. Aren't they? And if the statute could be read to include them, isn't it unconstitutionally vague?

The Supreme Court didn't think so. In its view, a "concealable" firearm was one that could be hidden on "an average person garbed in a manner to aid, rather than hinder, concealment of the weapons." The justices were satisfied that a sawed-off shotgun almost two feet long could be concealed on an average person if they

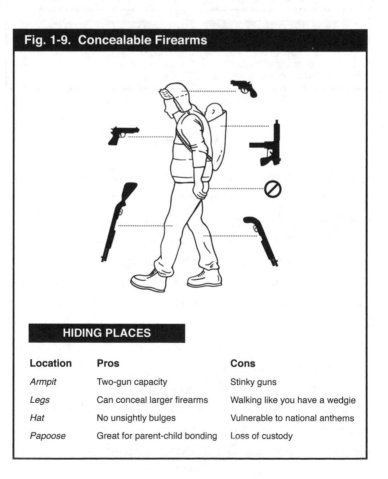

Fig. 1-9. Concealable Firearms

HIDING PLACES

Location	Pros	Cons
Armpit	Two-gun capacity	Stinky guns
Legs	Can conceal larger firearms	Walking like you have a wedgie
Hat	No unsightly bulges	Vulnerable to national anthems
Papoose	Great for parent-child bonding	Loss of custody

dressed appropriately—which is pretty rich, coming from nine people who wear flowing black robes to work.[7]

In any event, it's safe to say that the standard for concealability isn't what you can hide in a pair of yoga pants. After *Powell*, the analysis for a gun mailer is simple: Could an average-sized person—however creatively—hide the gun somewhere on their body with the appropriate wardrobe? (See Fig. 1-9.) If the answer is yes, it's a crime to mail.

THE DAY THE MAIL WENT POSTAL

Although the defendant in *Powell* mailed quite a care package—including a sawed-off shotgun, some shotgun shells, and "20 or 30 hacksaw blades" for good measure—at least the gun was unloaded. Compare that to the Idaho woman who in 2015 pleaded guilty to mailing a loaded .357 Magnum that managed to fire off a shot when a postal worker picked up the package at a processing facility.

Luckily, according to the Department of Justice's press release, nobody was hurt when the mail started shooting at people—not badly, anyway. One postal worker sought medical attention for ringing ears and stinging hands. The defendant was sentenced to two hundred hours of community service, $3,397.28 in restitution and a $1,000 fine. Powell, by contrast, was sentenced to two years in prison.

While the law doesn't distinguish between loaded and unloaded guns sent through the mail, the law does exempt certain people from criminal liability. Licensed gun dealers and manufacturers, as well as certain government employees, are allowed to mail handguns for approved purposes.

Fig. 1-10. Mailing a Gun

①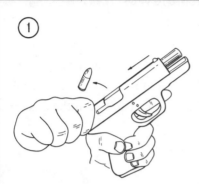

GET A GUN

Pistols, revolvers, and any gun that can be concealed on an average person who is dressed for concealment can all give rise to criminal liability if mailed.

Although the law doesn't distinguish between loaded and unloaded guns, at least one offender had her cover blown by mailing a loaded one.

②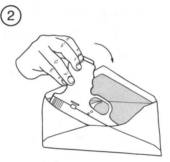

APPLY U.S. POSTAGE

The gun-mailing statute only applies to the U.S. mail and not other parcel services. However, other federal laws may prohibit sending guns even by these other means.

For example, transferring a firearm to a prohibited person—including users of marijuana—is also a federal crime.

③

PUT IT IN THE MAIL

The gun must be knowingly deposited in the mail for the crime to be complete.

This is the part where the mail has started exercising its Second Amendment rights in the past, so offenders and letter carriers alike should use great care around any gun-shaped mail.

MAILING NINJA WEAPONS INSTEAD

Congress hasn't always succeeded in banning weapons from the mail. In 1986, for example, Senators Ted Kennedy and Strom Thurmond cosponsored a bill to "prohibit the use of the mails to send dangerous martial arts weapons." The bill was left to die in committee and failed to become a law. But had it been enacted, it would have criminalized mailing ninja weapons into any state where those weapons were banned by state law. That included nunchaku (also known as "nunchuks"), shuriken (also known as "throwing stars"), and manrikigusari, which the bill described as "fighting chains" with weighted ends.

In hearings before the Senate Judiciary Committee, some members of the martial arts community opposed the bill.[8] They argued that the proposed law was discriminatory against Asian culture and posed a threat to the future of martial arts.

Other witnesses, however, said the bill didn't go far enough. Victoria Toensing, then a deputy assistant attorney general, testified that banning martial arts weapons from the mail was too narrow a prohibition. She argued that the law should be more like the Federal Switchblade Act, which broadly prohibited moving switchblade knives in "interstate commerce." Toensing explained that the martial arts weapons bill, if it were to become law, would leave companies free to circumvent the restriction by delivering throwing stars to kids through UPS or other commercial carriers. At least they'd be able to track their packages.

But how big of a problem was ninja mail? A member of the Boston Police Department testified that the risk posed by mail-order ninja weapons was real. He had recently been approached by a father who discovered his twelve-year-old son's cache of "throwing stars, nunchakus, and a double-edged throwing knife." When asked how he'd acquired them, the boy told his dad that he had simply "saved his allowance, filled out a coupon in a magazine and sent cash through the U.S. mail in return for [the] weapons." Another member of the Boston police force testified that he and his fellow officers had even come face-to-face with throwing stars in the line of duty. In 1974, during demonstrations against mandatory busing of schoolchildren to end segregation in schools, groups of angry youths had clashed with police and thrown shuriken at them.

And let's be honest: Who wouldn't have predicted that the weapon of choice for segregationist youth in 1970s New England was the Japanese throwing star?

The 1980s brought along a so-called ninja mania. *The Karate Kid* was a box-office hit. *Teenage Mutant Ninja Turtles* debuted on TV. Throwing stars were even turning up in grade-school backpacks.

This inspired a man named Larry Kelley to fight back against easy access to these weapons. Kelley was a black belt in karate, owner of a karate school in western Massachusetts, and voted "Best Kicker" in *Sport Karate* magazine. To get Congress's attention, he mailed a throwing star to each U.S. senator in an envelope that read "Illegal weapon, legally enclosed." When he was invited to Washington to testify in support of the bill, Kelley did what anyone would do: he gave the Judiciary Committee a live nunchaku demonstration in response to Senator Kennedy's request:

SENATOR KENNEDY: Do you want to just explain about the nun-chaku, to the extent that it is dangerous?

MR. KELLEY: Would you mind?

SENATOR KENNEDY: Sure, get up and show us. I do not see a volunteer Senator for you to demonstrate with—if there are any Republicans in the room. [Laughter.]

MR. KELLEY: These [demonstrating] can attain speeds of 100 miles per hour. So if you catch one of these in the side of the head—

which I will probably be doing in 1 second for you—and the thing is, if you are standing there like this, and a police officer walks up and sees you from this perspective, all he sees is about a 12-inch club. So the officer figures, "Well: I'm safe as long as I am 24 inches away, because that is only a 12-inch club"—and then, bang.

Surprisingly, Ted Kennedy didn't invite Kelley to demonstrate the throwing stars on any Republicans. But Kelley did explain that anyone capable of throwing a Frisbee could throw one and "it takes no skill whatsoever to make them stick." To really drive home how serious the problem was, Kelley held up a throwing star and told Congress that he had recently read in a magazine that ninjas "used to dip this in solid excretal waste in order to cause massive infection when it stuck in." He feared that with this information being made public "now all the little kids will be doing that."

Despite all of this, the bill failed to become law. Even so, America has somehow managed to avoid the plague of little kids going around dipping ninja stars in fecal matter and throwing them at people as Kelley had warned. So far, anyway.

Fig. 1-11. Banned or Restricted Weapons

Concealable Firearms
Banned from mail by 18 U.S.C. § 1715 with exceptions for some people.

Switchblade Knives
Can only be mailed to certain recipients under 15 U.S.C. § 1242 et seq.

Cockfighting Weapons
Banned under 7 U.S.C. § 2156.

Note: Live, unarmed, day-old poultry may be mailed.

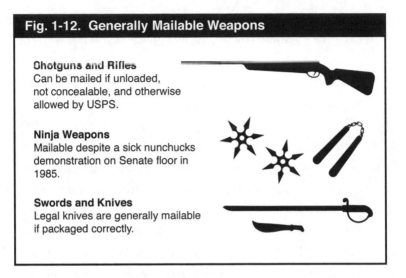

Fig. 1-12. Generally Mailable Weapons

Shotguns and Rifles
Can be mailed if unloaded,
not concealable, and otherwise
allowed by USPS.

Ninja Weapons
Mailable despite a sick nunchucks
demonstration on Senate floor in
1985.

Swords and Knives
Legal knives are generally mailable
if packaged correctly.

Mail a Threatening Letter to the Circus

Also known as the Animal Enterprise Terrorism Act (AETA), 18 U.S.C. § 43 prohibits all kinds of violent and threatening acts directed at "animal enterprises"—that is, businesses like animal research facilities, zoos, aquariums, and pet stores.

The law was passed in 2006 to strengthen an existing statute that already made it a federal crime to physically disrupt and cause economic damage to animal enterprises. According to lawmakers, animal rights activists had been exploiting a loophole in the existing law, directing their acts of intimidation and vandalism at employees and family members rather than the protected businesses themselves. The new law extended protections to these "secondary targets" and broadened criminal penalties for interfering with animal enterprises. Plus, the statute's new name allowed the government to call a whole new group of people "terrorists," which is one of its favorite things to do.

Given its history, most prosecutions under 18 U.S.C. § 43 have predictably involved animal rights activists. They have been charged for things like releasing thousands of minks from a mink farm and holding threatening demonstrations outside research facilities. But the law is broad enough to apply whether the offender has a pro-animal bent or not. It protects rodeos, fairs, and, yes, circuses. That means anti-clown radicals can also be charged.

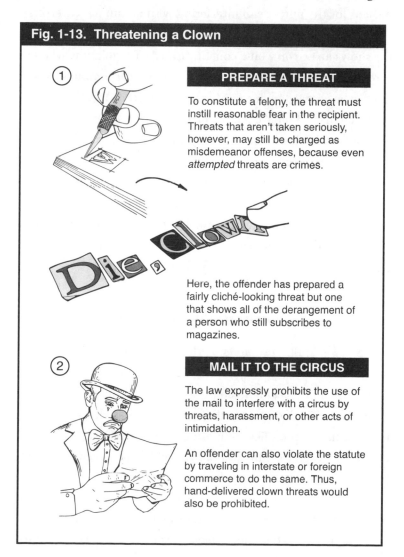

Fig. 1-13. Threatening a Clown

① PREPARE A THREAT

To constitute a felony, the threat must instill reasonable fear in the recipient. Threats that aren't taken seriously, however, may still be charged as misdemeanor offenses, because even *attempted* threats are crimes.

Here, the offender has prepared a fairly cliché-looking threat but one that shows all of the derangement of a person who still subscribes to magazines.

② MAIL IT TO THE CIRCUS

The law expressly prohibits the use of the mail to interfere with a circus by threats, harassment, or other acts of intimidation.

An offender can also violate the statute by traveling in interstate or foreign commerce to do the same. Thus, hand-delivered clown threats would also be prohibited.

Under subsection (a)(2)(B) of the statute, an offender can commit this crime by mailing a threat to anyone associated with an animal enterprise, their immediate family members, spouse, or intimate partner. The threat only needs to place its recipient in reasonable fear of death or serious bodily injury. It must also be sent for the purpose of interfering with an animal enterprise. For example, threatening a circus employee to the point where the show can't go on would constitute an AETA violation, whereas threatening that person's cousin or platonic roommate would have to be charged under a different statute. (See Fig. 1-13.)

Of course, criminal circus threats have become much more difficult and unlikely ever since the Ringling Brothers and Barnum & Bailey Circus closed its doors in 2017. Animal rights activists have also turned their focus to more pressing matters—like forcing Nabisco to redesign its animal cracker box to depict the cartoon animals freely roaming in cartoon habitats, rather than trapped in cartoon cages. Still, they can't stop you from slowly nibbling off the animal crackers' feet before biting off their heads. Never.

Mail a Miniature Spoon

21 U.S.C. § 863(a)(2) prohibits sending anything by mail that is determined to be "drug paraphernalia." This includes obvious things like bongs and "cocaine freebase kits" (they come in kits, apparently). It also includes other things that are less clearly intended for drug use—things like "miniature spoons with level capacities of one-tenth cubic centimeter or less," which are specifically identified as potential drug paraphernalia in the statute.

Adorable as they may be, it turns out that tiny spoons have a reputation as a convenient way to measure and snort cocaine. In fact, congressional testimony suggests that even McDonald's once

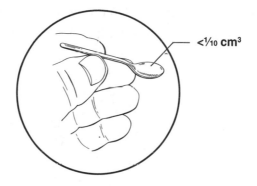

Fig. 1-14.

ceded to the demands of antidrug paraphernalia lobbyists by discontinuing its popular spoon-shaped coffee stirrers of the 1970s for precisely this reason.

In 1979, Joyce Nalepka of the "Coalition for Concern about Marihuana Use in Youth" testified before the Senate Judiciary Committee's Subcommittee on Criminal Justice. She described all sorts of makeshift drug paraphernalia that kids could readily get their hands on, including makeup mirrors, toilet paper rollers, a shoebox, and yes, "a coffee stirring spoon from our all-American Mc-Donald's."[9] Although Nalepka didn't describe exactly how to use a toilet paper rollers or a shoebox to do drugs (there was no demonstration on the Senate floor this time), she proudly announced the impending death of the "McSpoon," telling lawmakers that "last evening at 6 o'clock Mr. Edward Schmidt, president of McDonald's Restaurants, gave me permission to announce to you that McDonald's will either redesign or discontinue the item altogether."

That's how it came to be that we now stir our coffee with tiny little straws that could never, ever, ever be used to do drugs of any kind. Even though the McSpoon died in 1979, it wasn't until 1986 that Congress finally got around to enacting the Anti-Drug Abuse

Act. The new law made it a federal crime to mail drug paraphernalia like mini-spoons and "roach clips." (See Fig. 1-15.)

Fig. 1-15.

There are, however, ways to mail each of these things without becoming a federal criminal. In determining whether an item truly is drug paraphernalia, the statute considers a number of factors, including:

- the instructions provided with the item concerning its use;
- how the item is described, advertised, or displayed for sale;
- whether the owner is a legitimate supplier of like or related items to the community; and
- the existence and scope of legitimate uses of the item in the community.

Thus, mailing a miniature spoon with instructions that make clear the spoon is only to be used for eating miniature food would tend to weigh against a finding that it is drug paraphernalia. If it can be established that lots of people in the community use miniature spoons, the offender's defense just got even stronger.

Or consider roach clips, which are defined by law as "objects used to hold burning material, such as a marihuana cigarette, that has become too small or too short to be held in the hand." Things like bobby pins, surgical hemostats, "alligator clips," and other items resembling tweezers may each be presumed to be roach clips, but each has a legitimate, lawful use as well. Each can be mailed as non-paraphernalia depending on its true purpose.

The same is true of other items presumed to be drug paraphernalia. Take, for example, this totally legit flower vase:

Fig. 1-16. Totally a Vase.

Supposedly, flower vases like the one shown above can also be used to smoke tobacco or even other things. That's what people say, anyway. But you can't trust everything you learn in college.

SCORPIONS AND OTHER NONMAILABLE MATTER

Federal law also makes it a crime to mail certain other things classified as "nonmailable matter." This includes poisons, "infernal machines," "disease germs or scabs," and really anything that could kill or injure someone. Although an "infernal machine" may sound cool, it's really just a fancy way of saying "bomb." And while you might be wondering why a person would want to mail germs or scabs, the law allows doctors and scientists to send microbiological specimens to each other for research. But you're no scientist and you probably belong in prison if you're picking off scabs and mailing them to people.

But the injurious mail statute does have one exception that is sure to haunt your dreams. It permits live scorpions to be sent through the mail. That's right. Live. Scorpions.

Title 18, Section 1716(c) of the U.S. Code provides that "the Postal Service is authorized and directed to permit the transmission in the mails, under regulations to be prescribed by it, of live scorpions which are to be used for purposes of medical research or for the manufacture of antivenom."

Fig. 1-17. Noncompliant Scorpion Packaging.

Apparently recognizing that scorpions have no place in a civilized society, postal rules require scorpion shipments to be made in packaging that can't be punctured by a scorpion. All live scorpions must also be mailed in a box clearly marked "Live Scorpions," and that box must be placed inside yet another box that's also labeled "Live Scorpions."

Although most would agree that any box containing live scorpions should be securely sealed and promptly set on fire, the law doesn't go quite so far. Still, for purposes of federal law, live scorpions mailed in packaging that isn't scorpion-proof or isn't properly marked are considered nonmailable matter and, under Section 1716(j), mailing a noncompliant box of scorpions is punishable by up to a year in prison.

Mail a Mongoose

Mongooses are probably best known for their long-running beef with snakes. Less well-known is their decades-old feud with the federal government. Since the year 1900, the Lacey Act has classified mongooses as "injurious animals" and has banned them from importation into the United States. Some animals have come and gone from the Lacey Act's blacklist, but Congress has remained firm on its no-mongoose policy from the beginning.

One postal statute, 39 U.S.C. § 3015(a), provides that any injurious animal prohibited from importation under the Lacey Act is "nonmailable matter." Another statute, 18 U.S.C. § 1716D, makes it a federal crime to mail one. Mongoose mailers are subject to as much as a year in federal prison. That's twice the maximum sentence available for mongoose importers.

Committing this crime may seem simple enough: get a box, some postage, and a mongoose, then head to the post office. (See Fig. 1-18.) Avoiding this crime may also seem straightforward: just don't mail a mongoose. In fact, under the explicit text of the Lacey Act, only "the mongoose of the species *Herpestes auropunctatus*" is identified as an injurious animal, so maybe it's still okay to mail some mongooses, right?

Probably not, actually. A regulation issued under the Lacey Act prohibits the importation of "any species of mongoose or meerkat of the genera *Atilax, Cynictis, Helogale, Herpestes, Ichneumia,*

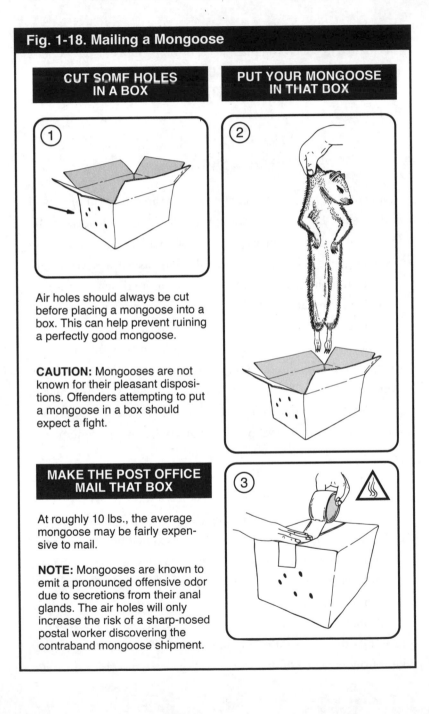

Fig. 1-18. Mailing a Mongoose

CUT SOME HOLES IN A BOX

① Air holes should always be cut before placing a mongoose into a box. This can help prevent ruining a perfectly good mongoose.

CAUTION: Mongooses are not known for their pleasant dispositions. Offenders attempting to put a mongoose in a box should expect a fight.

PUT YOUR MONGOOSE IN THAT BOX

②

MAKE THE POST OFFICE MAIL THAT BOX

At roughly 10 lbs., the average mongoose may be fairly expensive to mail.

NOTE: Mongooses are known to emit a pronounced offensive odor due to secretions from their anal glands. The air holes will only increase the risk of a sharp-nosed postal worker discovering the contraband mongoose shipment.

③

Mungos, and *Suricata . . ."* For those who are rusty on their taxonomy, it's probably safest to avoid mailing any mongooses or meerkats—and, honestly, prairie dogs, feral cats, and big squirrels may be better hand-delivered just to be safe.

This isn't to say that the feds can't be convinced to look the other way when it comes to mongoose crimes. In 1963 the secretary of the interior even issued a formal pardon to a mongoose named Mr. Magoo who had been imported to the U.S. mainland by a merchant seaman. When federal authorities caught wind that he was in the country, they threatened to deport him back to India or even to put him to death (the mongoose, not the merchant seaman). Following his pardon, Mr. Magoo lived out the rest of his days in the Duluth Zoo. The seaman remains at large.

Run a Mail-Order Denture Business

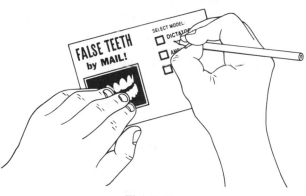

Fig. 1-19.

In the midst of World War II, dentists were fighting their own battle here on the home front. False teeth made by mail-order denture companies were freely flowing across state borders, and dentists were getting sick of it. At the time, forty-seven states prohibited denture-making by anyone but a dentist licensed in the state. Even though no state law expressly prohibited mail-order dentures, the whole thing was making dentists nervous.

Seeking to restore order, a collective of dentists lobbied Congress for a federal law. After days of congressional hearings, including tales of ill-fitting dentures showing up in mailboxes everywhere, the House and Senate agreed that the plight of dentists and America's toothless citizens was sufficiently serious to warrant an Act of Congress.[10] On Christmas Eve 1942, Congress approved the enactment of a federal statute making it a crime to mail dentures into a state if the dentures had been made by a person not licensed to practice dentistry in that state. To this day, the law, which appears at 18 U.S.C. § 1821, provides for a prison sentence of up to a year.

The law, however, was not without its skeptics. Before its enactment, Senator D. Worth Clark of Idaho questioned whether this type of denture-making by laypersons really needed to be a federal crime, particularly where mail-order dentures weren't actually violating any existing law. He thought Congress should give more consideration to a matter before making it a federal crime. He remarked:

> I think we are asked to write a very definite criminal statute under which and for violations thereof a man could be committed to jail. Apparently, such a statute is needed, or is asked for, because no law on the statute books today is being violated, at least no law under which a prosecution could be conducted. If you are going to put people in jail for doing something which they are doing legally now, you must write a new law. If you enact a law which will put a man in jail for doing something which he is doing legally now, I think you have to go into the entire merits of the subject.

Other senators were a little more relaxed about making new crimes. Senator Clyde Reed of Kansas explained that the law simply looked to the states to determine what denture mailings would be prohibited within their borders. If a state outlawed dentures made by a layperson, then the federal statute would permit a federal prosecution for mailing amateur dentures into the state.

Clark, however, urged a more discriminating approach to creating federal crimes. He asked:

SENATOR CLARK: Let us suppose that a State enacted a perfectly outrageous statute. This happens to be one of the things that is on the border line. Suppose the State of Idaho or the State of Kansas should prohibit something that was clearly outrageous. At least, in the opinion of some people, States have enacted such statutes. Suppose such a statute were enacted and we were called upon to write a Federal statute which would make it unlawful to transport in interstate commerce what a State said was unlawful to do in its own borders. In that case wouldn't you want to go beyond just merely the fact that the State had a law? Wouldn't you want to examine into the matter before you wrote a Federal statute?

SENATOR REED: I think not.

SENATOR CLARK: Then there is a sharp divergence of view.

Among the evidence submitted to the 77th Congress in support of the mail-order denture ban was an advertisement by the "United States Dental Company" based in Chicago. The company advertised various models of dentures, including "The President," "The Vice President," "The Ambassador," and a bold marketing choice for the early 1940s: "The Dictator." A full set of "Dictator" dentures cost $16.50, whereas "Ambassador" teeth ran as much as $87.50, presumably because Americans value diplomacy over autocracy or something.

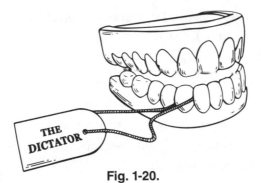

Fig. 1-20.

The real magic of any mail-order denture business, however, was the process for taking an impression of the customer's mouth. As summarized by Philip Traynor, a U.S. representative from Delaware and himself a dentist:

> *Their scheme is to send a gob of wax to a person who answers their advertisement and let him take his own impression…*
>
> *The patient is instructed to take the gob of wax, put it in hot water for a few minutes, then take and put it in their mouth and hold it in their mouth for a minute and a half, thereby supposing that they get the first impression that they can work with. That is sent back and with instructions they are supposed to send $2 with that gob of wax that has been in their mouth. I do not know whether it is worth $2 to put it in their mouth or not; but they send on the impression, and then they will send more wax with instructions to go ahead and take the second impression, from which they go ahead and make the set of teeth.*

Written submissions to Congress claimed that "if a patient obtains satisfactory dentures by his own manipulations, the result is due to pure chance." Actual customers, however, begged to differ.

In a letter addressed to a Cleveland mail-order denture company, one bedentured Brooklynite said of his dentures that he "would not part with them for a thousand dollars." The customer did confess, though, that when biting into the heated gob of wax "[i]t stuck to the roof of [his] mouth so tight that [he] was terrified . . ." And that's saying a lot, because a person who's perfectly happy to take a gob of wax that shows up in his mailbox from a stranger, heat it up, and cram it into his mouth isn't usually the type to scare easily.

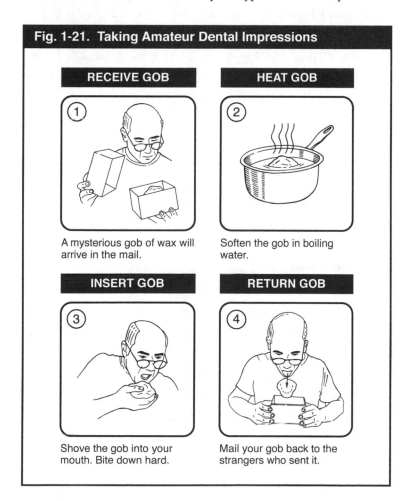

Fig. 1-21. Taking Amateur Dental Impressions

RECEIVE GOB

① A mysterious gob of wax will arrive in the mail.

HEAT GOB

② Soften the gob in boiling water.

INSERT GOB

③ Shove the gob into your mouth. Bite down hard.

RETURN GOB

④ Mail your gob back to the strangers who sent it.

The Chicago-based United States Dental Company wasn't only a pioneer in the marketing and naming of false teeth; it was also the first to test out the new criminal denture statute less than a year after it became law. In 1943, federal prosecutors charged Margaret Johnson and Mary Layton, both executives of United States Dental Company, with mailing prohibited dentures from Illinois to Delaware.

But the case had one wrinkle. It was prosecutors in Delaware, not Illinois, who brought the case. Johnson and Layton argued that the new denture law didn't permit prosecution in the district where the offending dentures were received but only in the district where they were put in the mail. The text of the law prohibited the "use" of the mails to send prohibited dentures, not the "transportation" of them. They moved to dismiss the charges and won.

In a humiliating defeat, the government had lost its first-ever prosecution under the mail-order denture law. The government appealed the case all the way to the Supreme Court and lost. Johnson and Layton were free to mail dentures another day.

Eventually, however, the law caught up with them. They were charged in Illinois, convicted, and fined $1,000 each. On appeal, the Seventh Circuit Court admonished them for failing to see "the necessity for intelligent and skilled construction of artificial teeth" and noted that the wisdom of the Denture Act was obvious. The court explained that "it falls within the category of legislation for the public health which is a prime, as well as a worthy, purpose of government. That the Federal Government, under its interstate commerce power may aid such state legislation, is not debatable."[11]

This time the Supreme Court wasn't interested in their appeal and declined to hear their case, leaving their denture-mailing convictions undisturbed.

Chapter 2

HOW TO BECOME A FEDERAL CRIMINAL

WITH ANIMALS

I n 1971, Congress officially declared wild, free-roaming burros to be "living symbols of the historic and pioneer spirit of
the West."[1] And when a donkey is that good, you pass a law. So
Congress enacted the Wild Free-Roaming Horse and Burros Act,
making it a crime to infringe upon the civil liberties of all those
diminutive wild donkeys.

That wasn't the first time Congress had federally protected an
animal. Since 1918, federal law has protected a long list of "migratory" birds. In 1940, bald eagles got their own set of federal statutes too. In 1972, it was marine mammals. And in 1973, Congress

49

passed the Endangered Species Act, which protects a wide range of other animals at risk of extinction.

However, you don't need to kill a bird or harass a wild little donkey to become a federal criminal. There are plenty of nonviolent ways to land in federal prison with animals.

MIGRATORY BIRDS

Blue-footed boobies, bushtits, and hundreds of other bird species with names that you can say around kids are legally protected by the Migratory Bird Treaty Act (MBTA), which broadly implements bird treaties between the United States and Canada, Mexico, Japan, and Russia. The MBTA prohibits pursuing, taking, killing, possessing, selling, and transporting migratory birds unless done in strict compliance with federal bird law.

Fig. 2-1. American Bushtit (A Nonmigratory "Migratory" Bird).

Don't let the name of the law confuse you, though. A bird doesn't actually need to be migratory to be on the list of "migratory" birds. (See, for example, Fig. 2-1.) Even when scientists haven't quite figured out if a particular bird migrates or not, chances are good that it's still on the list. So, yes, it really is a federal crime to kill a mockingbird.

Naturally, you might be wondering whether it's necessary to put on hunting gear, grab a shotgun, and go poach a few pigeons or tufted puffins (both protected) in order to add a migratory bird conviction to your rap sheet. After all, the statute does say that it's unlawful to do any of the things that the act prohibits "at any time, by any means or in any manner." Surely that must include more creative bird crimes than just illegal hunting.

Say, for example, you've attained streak-free plate glass windows and an egret happens to meet its abrupt demise flying into one of them. Are you a federal criminal? The U.S. Court of Appeals for the Second Circuit once held that it "would offend reason and common sense" to convict someone for that kind of bird death. Still, the court held that "[s]uch situations properly can be left to the sound discretion of prosecutors and the courts."[2] In other words, you *can* be federally charged with causing a bird death even if your only weapon is a bottle of glass cleaner, but you should just trust that prosecutors will use appropriate discretion in deciding whether to indict you or not.

In fact, accidental bird killers have been charged. In 2013, North Carolina utility giant Duke Energy was criminally charged for failing to prevent the deaths of birds in the blades of its bloodthirsty wind turbines. (See Fig. 2-2.) Even though the company hadn't planned to kill the birds, its operations resulted in the "incidental take" of at least 163 migratory birds. Duke pleaded guilty and, at long last, the hundreds of thousands of birds pureed in wind turbines each year were finally recognized as crime victims. That's what you get for trying to save the planet.

In January 2017, about ten days before Donald Trump was inaugurated, Barack Obama's Department of the Interior issued a thirty-page opinion affirming that this kind of "incidental take" was indeed a crime under the MBTA and that prosecutors should be trusted not to charge absurd cases. Almost immediately, however, the new Trump administration suspended that interpretation, and, in late December 2017, it issued a new opinion permanently withdrawing and replacing it.

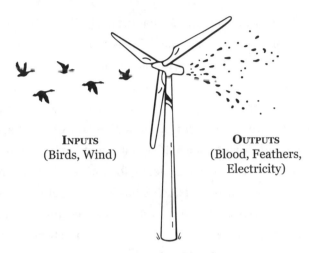

INPUTS
(Birds, Wind)

OUTPUTS
(Blood, Feathers,
Electricity)

Fig. 2-2. A Bird Blender.

The new opinion called the MBTA "the epitome of vague law" and noted that earlier interpretations made it "literally impossible for individuals and companies to know what is required of them under the law when otherwise lawful activities necessarily result in some accidental bird deaths. Even if they comply with everything requested of them by the Fish and Wildlife Service, they may still be prosecuted, and still found guilty of criminal conduct."

The bottom line is that you either will or won't be indicted for accidentally killing a bird depending on who is president, who is a federal prosecutor, and—most importantly—if anyone finds out. But there's no sense in worrying about all that. Even without killing a single bird, there are plenty of other ways to become a criminal under the MBTA.

Violating or failing to comply with *any regulation* made under the act is a federal misdemeanor and punishable by fines and imprisonment. Lucky for would-be bird offenders everywhere, there are hundreds of regulations issued under the act. Here are a few.

Shoot Canada Geese from a Sailboat with the Sails Unfurled

In 2005, the U.S. Fish and Wildlife Service determined that conflicts between geese and people had become a public health problem. Interspecies relations had apparently grown considerably worse since George W. Bush optimistically proclaimed in a 2000 speech: "I know the human being and fish can coexist peacefully." Not so with geese.

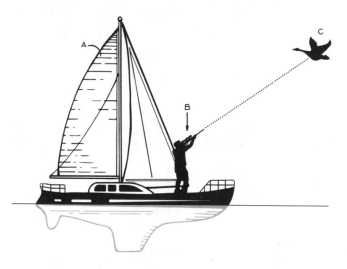

Fig. 2-3.

To address the problem, federal regulators created the "resident Canada goose population control program." It allows hunters to kill Canada geese without risk of prosecution under the Migratory Bird Treaty Act, provided they get a permit. But even with a permit, there are limits. For example, under 50 C.F.R. § 21.61(e)(4)(iv), it's still a federal crime to shoot a Canada goose from a sailboat if the sails are unfurled. (See Fig. 2-3.)

A person can also become a federal criminal by killing a type of goose that's not covered by the program. Only a *resident* Canada goose may be hunted under a population control permit, which the law defines as a Canada goose who nests in the lower forty-eight states in the months of March, April, May, or June, or resides within the lower forty-eight states and the District of Columbia in the months of April, May, June, July, or August.

If you should happen to shoot a Canada goose without first asking its place of residence and travel habits, you risk killing a goose who is just vacationing. That, too, would constitute a criminal violation of the MBTA, whether your sails are unfurled or not.

In addition to these offenses, the goose population control program imposes strict limitations on the types of weapons that can be used to knock off a goose. (See Fig. 2-4.)

Fig. 2-4. Prohibited Goose Killers

Machine Guns
Effective for rapid goose control.
May expose the offender to additional criminal charges under federal firearms laws.

Explosives
Ideal for times when aim and patience are in short supply. Subject to additional criminal penalties discussed in Chapter 8.

Poison
An up-close-and-personal approach to killing geese. Requires stealthiness to properly administer.

Other goose-killing weapons prohibited by law are punt guns, electricity, and any "stupefying substance."

Use a Falconry Bird in a Movie That
Isn't About Falconry

The Migratory Bird Treaty Act addresses certain situations where people and birds happen to get along. Unlike geese, it turns out that some birds actually like hanging out with people. Take falcons for instance, and the ancient art of falconry.

Federal regulations define falconry as "caring for and training raptors for pursuit of wild game, and hunting wild game with raptors." In plain English, though, falconry is when a person trains a bird of prey to kill on command and generally do their murderous bidding. For purposes of federal falconry law, a "raptor" is a migratory bird of the Order Accipitriformes, the Order Falconiformes, or the Order Strigiformes, if listed on the List of Migratory Birds, and it includes bald eagles (Haliaeetus leucocephalus) and golden eagles (Aquila chrysaetos). You might know them better as hawks, vultures, eagles, owls, and falcons. It does not include velociraptors.

Under regulations issued under the MBTA, falconers have limits on how many raptors they can keep, what kind, and even how long they can let their raptor stay with a non-falconer friend (forty-five days, in case you were wondering). One deeply unfair facet of federal falconry law, however, forbids falconers from letting their falcons appear in films that aren't about falconry. Aside from being hard to say ten times fast, it also happens to be a federal crime.

Falconers are only allowed to let their falconry birds appear in movies that are about falconry or "the biology, ecological roles, and conservation needs of raptors and other migratory birds." Even then, falconers can't be paid for the performance.[3]

Although this rule has just led movie studios to use look-alike birds or digital effects to meet their cinematic bird needs, how can we be sure that great unseen films featuring falcons haven't been

Fig. 2-5. Making a Non-Falconry Movie

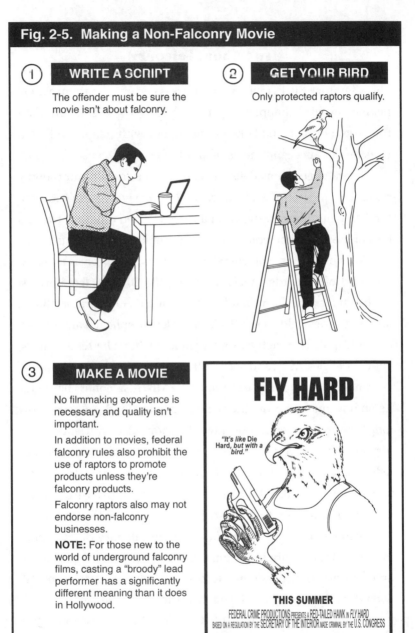

① WRITE A SCRIPT

The offender must be sure the movie isn't about falconry.

② GET YOUR BIRD

Only protected raptors qualify.

③ MAKE A MOVIE

No filmmaking experience is necessary and quality isn't important.

In addition to movies, federal falconry rules also prohibit the use of raptors to promote products unless they're falconry products.

Falconry raptors also may not endorse non-falconry businesses.

NOTE: For those new to the world of underground falconry films, casting a "broody" lead performer has a significantly different meaning than it does in Hollywood.

FLY HARD

"It's like Die Hard, *but with a bird."*

THIS SUMMER

FEDERAL CRIME PRODUCTIONS PRESENTS A RED-TAILED HAWK IN FLY HARD
BASED ON A REGULATION BY THE SECRETARY OF THE INTERIOR MADE CRIMINAL BY THE U.S. CONGRESS

scrapped because of oppressive government regulation? How many talented kestrels have given up on their silver-screen dreams? And how is a bird supposed to make a buck in show business with all this regulation? The answer, of course, is by breaking the law and making an illicit bird movie.

Barter for a Flamingo

The ancient art of barter involves the exchange of goods or services without using money. Under 16 U.S.C. § 707(b)(2) of the MBTA, it's also one of several prohibited ways for a person to acquire or get rid of a migratory bird. That includes flamingos.

To engage in criminal flamingo bartering, the offender only needs a lead on a flamingo and something of roughly equivalent value to trade for it. (See Fig. 2-6.) And while that may already seem shockingly straightforward, committing the offense is made easier by the fact that even a mere *offer* to barter for a flamingo is a crime. The same is true of more traditional offers to buy or sell flamingos and other migratory birds.

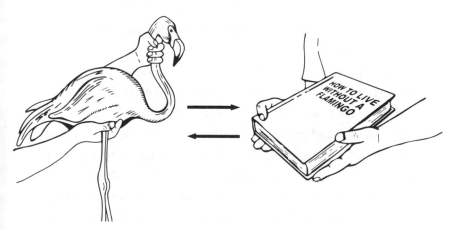

Fig. 2-6. Flamingo Bartering.

Although the ease with which this offense can be committed may be good news for aspiring offenders, it's bad news for black market bird dealers trying to stay out of prison. For them, the illicit bird trade has been made even more perilous ever since undercover bird cops started conducting undercover flamingo busts.

A FEDERAL FLAMINGO STING

In 1980, a Colorado man learned how seriously the government takes flamingo crimes when he took out an ad in a magazine offering various exotic birds for sale. Not long after he ran the ad, a couple of prospective buyers contacted him and went to his home to check out the merchandise. Unbeknownst to him, he wasn't dealing with authentic flamingophiles. The buyers were actually a pair of federal bird narcs conducting a sting.

After some initial haggling with the undercover Fish and Wildlife agents, the bird dealer agreed to sell a pair of flamingos for $2,500. Although the agents could have arrested him right then and there, they wanted to build as strong a flamingo-selling case as possible. They put down a $200 deposit on the flamingos and agreed to return with the balance.

When the agents came back, they brought two things with them: a birdcage and an arrest warrant. But before they whipped out the warrant and made the bust, they helped their target catch the flamingos and put them into their van, just the way a normal flamingo buy is supposed to go down. The agents then paid the $2,300 they still owed and promptly arrested the bird perp.

As strong as the government's case was, however, flamingo law is complicated. The bird dealer filed a motion to suppress the flamingos, arguing that the agents waited too long to execute the arrest warrant. It wasn't fair, he argued, because the agents waited to arrest him until after he had wrangled the flamingos into their van and only after they conducted the controlled buy. Believe it or not, the trial judge actually agreed. The judge suppressed the flamingos and dismissed the indictment.

In what was probably the first and only successful motion to suppress flamingos in the history of American jurisprudence, a defendant was about to walk free because of a flamingo deal gone bad. But the government appealed and ultimately prevailed. The Tenth Circuit Court of Appeals found that the flamingos should not have been suppressed and even acknowledged the agents' honorable efforts to "obtain peaceful possession of the birds."[4]

Import a Pregnant Polar Bear

Migratory birds aren't the only beneficiaries of a strong lobby in Washington. Sea otters, walruses, some kinds of manatees, and even polar bears are all "marine mammals" protected by federal law. Since 1972 the Marine Mammal Protection Act (MMPA) has made it a crime to hunt, capture, or kill them. The act also strictly prohibits buying them for any reason other than public display, scientific research, or preservation of the species.

This may explain why the rate of private walrus ownership continues to be extremely low in the United States year after year. It also explains why it's so hard to get your hands on a polar bear no matter how bad you might want one.

To be fair, though, the law was enacted in an effort to put an end to some of the more brutal human practices directed toward marine animals. As lawmakers explained when the law was being drafted, marine mammals had been "shot, blown up, clubbed to death, run down by boats, poisoned, and exposed to a multitude of other indignities."[5] But the law also made it a crime to do non-violent things involving marine mammals—things like importing a pregnant polar bear, which is prohibited by 50 C.F.R. §18.12(c)(1). Knowing violations are made criminal by 16 U.S.C. § 1375(h).

Interestingly, for a Congress that so often gets criticized when it comes to laws governing human reproduction, the legislative history of the MMPA reflects an impressive degree of familiarity with the intricacies of marine mammal pregnancy. As lawmakers explained:

> *It is known that some marine mammals are technically pregnant almost year-round, and in the cases of others, it is extremely difficult for even trained observers to detect pregnancy except in the latter stages or in seasons when such animals are known to give birth. It is the intent of the conferees that the term "pregnant" be interpreted as referring to animals pregnant near term or suspected of being pregnant near term as the case may be.*[6]

Thus, to criminally import a pregnant polar bear or any expectant marine mammal, offenders need to confirm, or at least suspect, a near-term pregnancy.

MAKING SURE THE POLAR BEAR IS PREGNANT

Unfortunately, there is currently no definitive polar bear pregnancy test on the market, despite scientists' best efforts to create one. Although a research team at the Cincinnati Zoo has been working to develop one since 2008, its biggest achievement so far has been training a beagle named Elvis to sniff out pregnancies in polar bear poop with a questionable degree of accuracy.[7]

Assuming an offender doesn't have access to a pregnancy-sniffing beagle or an ultrasound machine suitable for a polar bear, testing a bear's hormone levels may be the next best option. (See Fig. 2-7.) Even then, however, the results may be vague, because polar bears are known to have "pseudo-pregnancies," and a positive result may not indicate an actual pregnancy.

CAUTION:
Risk of being mauled during
administration of pregnancy test
is moderate to high.

Fig. 2-7.

Male offenders should also be reminded that it's never ever appropriate to ask a polar bear if she's pregnant.

Despite these challenges, the law is unforgiving. Because 16 U.S.C. § 1375(b) requires a person to *knowingly* import a pregnant polar bear before they can be convicted, confirmation or at least a strong suspicion of pregnancy is essential.

OTHER POLAR BEAR OFFENSES

For those who might not like polar bears enough to try to import one, Title 50, Section 18.34, of the C.F.R. provides guidance on how to safely deter polar bears who might be messing around with your private property. Honking a car horn at a polar bear is allowed but only if the honking doesn't last more than thirty seconds at a time. The law also allows the use of commercial air horns to scare off polar bears, so long as they aren't louder than 140 decibels.

Fig. 2-8.

Sadly, the gentleman in Fig. 2-8 didn't make it. But there are other bear deterrence measures that can lawfully be taken while still giving the offender a fighting chance. Driving in circles around your property in a truck or ATV, for example, is expressly permitted under 50 C.F.R. § 18.34. Don't get carried away, though. Chasing a polar bear in a truck is strictly prohibited. Engaging in prohibited polar bear deterrence measures may be considered an act of "take," subjecting the offender to criminal prosecution.

Ride a Manatee

The Marine Mammal Protection Act makes it a crime to do anything that could injure, disturb, or otherwise annoy a marine mammal in the wild, pregnant or not. On its own, this blanket ban on harassing marine mammals may seem vague, but federal regulations issued under the MMPA shed light on the kinds of things that people apparently need to be told to not do with marine mammals. Things like riding a manatee.

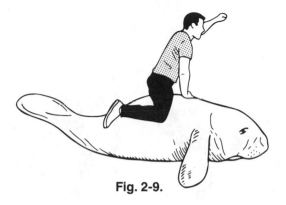

Fig. 2-9.

Under the MMPA, any kind of manatee harassment is generally prohibited. But in Florida's Kings Bay Manatee Refuge, it somehow became necessary for the director of Fish and Wildlife to get a little more explicit and expressly ban riding a manatee.

Worse, the director had to make it crystal clear through other provisions in 50 C.F.R. § 17.108(c)(14)(ix) that pinching, poking, standing on, diving on, chasing, cornering, or giving food or a drink to a manatee are also not okay.

In addition to violating federal law, manatee rides are also prohibited under the Florida Manatee Sanctuary Act, a state law with its own criminal penalties. While that means some manatee riders may get off without federal charges, if the feds do get interested, manatee harassers are subject to fines of up to $10,000 and as much as one year in prison under 16 U.S.C. § 1375(b).

Have a Contact Visit with Your Quarantined Llama Without Permission

Let's face it: it can get really lonely when you miss your llama. It's even worse when your llama finally arrives in the United States and immediately gets put in federal quarantine for a month. As

Fig. 2-10.

far as federal law is concerned, however, that doesn't give you a right to just stop in and visit whenever you feel like it.

The Animal Health Protection Act authorizes the secretary of agriculture to quarantine animals imported into the United States. For foreign llamas, that means a mandatory thirty-day stay in quarantine. Under 9 C.F.R. § 93.413, visitors of quarantined llamas are not permitted in quarantine enclosures unless a federal Animal and Plant Health Inspection Service representative or inspector in charge specifically grants permission. Because 7 U.S.C. § 8313 makes it a crime to violate the provisions of federal animal quarantine law, sneaking a little unpermitted contact with your llama before his time in lockup is done may be enough to get you locked up as well. But the heart wants what it wants.

Llamas aren't the only ones. 9 C.F.R. § 93.400 provides that the visitation rule applies to all ruminants, which includes all animals that "chew the cud, such as cattle, buffaloes, sheep, goats, deer, antelopes, camels, llamas and giraffes." There are similar restrictions for visitation of quarantined chickens, horses, and cattle as well.

The goal of all this is to see if the animal is showing signs of any communicable disease before it goes off and starts fraternizing with others. That's a good thing for everyone's safety. Nobody wants to catch llama pox or whatever it is that llamas get. Of course, safety doesn't make it any easier for those llama owners forced to go home alone each night.

CONTRABAND LLAMA POOP

Even if a llama owner does get a chance to visit his llama while in quarantine, taking souvenirs home can also give rise to criminal charges. Under 9 C.F.R. § 93.415, removing llama manure from a quarantine facility is strictly prohibited unless and until the llama who made the manure has been released.

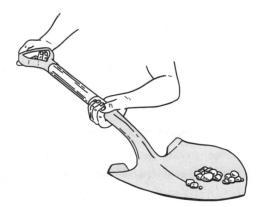

Fig. 2-11. Llamanure.

Although 7 U.S.C. § 8313(a)(1)(A) allows for a penalty of up to a year in prison for violations of these and other animal health protection laws, Section 8313(a)(1)(B) allows for a sentence of up to five years for illegally selling any animal or restricted animal article. In other words, taking home quarantined llama poop can result in an even stiffer sentence if you turn around and sell it. The same goes for llama milk.

Feed Garbage to a Pig Without Cooking It to a Boil

Federal quarantine laws don't just regulate the visitation of quarantined llamas and other cud-chewing ruminants—they also control a wide range of things involving the movement of animals and animal products from state to state. One of those things is the kind of garbage that you can feed to a pig.

To be clear, it's totally okay to feed garbage to a pig. It is America, after all. And who doesn't love the idea of garbage-fed pork? But we get many of our laws from people doing dumb, gross, and dangerous things. So the feds were forced to make it a federal crime to feed garbage to swine unless it has been cooked to a boil first.

The law is designed to prevent the spread of some pretty horrific diseases caused by feeding raw meat and other food waste to pigs—exciting-sounding stuff like foot-and-mouth disease, African swine fever, hog cholera, and swine vesicular diseases.

The Swine Health Protection Act prohibits feeding garbage to a pig, unless the garbage has been cooked by a garbage cooker who holds a garbage-cooking permit. The FDA has its own rule, 21 C.F.R. § 1240.75, but it doesn't expressly require garbage cookers to have permits and it only prohibits feeding uncooked garbage to a pig if the garbage came from out of state or it traveled through another state before being fed to a pig.

Even offenders who don't have pigs of their own can be charged. Under the FDA's rule, it's a federal crime to deliver out-of-state garbage to someone if you know they are going to feed it to a pig without cooking it or they have a known practice of doing so. Of course, if you're the kind of person whose friends habitually feed uncooked garbage to pigs, it's time to get new friends.

Fig. 2-12. Feeding Garbage to a Pig

GET GARBAGE

First, the offender must acquire some uncooked garbage. By law, "garbage" can include typical food waste from houses, restaurants, and other places (A). That includes meat in general and pork in particular (B).

NOTE: Pigs may not be fed other non-food things more commonly thought of as garbage (even hot garbage), like a DVD of *Star Wars: Episode I — The Phantom Menace* (C).

DON'T COOK IT

The law requires that all garbage be subjected to "minimum heat treatment" before feeding it to a pig. That means boiling it for at least 30 minutes.

MARRIAGE TIP: Don't use the nice cookware if you do decide to boil up some garbage for a pig.

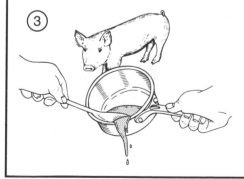

FEED IT TO A PIG

Although a person can be criminally convicted for running an unlicensed garbage-cooking operation, the focus of the Swine Protection Act and the federal quarantine laws is the feeding of garbage to swine. There is, however, no prohibition on tasting a little yourself.

Remove a Bald Eagle from Your House Without a Permit

Coming home to find that a bald eagle has taken up roost in your home can be a confusing time. It's simultaneously a patriotic milestone and a nightmare of Hitchcockian proportions. If this should happen to you, many questions may come to mind: Am I in the right house? Do I even know this eagle? How bad do I really need a house, anyway? What's the penalty for arson?

Faced with this predicament, a few brave souls might consider attempting a self-help eviction of the eagle. After all, it is your home. How sharp can those talons really be? Eagles are basically just large pigeons with a strong sense of country. Right?

Luckily, the federal government has regulated this precise situation, making the legality of your next steps as clear as possible. Title 50, Section 21.12(d), of the Code of Federal Regulations provides that most migratory birds may be removed from a building

Fig. 2-13. Cohabitation with Bald Eagle.

if they are attacking humans, pose a risk to food or merchandise, or are a threat to human safety because of their behavior, including if the birds are "opening and closing automatic doors." But the rule makes very clear that "you *must* have a permit from your Regional migratory bird permits office to remove a bald eagle or a golden eagle from a building . . ." (emphasis added).

To legally remove a bald eagle from your home or business, you'll need to apply for an eagle removal permit and propose a method for removing the eagle. Even then, there's no guarantee your application will be granted quickly—or ever.

In the meantime, if you're the law-abiding type, here are a few steps to follow when faced with a new eagle squatting in your home:

THE LAWFUL APPROACH

Step 1: *Panic.* This is healthy, and it's a natural part of the process. Don't forget, you have an eagle in your house.

Step 2: *Cry a little.* Remember: eagle in the house.

Step 3: *Apply for your permit.*

Step 4: *Wait for a decision.* By law, the regional migratory bird permit office will not issue a permit unless the director determines that your removal of the eagle is "compatible with the preservation of the bald or golden eagle." If the director decides the eagle is better off living with you for a while, move on to Step 5.

Step 5: *Accept it.* You live with a bald eagle now. Try to make the best of it and respect each other's space. (See Fig. 2-13.)

THE CRIMINAL APPROACH

Most states endorse some form of the "castle doctrine," which permits a homeowner to use deadly force against a violent intruder in his or her home. But this is a bald eagle we're talking about, not just

Fig. 2-14. Eagle Removal Gear.

some stupid person, so that defense doesn't apply. Getting rid of this intruder without a permit can't be done without a little law-breaking.

Unfortunately, Wikipedia doesn't have an entry for "eagle removal," so it's really anybody's guess on how to go about the removal or what constitutes appropriate eagle-removal gear. Presumably, though, offenders will at least want to have eye protection and some rubber gloves. Coupled with some sort of implement for guiding the eagle out of the house, this makeshift setup may give you just the right level of confidence to calmly approach an eagle and bring the situation to a peaceful end.

But none of that is realistic. If you try to remove an eagle from your house, it's totally going to attack you. (See Fig. 2-15.) Even if the risk of federal charges wasn't enough to deter you from this plan, knowing the pain of eight razor-sharp raptor talons in your back probably would have done it. But it's too late now. This is why it's important to always read ahead.

Fig. 2-15. You Had This Coming.

Anyway, the good news is that you'll probably pass out shortly into your tangle with the eagle, either from panic or blood loss. Eventually the eagle will have had enough of your pathetic display and leave through whatever window it was that you stupidly left open in the first place. Problem solved.

Mess with a Wild Little Donkey on Federal Land

Burros, which are basically just wild little donkeys who freely roam federal land without paying taxes, are statutorily designated as a national treasure. That means you have to love them. It's the law.

Because there's no limit to how awful people can be to animals, burros, along with wild horses, enjoy strong federal protections. In the 1950s, Congress learned that some actual asses out west had been turning them into dog food and using them for target practice. After passing an early burro protection law in 1959, Congress strengthened federal donkey law in 1971 with the Wild Free-Roaming Horses and Burros Act.

To briefly summarize, 16 U.S.C. § 1338(a) makes it a crime to:

(1) willfully remove, or try to remove, a burro from federal land;

(2) convert a wild burro into a private burro;

(3) maliciously kill or harass a burro;

(4) make products from the remains of dead burros; or

(5) sell a wild burro that wandered onto private land.

Like many other federal criminal statutes, the Wild Free-Roaming Horses and Burros Act also contains a catchall provision making it a crime to violate any burro regulation issued under the authority of the statute. That includes things like using a wild burro as a rodeo animal, which is expressly prohibited under 43 C.F.R. § 9264.7(a)(8).

Importantly, though, the statute's catchall provision requires that a person *willfully* violate a burro regulation before being criminally charged. Congress took care to ensure accidental or good-faith burro removals wouldn't be prosecuted. Even so, it's always good practice for anyone hoping to avoid criminal charges to check for burro stowaways when leaving federal land.

For those offenders with a little more disposable income, another criminal burro law, 18 U.S.C. § 47(a), makes it a crime to hunt burros using an airplane (the offender is the one using the

Fig. 2-16. Wild Donkey Crimes

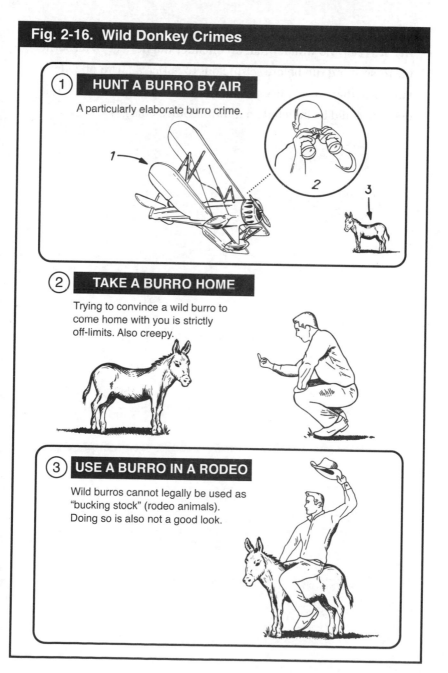

① HUNT A BURRO BY AIR

A particularly elaborate burro crime.

② TAKE A BURRO HOME

Trying to convince a wild burro to come home with you is strictly off-limits. Also creepy.

③ USE A BURRO IN A RODEO

Wild burros cannot legally be used as "bucking stock" (rodeo animals). Doing so is also not a good look.

airplane, not the burro). Given the vastness of the American fron-
tier, it's really no wonder that an offender might take an airborne
burro-spotting run before setting out to entice a burro off federal
land, whether to sell, use privately, or ride in a rodeo. But if he
does, he could be indicted on multiple burro charges.

Chapter 3

HOW TO BECOME A FEDERAL CRIMINAL

WITH MONEY

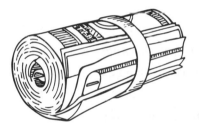

B enjamin Franklin is known to many Americans as the face of the $100 bill. Others "know" him as one of America's greatest presidents. Readers of *this* book, however, probably know him best as the author of "Fart Proudly," an eloquent essay about flatulence.

Franklin is also notable for his innovative anticounterfeiting efforts in the 1730s. At his Pennsylvania printing company, Franklin is credited with designing some of the earliest security features on paper money, including highly detailed images intended to thwart counterfeiters who lacked the ability to faithfully reproduce them. This early Colonial money also carried a stern warning: "To counterfeit is death."[1]

Today, counterfeiting money is no longer a capital offense, but there remain dozens of ways to become a federal criminal with U.S. currency. Most don't require the time and overhead of a full-blown counterfeiting operation. In fact, many can be committed for as little as one cent.

Mutilate a Coin

In 2010, Barack Obama pardoned a man named Ronald Foster who had been convicted of a federal crime more than forty years earlier. His offense? He cut the edges off pennies to trick vending machines into accepting them as dimes. Foster pleaded guilty, was sentenced to a $20 fine and a year of probation, and promptly forgot about the whole thing.

About forty-five years later, however, Foster applied for a pistol permit and was denied. That's how he first learned his youthful indiscretion had actually made him a convicted felon for all those years.

It turned out that the eighteen-year-old Foster—then a young marine at Camp Lejeune—had pleaded guilty to violating 18 U.S.C. § 331, which makes it a federal crime to fraudulently alter, deface, mutilate, impair, diminish, falsify, scale, or lighten U.S. coins. He had altered pennies in order to commit a nine-cent fraud each time he used one as a dime.[2] Lucky for him, President Obama was feeling sympathetic.

COIN CLIPPING

Coin clipping is a centuries-old practice in which the offender cuts or files down the edges of coins to collect the valuable metal shavings while still using the lightened coins at face value. (See Fig. 3-1.) Although this practice would surely constitute a violation of Section 331 today, it was more prevalent when coins were still made of

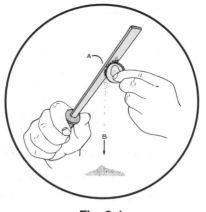

Fig. 3-1.

precious metals. U.S. coins in common circulation are now mostly made from metals like copper and zinc, meaning an offender would need to clip a huge number of coins to turn even a small profit.

FAKE COLLECTIBLES

Altering a coin to pass it off as a collectible can also be a crime. For example, "error coins" are highly collectible coins with mint-made errors like missing letters or double-struck images. Coin collectors are probably drawn to these coins because they find screwups highly relatable. But whatever the appeal of these rare coins may be, some fraudsters have been known to manipulate perfectly normal coins in order to pass them off to collectors as genuine error coins.

In 1966, two men were indicted for making and selling hundreds of fake double-struck pennies that they claimed had been "discovered" in sealed bags of bulk pennies purchased from the Federal Reserve. The men were ultimately caught when they tried to prove their claims by opening one of the "sealed" treasury bags in front of the audience at a private coin show. They unveiled a supposedly unopened treasury bag they conveniently already knew would contain error coins.[3] What they didn't count on was the Secret Service agent in the audience.

FLATTENING COINS

There are some perfectly legal ways to mutilate coins. Because Section 331 requires fraudulent intent, purely recreational coin mutilation is not prohibited by law. Thus, contrary to popular belief, flattening a penny on railroad tracks or in a penny press machine is not a crime under the mutilation statute.

Defacing Paper Money

In late 2007, Hillary Clinton narrowly avoided committing a federal crime—or at least, that's what she thought. At a campaign stop in Iowa, a potential voter asked for her autograph on a dollar bill. Clinton responded: "I can't sign money. That's illegal."

In fact, 18 U.S.C. § 333 does prohibit defacing, mutilating, disfiguring, or otherwise destroying Federal Reserve notes, and violators are exposed to stiff fines and imprisonment. But in order to be guilty, a person must act with the intent to render a bill "unfit to be reissued." That's probably good news for Bill Clinton, who reportedly had already signed the dollar in question without protest.[4] So far, neither Clinton has been charged.

Rendering a Bill "Unfit to Be Reissued"

Although the statute is silent on exactly what it takes to render a bill "unfit to be reissued," the Federal Reserve defines "unfit currency" as "a note that is not suitable for further circulation because of its physical condition, such as torn, dirty, limp, worn, or defaced."[5] A bill is unfit if it has excessive holes, tears, tape, or excessive graffiti.

EXCESSIVE HOLES

A bill has "excessive holes" if it has a "total holes area" of more than 15 square millimeters.

While a single hole bigger than 15 square millimeters will do the trick, the hole limit is additive, so many smaller holes will also render the bill unfit. (See, for example, Fig. 3-2.)

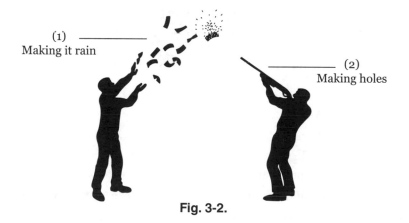

(1) _____
Making it rain

_____ (2)
Making holes

Fig. 3-2.

EXCESSIVE GRAFFITI

A bill can be rendered unfit due to "excessive graffiti," which means more than 40 square millimeters of the front or back are covered with visible, dark markings. To put that into perspective, Andrew Jackson's portrait on a $20 bill could accommodate a teardrop tattoo commemorating his killing of Charles Dickinson in an 1806 duel using only about 6 square millimeters of space. A patriotic yet tasteful forehead tattoo would occupy well over

75 square millimeters, and a full beard consistent with Jackson's iconic mussy hairstyle would easily exceed 400 square millimeters. (See Fig. 3-3.)

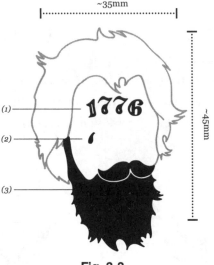

~35mm

~45mm

(1)

(2)

(3)

Fig. 3-3.

MISSING PIECES

In addition to holes and graffiti, a bill will be considered unfit for circulation if it has at least one missing corner. As explained in the following section, removing pieces of bills—particularly their corners—may also be evidence of other federal money crimes.

Attach Part of One Bill to Part of Another Bill to Make One Bill

18 U.S.C. § 484 is entitled "Connecting parts of different notes," and it basically prohibits exactly that. The statute makes it a federal crime to place or connect together "different parts of two or

more notes, bills, or other genuine instruments issued under the authority of the United States" in order to "produce one instrument."

The law doesn't prohibit innocently fixing a torn dollar bill. It requires that the person connecting the pieces of money do so "with intent to defraud" before making a criminal out of them. But how exactly does a person defraud someone with a couple of dollar bills cobbled together? The 1991 case of *United States v. Kenneth Michael Brown* illustrates one possible way.

In *Brown*, the defendant and his accomplice entered a convenience store in New Hampshire looking to buy cigarettes with what appeared to be a pair of $20 bills. At first, everything seemed normal. But after studying one of the bills, the clerk grew suspicious. The supposed $20 bill that the defendant handed to her said "20" in the corners, but showed George Washington's portrait, not Andrew Jackson's. The clerk handed the bills back, waited for the men to leave, and called the police.

Police determined that the defendant had tried to use two "raised" bills, made by taping the corners of genuine $20 bills to the bodies of genuine $1 bills. (See Fig. 3-4.) After ripping the corners off the real twenties, the torn bills were exchanged for new ones at a local bank and the raised bill was then passed as a real $20 bill in the hopes that nobody would notice. The whole scheme could have worked too—that is, if the clerk hadn't known her presidents.

When Brown was later arrested and brought to jail, a search for contraband revealed "two torn twenty dollar bills secreted in [his] rectal cavity." And while it's possible he just missed his wallet by a few inches, the court thought the location of the two Brown bills was incriminating. Brown was convicted of connecting parts of different notes in violation of 18 U.S.C. § 484.[6]

Fig. 3-4. Attaching Parts of Different Bills

①

DIVIDE MULTIPLE BILLS

As in the *Brown* case, a typical bill-cobbling offense involves cutting the corners off a large-denomination bill and attaching them to the body of a small-denomination bill.

②

ATTACH THE PIECES

Next, the offender connects the parts together to make one bill.

Glue, transparent tape, and other inconspicuous attachment methods are probably most commonly used, but there is no reason a real hack job with staples or duct tape couldn't result in criminal charges.

③

INTEND TO USE IT

Finally, the offender must intend to use the bill fraudulently as the defendant did in *Brown*. However, there is no need to insert the bill into your rectum.

Leave the Country with Too Many Nickels in Your Pockets

Even traveling with a little too much pocket change can get a person convicted of a federal crime. Since 2006 a federal regulation has prohibited exporting pennies or nickels from the United States without a special license from the U.S. Mint. Under 31 U.S.C. § 5111(d)(2), doing so knowingly is a federal crime and is punishable by up to five years in prison.

If the government had stopped there, it would be a federal crime to leave the country with *any* amount of nickels or pennies. In an effort to show its capacity for fairness and generosity, however, our benevolent regulators made an exception to that rule. The exception, found in 31 C.F.R. § 82.2, provides that people may legally travel abroad with up to $5 in pennies or nickels, or even as much as $25, so long as it's clear that the coins are for a "legitimate personal numismatic, amusement, or recreational use." In other words, if you want to leave the country with between $5 and $25 in small coins, you'd better be able to show you're either a genuine coin collector or that you're planning to have some fun with your nickels. Not too much fun, though: there is no allowance made for personally carrying more than $25 in pennies or nickels out of the country without a license.

THE OPPOSITION

Believe it or not, the penny and nickel export ban had some vocal opponents when the United States Mint considered comments from the public on whether to make an interim version of the rule final. According to the *Federal Register*, the Mint received thirty-one comments on the proposed rule, eighteen of them opposing it.

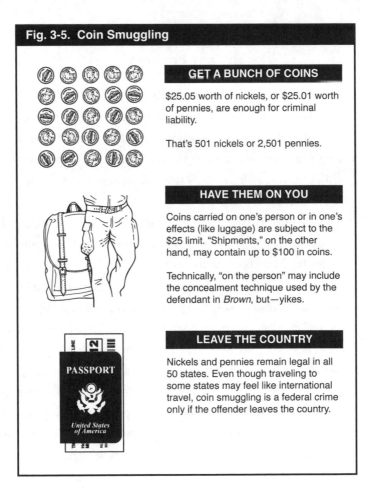

Fig. 3-5. Coin Smuggling

GET A BUNCH OF COINS

$25.05 worth of nickels, or $25.01 worth of pennies, are enough for criminal liability.

That's 501 nickels or 2,501 pennies.

HAVE THEM ON YOU

Coins carried on one's person or in one's effects (like luggage) are subject to the $25 limit. "Shipments," on the other hand, may contain up to $100 in coins.

Technically, "on the person" may include the concealment technique used by the defendant in *Brown*, but—yikes.

LEAVE THE COUNTRY

Nickels and pennies remain legal in all 50 states. Even though traveling to some states may feel like international travel, coin smuggling is a federal crime only if the offender leaves the country.

The reasons for opposing the export ban varied. Some members of the public even took the opportunity to propose getting rid of pennies and nickels entirely because they "waste pocket space" and people just throw them away. Others believed the cost of enforcing the rule would exceed the cost of minting new coins to replace those that might be lost to exportation. Then there were those who objected to the rule because they thought the penalties were too harsh. But one commenter wrote to oppose the rule for a more personal reason: it would prevent Americans from crossing the border into Canada with sufficient coins to play "nickel slot" machines or "penny-ante" poker.

In adopting the final rule, regulators acknowledged that five years in prison and hefty fines were available by law, but they were unmoved by the plight of penny-ante poker players looking for a good time in Canada. The final rule went into effect in April 2007 and remains in place, forcing nickel smugglers into the shadows once and for all.

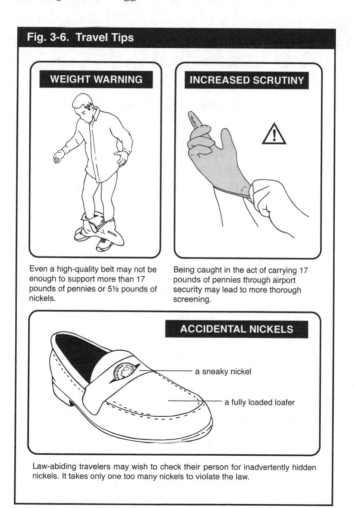

Fig. 3-6. Travel Tips

WEIGHT WARNING

Even a high-quality belt may not be enough to support more than 17 pounds of pennies or 5½ pounds of nickels.

INCREASED SCRUTINY

Being caught in the act of carrying 17 pounds of pennies through airport security may lead to more thorough screening.

ACCIDENTAL NICKELS

— a sneaky nickel

— a fully loaded loafer

Law-abiding travelers may wish to check their person for inadvertently hidden nickels. It takes only one too many nickels to violate the law.

THE WORLD WAR II NICKEL EXCEPTION

Even if a nickel smuggler is caught red-handed with more than five hundred nickels on his way out of the country, he may still be innocent, depending on the particular nickels he uses. Under 31 C.F.R. § 82.2(d), exporting nickels minted in 1942, 1943, 1944, or 1945 is not prohibited by law. That's because the nickel export ban was always intended to prevent coins from being taken abroad and hoarded or melted down for their metal value, which can significantly exceed the face value of the coins themselves. Nickels minted during World War II, however, contain no nickel. Instead, they were made from a less valuable alloy of copper, silver, and manganese in order to preserve nickel for armor plating during the war effort.

For a would-be offender who gets cold feet when the cuffs go on and the glove comes out, a quick scramble to find enough World War II nickels among the bunch may provide a defense.

CASH

Although the export ban on nickels and pennies can send a person to prison, a far more common occurrence at America's ports is the seizure of cash from international travelers. Under federal law, anyone traveling into or out of the United States with more than $10,000 in cash can be detained, searched, and have their money seized, all because they neglected to fill out a form reporting the cash to the government. It's a requirement buried in the Code of Federal Regulations and one that many travelers have never heard of.

No, the government doesn't need proof that the money is stolen, drug money, money for terrorists, or anything of the sort. Not initially, anyway. All that the customs agent needs is a traveler who didn't fill out a government form and who happens to be carrying too much money according to an arbitrary standard set by the feds. The government seizes millions of dollars each year this way, frequently confiscating perfectly legal money and making the owner fight to get it back.

The government can even criminally charge these travelers with failing to report the money or "bulk cash smuggling": for knowingly concealing more than $10,000 in their luggage or clothes with the intention of not reporting it. The penalty is up to five years in prison, which is the same amount of time a person can get for exporting too many nickels or pennies.

Write a Check for Less Than $1

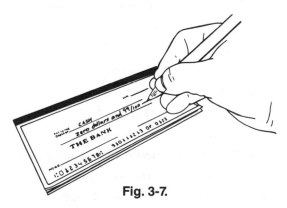

Fig. 3-7.

A personal check—which is basically just an IOU with consequences—is not a method of payment known for its efficiency. You need a pen, there's writing involved, and apparently you're actually supposed to have the money in an account before you write one. The only real advantages of using personal checks are learning how to spell out things like "forty-eight" and practicing your fractions.

But one curious federal statute, 18 U.S.C. § 336, has long made it a federal crime to issue "any note, *check*, memorandum, token, or other obligation for a less sum than $1" (emphasis added) if it's intended to "circulate as money" or be used "in lieu of lawful money of the United States." This statute has led some to wonder if writing a personal check for ninety-nine cents or less might actually be a federal crime.

Unfortunately for the people behind you in the checkout line, the history of Section 336 suggests that it probably isn't a crime. Congress enacted the statute in 1862, at a time when inflation had caused the metal value of coins to exceed their face value. That led people to start hoarding the increasingly valuable coins, which in turn led to a shortage of coins in circulation.

To keep business moving during the coin shortage, some retailers responded by issuing their own notes and tokens in small denominations for use as change. But the government didn't take kindly to the idea of competing currencies, so Congress passed the Stamp Payments Act, making the issuance of private small denomination currency a federal crime.

Like a government with a new statute, the feds didn't wait long to use it. In 1874, prosecutors indicted an employee of a furnace store in Michigan for circulating notes issued by his employer that read: "The Bangor Furnace Company will pay the bearer, on demand, fifty cents, in goods, at their store, in Bangor, Mich."

That's right: the furnace store employee was charged with a federal crime because of fifty cents in store credit. He challenged his indictment and ultimately appealed his case all the way to the Supreme Court. In the end, the justices held that the statute didn't apply to notes or obligations payable in goods but was intended only to prevent the circulation of a private currency whose value was payable in fractions of a dollar.[7]

More recently, the statute has garnered attention because of its potential applicability to cryptocurrencies like Bitcoin. Some scholars have suggested that the ability to exchange cryptocurrencies in amounts less than $1 brings it within the prohibition on issuing circulating obligations designed to compete with U.S. currency. However, others have pointed out that the statute refers only to physical things like tokens, coins, checks, and notes designed to circulate. That's why the Congressional Research Service determined that "it does not seem likely" that a non-physical currency would be covered by the Stamp Payments Act. But, like the furnace store debacle in 1874, someone may just need to be charged, convicted, and have their case heard by the Supreme Court before we can know if it's a crime for sure. And if that's what it takes to get people to shut up about Bitcoin already, it wouldn't be the worst thing.

Make Your Own Coins

Typical counterfeiting is pretty boring. Take a coin or paper bill, copy it as closely as possible, and you're done. The idea is to make a good enough duplicate to pass it off as real money.

The problem, of course, is that even the most creative counterfeiter is stuck with the same old designs that the U.S. Mint has been using for decades. That means lots of Lincolns, Jeffersons, Washingtons, FDRs, and the occasional JFK. What do offenders do when they've grown tired of using coins struck with the busts of dead presidents? What if they want to design their own currency? Well, that's probably a crime too.

18 U.S.C. § 485 and § 486 each prohibit some form of private coin making, depending on the circumstances. The first one, Section 485, prohibits "falsely mak[ing], forg[ing], or counterfeit[ing]

any coin or bar in resemblance or similitude of any coin of denomination higher than 5 cents." That's your standard non-penny coin counterfeiting statute, which is why it requires "similitude." Section 486, on the other hand, punishes those offenders with a more creative flair. It prohibits making or using fake coins "whether in the resemblance of coins of the United States or of foreign countries, *or of original design*" (emphasis added).

In 2009, a grand jury indicted a man named Bernard von NotHaus under both statutes.[8] Despite his name, von NotHaus wasn't indicted for being a Bond villain. The government alleged that he had minted coins of his own design called "Liberty Dollars" and that they were made to look like U.S. coins. The indictment also alleged that von NotHaus intended to introduce the Liberty Dollar coins into the U.S. economy in order to compete with U.S. currency. The government didn't like that, so it charged him under both Section 485 and Section 486.

At trial, the government called a professional numismatist as an expert witness to weigh in on the similarities between the Liberty Dollars and genuine U.S. coins. He noted the use of reeded edges, a serif font, phrases like "In God We Trust," and the word "Liberty" were all attributes shared by the coins.

Also important was the Liberty Dollar's use of the Statue of Liberty on one of its sides. That iconic symbol of liberty, coupled with the other factors the government numismatist identified, were sufficient for a finding that von NotHaus had made coins with sufficient "similitude" to authentic U.S. coins. The jury found von NotHaus guilty on all counts of the indictment.

As in *United States v. von NotHaus*, employing design elements similar to those used in minting U.S. coins can go a long way toward a finding of guilt:

Fig. 3-8. Anatomy of a Crime Coin

Design features used by the secretary of the treasury in minting real U.S. coins pursuant to 31 U.S.C. § 5112 include:

(1) reference to the "United States of America";

(2) words like "Liberty";

(3) a depiction of something symbolic of liberty (e.g., freedom fries);

(4) reeded edges;

(5) the phrase "In God We Trust";

(6) the year of minting, issuance, or a president's term of office. (As to this last element, the coin shown uses the years during which french fries were called "freedom fries" in the cafeteria at the U.S. Capitol.)

Chapter 4

HOW TO BECOME A FEDERAL CRIMINAL

WITH FOOD

I n 1923, Congress enacted the Filled Milk Act, prohibiting the
interstate sale of any "imitation or semblance of milk, cream,
or skimmed milk." Apparently, fake milk was a big problem. Such
a problem, in fact, that in *United States v. Carolene Products Co.*
(1938), the Supreme Court upheld criminal charges against a
company for selling "Milnut," a milk-like mixture of condensed
skimmed milk and coconut oil. Delicious.

In 1937, however, things got serious. A Tennessee company decided to sell a drug for treating strep infections without bothering
to test if it was toxic first. As it turned out, the drug contained a

poisonous ingredient used in antifreeze. Seventy-one adults and thirty-four children died.

Congress responded with the Food, Drug and Cosmetic Act of 1938. It aimed to keep America's food and drug supply safe. Since then, however, Title 21 of the United States Code and related regulations have expanded significantly, creating countless ways to commit a federal crime with food.

FOOD CRIMES: A PRIMER

There are a few key statutes that any potential food criminal must know. Perhaps most important is 21 U.S.C. § 331 of the Food, Drug, and Cosmetic Act, which makes it unlawful to introduce "adulterated," "misbranded," or otherwise prohibited food products into interstate commerce. Under 21 U.S.C. § 333, these prohibited food transactions are punishable by fines and imprisonment.

ADULTERATED FOOD

Under 21 U.S.C. § 342, food is considered "adulterated" when it is poisonous, contaminated, or contains any substance that will be injurious to the consumer's health. But not all filth makes food adulterated. Far from it, actually. The FDA has issued an entire set of "defect action levels," allowing things like insect parts, mammal feces, and maggots in certain amounts, depending on the food product. The FDA gets the last word on just how much mammal feces is too much mammal feces in your food.

MISBRANDED FOOD

A little less disgusting is "misbranded" food. Food falls into this category if its labeling is false or misleading or if the food itself doesn't meet federally mandated food specifications called "standards of identity." As one example, the FDA has decreed that a "frozen cherry tart" may not be more than four inches in diameter. Any larger and it must be called a "frozen cherry pie," even though tarts and pies are different in other important ways left unaddressed by federal law.[1] Another standard of identity specifies that "mixed fruit jelly" can only be a mix of up to five fruits.[2] There are dozens of these standards of identity, and they create dozens of potential food crimes involving everything from canned asparagus to sherbet.

To help navigate this tangled web of federal food crimes, the food crime pyramid (See Fig. 4-1.) organizes them into familiar food-based categories. The pyramid can be used to quickly find a food crime to meet anyone's personal tastes or dietary restrictions. Plus, unlike the USDA's food pyramid from 1992, this one won't try to guilt you into eating less butter.

It's not just the Food, Drug, and Cosmetic Act that makes violations of food regulations into food crimes. 21 U.S.C. § 676 of the Meat Inspection Act creates a broad-sweeping criminal penalty for selling noncompliant meat. Similarly, 21 U.S.C. § 1041 of the Egg Products Inspection Act does the same for eggs. And 7 U.S.C. § 1622 of the Agricultural Marketing Act makes it a crime to mark food products "USDA Certified" if they aren't.

Regulations issued under these statutes ensure that anyone in this country who is brave enough to buy something called "Sauerkraut with Wieners and Juice" is getting at least 20 percent wieners by weight.[3] Bacon sellers can be criminally charged for selling shingle-packed bacon if consumers can't see at least 70 percent of a "representative slice" through that little window in the package.[4] (See Fig. 4-2.) Egg handlers aren't allowed to handle your egg products without wearing a hairnet.[5] And if you're

Fig. 4-1. The Food Crime Pyramid

(1) Margarine and Butter Crimes
21 U.S.C. §§ 331 & 347—Prohibits the interstate sale of yellow margarine that fails to meet stringent labeling, packaging, and form requirements.

(2) & (3) Fruit and Vegetable Crimes
21 C.F.R., Part 145—Sets federal requirements for canned fruits.
21 C.F.R., Part 155—Sets federal requirements for canned vegetables.
21 C.F.R., Part 158—Sets federal requirements for frozen vegetables.
7 C.F.R., Part 319—Regulates imported fruits and vegetables.

(4) & (5) Meat, Egg, and Dairy Crimes
21 U.S.C. §§ 610 & 676—Prohibits the sale of noncompliant meat products.
21 U.S.C. § 1037 & 21 CFR, Part 160—Regulates the handling and sale of eggs.
21 C.F.R., Part 131—Sets federal regulations for milk and cream products.
21 C.F.R., Part 133 & 7 U.S.C., Part 58—Regulates cheese products.

(6) Bread and Pasta Crimes
21 C.F.R., Part 136—Sets federal standards for bakery products.
21 C.F.R., Part 139—Regulates macaroni products.

buying USDA-certified ice cream, the law requires that someone has already determined it meets the government's standards—including that it's "attractive" and has a firm body.[6] Perhaps one day there will be a Federal Online Dating Act with similar safeguards.

70%

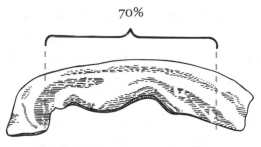

Fig. 4-2. A Representative Slice.

It's no secret why many of these things are regulated in such detail. Consumers want to know that when they buy something that claims to be "Lima Beans with Ham in Sauce," they aren't getting all sauce and no ham. And if Big Bacon could get away with always just putting the show bacon on the top of a pack without the window of truth, how could the consumer ever really know if he was getting duped into buying a package full of fat strips?

But remember: these things aren't just regulated; they can all be charged as federal crimes.

HOME COOKING

It bears mentioning that even federally regulated foods are generally not criminal unless they are made, sold, transported, or received in "interstate commerce." So before you go reporting your mother-in-law to the FBI and USDA for her misshapen old-fashioned meat loaf—which 9 C.F.R. § 317.8(b)(9)(iii) usually requires to be "in a traditional form, such as rectangular with rounded top or circular with flat bottom and rounded top"—know that even terrible home cooking for purely private consumption is probably not a crime.

NONCRIMINAL RESOLUTIONS

One of the reasons that our prisons aren't yet full of food criminals is that the FDA and USDA like to handle things their own way. Violations of food regulations are often addressed out of court by a strongly worded letter to the food maker telling them to get their act together or else.

In late 2017 a Massachusetts bakery learned this the hard way after it had the temerity to list "love" as an ingredient in its granola bars. The FDA sent the bakery a letter warning that "'Love' is not a common or usual name of an ingredient, and is considered to be intervening material because it is not part of the common or usual name of the ingredient." According to the FDA, this rendered the granola bars misbranded under the Food, Drug, and Cosmetic Act and subjected the bakery to sanctions. The FDA stopped short of noting that listing "love" as an ingredient could also be charged as a federal crime.[7]

The moral of the story, of course, is that if you're going to make your food with love, the FDA wants you to please just shut up about it. And if "love" is a euphemism for some other ingredient, you'd better tell us what it is right now.

Yet, even if the FDA's granola letter demonstrated its deep disdain for love, another of its warning letters revealed that the agency might actually have a soft spot, and that soft spot is mayonnaise. In mid-2015 the FDA issued a warning to a company for selling vegan "mayo." According to the FDA, it was necessarily misbranded because real mayonnaise contains eggs, and vegan mayonnaise is made out of whatever the heck vegan mayonnaise is made out of. In a heartwarming twist, however, the FDA and the mayo company later announced that they had "met to discuss the issues cited in the warning letter and worked together to address them."[8]

FEDERAL JURISDICTION OVER A HAM-AND-CHEESE SANDWICH

Committing a federal food crime is one thing. Getting *charged* with one is an entirely different matter. That's why it helps to know who the federal food cops are and to understand their investigative authority.

At the federal level, the two main regulators of food are the Food and Drug Administration (FDA) and the United States Department of Agriculture (USDA). According to the FDA, it regulates 75 percent of the American food supply, including "everything we eat except for meat, poultry, and some egg products," with the USDA handling the rest.[9]

In truth, the jurisdiction of the two agencies is somewhat more complex and the divisions in their investigative authority isn't always clear. As shown in Figure 4-3, shell eggs are the responsibility of the FDA, while liquid eggs belong to the USDA. In the fried-foods category, alligator nuggets, which apparently exist, are an FDA concern. Corn dogs, on the other hand, are the USDA's business. In fact, while the USDA investigates most meat crimes, its jurisdiction is limited to those involving meat from cows, pigs, goats, and other traditional meat animals. The FDA oversees "non-specified red meats," including "zoo animals."

Yes, zoo animals. Meat from zoo animals.

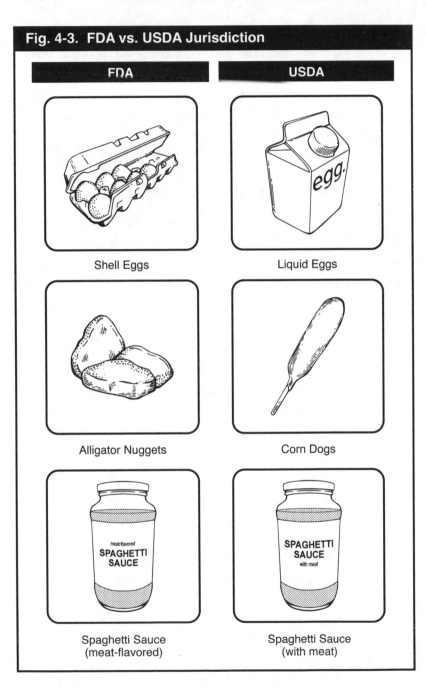

Fig. 4-3. FDA vs. USDA Jurisdiction

FDA

USDA

Shell Eggs

Liquid Eggs

Alligator Nuggets

Corn Dogs

Spaghetti Sauce
(meat-flavored)

Spaghetti Sauce
(with meat)

Meat-*flavored* spaghetti sauce versus spaghetti sauce with meat; cheese pizza versus pepperoni pizza; and chicken-flavored noodle soup versus chicken noodle soup each fall on opposite sides of the divide between FDA and USDA authority. But it's not at all clear who regulates pizza with zoo animal sausage.

Or consider the humble ham-and-cheese sandwich. Depending on where it is in its life span or what final form it takes, a sandwich-monger may be up against both federal agencies.[10]

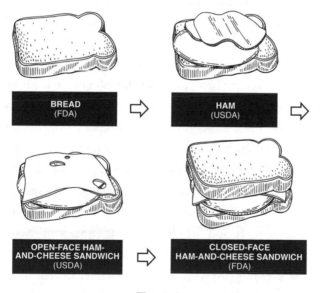

Fig. 4-4.

We begin with the bread, the foundation of any ham and cheese sandwich. Bakery products fall squarely in FDA jurisdiction.

One regulation promulgated by the FDA, Title 21, Section 136.110, of the Code of Federal Regulations, is appropriately entitled "Bread, rolls and buns." It sets the requirements for the most basic of bread products. For example, if the sandwich is going to be served on "egg bread," the FDA is of the view that the bread had better contain at least 2.56 percent egg solids by weight. There are also other more nuanced bread regulations, like how raisin-y "raisin bread" must be (at least 50 parts by weight for each 100 parts by weight of flour), and that "milk buns" can't contain any buttermilk.

Then comes the ham. Without it, we're just going to end up with a cold cheese sandwich on our hands, and that would be sad. But this is also where the USDA enters the picture.

Ham is a meat product subject to regulation by the USDA under Title 9 of the C.F.R. Before it leaves the slaughterhouse, the ham has to be inspected by the USDA and approved for human consumption. Say, for example, that the ham came from the carcass of a pig that happened to be giving off a "pronounced sexual odor." By law, that carcass was required to be condemned and is considered adulterated. Ignoring that requirement and using the sexual-smelling ham in our sandwich is a prohibited act under the federal Meat Inspection Act and chargeable as a federal crime. Don't worry, we'll discuss sexual pig odors in greater detail later.

Next, it's time to add the cheese to our crime sandwich. There are dozens of regulations governing the cheese itself. But whether the cheese is compliant with the federal regulations or not is only part of our concern. One slice of bread, some ham, and a piece of cheese technically make an open-face ham-and-cheese sandwich. Pursuant to the FDA's *Investigations Operations Manual*, open-face sandwiches are in the investigative jurisdiction of the USDA. Once the meat-to-bread ratio hits 50:50 on a single slice of bread, the USDA calls the shots. Add a second slice of bread, however, and you now have a closed-face sandwich, and you're back in FDA jurisdiction.

MARGARINE CRIMES

Margarine—the gateway condiment for food criminals—is one place where America's rich tradition of food crimes truly began. Margarine prosecutions were some of the earliest examples of people being charged for conduct prohibited by agency regulations rather than criminal statutes alone.

In 1888, for example, a grand jury returned a criminal indictment against a Massachusetts margarine seller named George R. Eaton for selling margarine without keeping logs of his margarine sales. Congress had just passed its legislative masterpiece, "an act defining 'butter,'" in which it gave the commissioner of internal revenue the authority to make rules governing the sale of butter and margarine. By statute, Congress broadly made it a crime for a margarine seller to fail "to do a thing required by law in the carrying on or conducting of his business." Drunk with power, the commissioner issued a regulation requiring margarine sellers to keep a logbook of all margarine sales, including who the margarine was sold to and where it came from.

Like any good margarine dealer, however, George Eaton was no snitch. He didn't think the feds had any business knowing who his margarine supplier was or who his buyers were, so he didn't keep the required logbook (or at least he didn't turn it over when the feds came knocking).

When he was indicted, Eaton moved to dismiss the charges on the grounds that he hadn't committed a crime but merely a regulatory violation. His motion was denied, he was tried, and he was convicted. Eventually, Eaton's appeal reached the Supreme Court, where the justices actually agreed with him. The court held that violating the margarine records rule couldn't be a crime, even if the regulations did have the force of law. In the court's words: "It does not follow that a thing required by [regulations] is a thing so required by law as to make the neglect to do the thing a criminal offense in a citizen, where a statute does not distinctly make the neglect in question a criminal offense."[11]

In other words, if Congress wanted the failure to keep margarine records to be a federal crime, it had to say so clearly.

Eaton wasn't alone. In 1896, another margarine dealer was convicted of violating federal margarine law. The government charged Israel C. Kollock with selling half-pound containers of margarine without putting his name and address on the containers and without printing the quantity of margarine in "letters not less than one-quarter of an inch square" as required by regulation.[12] In other words, he was charged with not using an eighteen-point font.

Kollock, like Eaton before him, moved to dismiss his indictment on the ground that Congress couldn't constitutionally give an executive branch official the power to make federal crimes. This time, however, the Supreme Court didn't buy the argument.

The court was of the view that Congress had properly made it a crime by statute to sell packages of margarine if they didn't have the "marks and characters" required by law. The commissioner's authority to specify *which* marks and characters were required, however, was "merely in the discharge of an administrative function" and properly delegated to him. Put simply, Kollock could be convicted for selling improperly labeled margarine because the regulation just "filled in the details" of what Congress had already made a crime. Thus, Kollock became one of America's earliest margarine criminals.

PINK MARGARINE

Even without federal butter control, things were already bad enough for margarine dealers under state law. In 1898 an agent of Swift & Company named Collins was charged and convicted in New Hampshire for selling margarine that wasn't pink. Yes, selling non-pink margarine was once a crime in the Live Free or Die state and people could actually be locked up for it. The law required margarine to be dyed pink if it was being sold as a substitute for butter, which is sort of margarine's whole thing.[13]

The case was *Collins v. State of New Hampshire*, and the defendant had the gall to sell margarine that was the same color as butter. Never shying away from a good margarine case, the U.S. Supreme Court agreed to hear Collins's appeal. In a 7–2 decision, the justices concluded that the plain purpose of the pink margarine law was to make would-be consumers feel a "repugnance up to the point of a positive and absolute refusal to purchase the article at any price." They struck down the pink margarine law as unconstitutional and, from that point forward, lawmakers could no longer require that margarine be pink. More importantly, selling butter-colored margarine was no longer a ticket to prison.

The decision in *Collins* represented one of the parting shots in a dark part of American history. Excessive taxes on margarine, smear campaigns by Big Butter, and hard-fought lobbying efforts to preserve butter's place on America's toast may now seem like a distant memory. But neither the Supreme Court nor Congress ever truly closed the door on federal margarine crimes.

Even after the Supreme Court decided *Collins*, *Eaton*, and *Kollock*, debate in Congress continued to rage. In 1901, a man named Rathbone Gardner stormed down to Washington on behalf of a Rhode Island margarine maker to testify before the House of Representatives. Gardner railed against onerous margarine regulations and even called out the injustice of pink margarine laws. He testified that the purpose behind the law was clear, since "it is absolutely certain that no man would spread upon his bread any pink substance." Mostly, however, margarine makers were mad about the oppressive federal tax imposed on margarine. They felt it was nothing more than an effort to make all margarine purchases cost prohibitive and a further attempt to wipe butter alternatives out of existence. Still, Gardner really seemed to have a pretty serious machismo problem when it came to pink condiments.

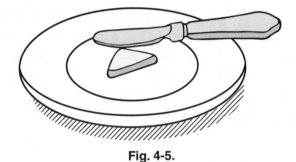

Fig. 4-5.

TRIANGULAR MARGARINE

Although the federal tax on margarine was finally repealed in the 1940s, federal law is still full of provisions with a clear anti-margarine bias. Under 21 U.S.C. § 347(c), it's a federal crime to serve margarine in a public eating place unless it's either conspicuously labeled as margarine or each serving is "triangular in shape." A number of states have their own triangular margarine laws. In fact, in 1952 a restaurant owner named Joseph Trewasky was arrested in Hartford, Connecticut, for serving square pats of margarine to his customers. He'd reportedly already been warned once to cut them into triangles.[14]

Section 347(e) even goes so far as to specify just how yellow "colored margarine" is. Specifically, it's "more than one and six-tenths degrees of yellow, or of yellow and red collectively, but with an excess of yellow over red, measured in terms of Lovibond tintometer scale or its equivalent."

LOOSE MARGARINE

Title 21, Section 347(b)(1), of the United States Code prohibits selling, or offering for sale, colored margarine "unless ... such oleomargarine or margarine is packaged." Doing so requires little more than a pair of hands and a generous wad of loose, unpackaged margarine. (See Fig. 4-6.) Violating Section 347(b)(1)'s packaging requirement constitutes a prohibited act under 21 U.S.C. § 331(m), which, under 21 U.S.C. § 333, is a federal crime punishable by up to a year in prison.

Fig. 4-6.

Even for an offender who does package his margarine like a civilized human being, there are still a number of other ways to earn a margarine conviction. As Israel Kollock learned in the 1890s, the federal government has long felt very strongly about labeling containers of margarine, right down to font size.

Fig. 4-7. Tub Law

- The net weight (if sold in a retail establishment) must be one pound or less (A);

- The word "margarine" must be written in letters at least as large as any other type or lettering on the label (compare B and C); and

- The word "oleomargarine" or "margarine" may not be in smaller than 20-point type or lettering (C).

FRUITS AND VEGETABLES

Few things are as wholesome as a farm stand selling ears of corn on the side of a bucolic country road. Whether it's the unattended money box operating on the honor system, the trendiness of farm-to-table eating, or the thrill of not knowing how many roadside strangers have fondled your food before you eat it, the appeal is undeniable. But if that farm stand is in the state of New York, it may also present an opportunity to commit one of many vegetable crimes under federal law.

Since 1972, New York has been under a federal quarantine order issued by the secretary of agriculture, which prohibits anyone from moving an unshucked ear of corn out of the state. That same regulation, 7 C.F.R. § 301.85, also makes it unlawful to move Irish potatoes under 1½ inches in diameter, used burlap bags, farm tools, and "muck" out of New York. Anyone who knowingly leaves the state with any of those things violates not only the quarantine regulation but also the criminal provisions of 7 U.S.C.

§ 7734(a). If convicted, the offender faces a prison sentence of up to five years.

If you should find yourself speeding across the border with an ear of corn on your passenger seat and red and blue lights flashing in your rearview mirror, remember: it's too late to shuck the corn now. When the feds see corn husks flying out of your car window, they'll know they have a corn smuggler on their hands. Just stay calm and get the best veggie lawyer money can buy.

Fig. 4-8.

Agricultural quarantine laws like that one also restrict the movement of all kinds of fruits and vegetables into and throughout the United States. Until 2018, federal regulations said that baby carrots from Zambia and potatoes from Mexico couldn't be imported if they had dirt on them. Avocados from Spain, Peru, and Mexico were prohibited from entry if they fell off the tree before the harvest. These kinds of rules are intended to keep invasive pests like the golden nematode and Mediterranean fruit fly from spreading in the United States. But unless you have a passport, lots of frequent-flier miles, and a hot tip on an untended Peruvian avocado grove, many of these crimes may be hard to commit if you're not a commercial importer.

Other fruit and vegetable crimes are similarly difficult because they require membership in special societies like the Popcorn Board or the Mushroom Council, both of which are totally real things. For example, 7 U.S.C. § 6104(i) makes it a crime for employees of the nine-member Mushroom Council to leak confidential mushroom information. Popcorn information is similarly protected from disclosure. Even revealing how an avocado producer voted in an avocado referendum is a federal crime.

THE FRUIT DUMPING LAW

In 1926, Congress held days of hearings on a proposed bill "to prevent the destruction or dumping, without good and sufficient cause therefor, of farm produce received in interstate commerce by commission merchants and others and to require them truly and correctly to account for all farm produce received by them." You see, back then, lawmakers didn't waste time with catchy titles or acronyms for laws. In fact, after reading the title of the fruit dumping bill, there was very little the text of the law itself could even add.

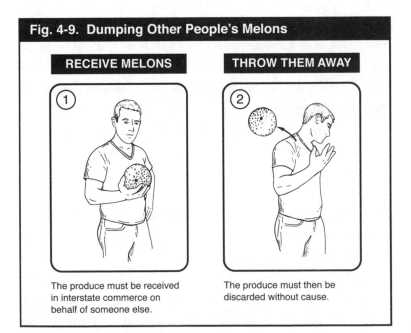

Fig. 4-9. Dumping Other People's Melons

RECEIVE MELONS

① The produce must be received in interstate commerce on behalf of someone else.

THROW THEM AWAY

② The produce must then be discarded without cause.

As the congressional testimony reflects, 1920s America had a problem with unscrupulous fruit merchants. One congressman recounted a tale of sweet potato shipments being fraudulently discarded. Another lamented mysterious losses of melons. Edward Ross from Pocomoke City, Maryland, shared his story of an ill-fated shipment of strawberries sent to a fruit merchant in Ohio that sparked a cross-country investigation and, ultimately, the federal law.

According to his congressional testimony, Ross's company had agreed to sell a shipment of strawberries to an Ohio fruit merchant for a set price. The company shipped $1,400 worth of strawberries and waited to hear if they arrived in Ohio safely. A few days later, however, Ross received a wire saying the shipment had been refused due to "decay." Knowing that strawberries wouldn't survive a shipment elsewhere, the company sold the strawberries to the merchant at a deep discount. But Ross was suspicious, so he packed up and went to Ohio to investigate.

Unfortunately, the trail had gone cold. There were no records, no witnesses, and, according to Ross, not a single "straight" lawyer in all of Columbus who would take his case against the fruit merchant. He suspected he'd been the victim of a berry heist. He just couldn't prove it. Undaunted, he went to Washington and urged Congress to do something.

Ross's strawberry caper compelled Congress to enact a criminal law prohibiting fruit merchants from failing to keep records or destroying produce for no good reason. As drafted, however, the law doesn't just apply to fruit merchants. Anyone who receives fruits, vegetables, melons, and other farm products on behalf of another person in interstate commerce can be convicted for throwing them away without good cause.

Sell a Barrel of Fruit with a Bulge
That's Too Small

Long before congressmen were focused on melons, they were concerned about bulge size. In 1912, the House of Representatives held hearings on a bill that would set mandatory dimensions for apple barrels, including a federally prescribed circumference for their bulges. The law was championed by buyers and sellers in the apple industry who were worried that lack of uniformity in barrel size posed a risk of fraud and deception. As one witness testified, the capacity of apple barrels could easily vary from 10 pecks to 3 bushels, whatever that means.

Title 15, Sections 231 through 242, of the U.S. Code specify the dimensions for fruit and vegetable barrels and impose criminal penalties for selling undersized barrels.

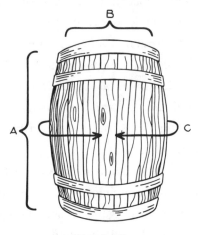

Fig. 4-10.

For barrels of fruits, vegetables, and other dry commodities other than cranberries, Section 243 requires that the distance between the barrel heads (A) be 26 inches. The heads themselves (B) must have a diameter of 17⅛ inches. Critically, though, the circumference of the bulge (C) must be 64 inches. Cranberry barrels can have a smaller bulge, of just 58½ inches.

Selling an undersized barrel of fruit or vegetables is punishable by a fine of up to $500 and imprisonment of up to six months. Importantly, the criminal penalty applies only if a barrel actually has too small a capacity. Noncompliant bulge size alone probably isn't a crime, but small bulges are likely to catch the government's eye.

Sell Runny Ketchup

Amazingly, putting ketchup on a hot dog is still completely legal in America. Neither Congress nor the FDA has yet mustered up the courage to outlaw that obscene practice once and for all.

Fig. 4-11. A Travesty.

For those of us refined enough to know when and where to use ketchup properly, there is some good news: federal regulations classify ketchup as a vegetable. That makes it a lot easier to justify a pile of french fries as a healthy choice.

Although federal law may not regulate the appropriate uses of ketchup, it does regulate its consistency. Specifically, 21 C.F.R. § 155.194 provides that ketchup may not flow at a rate faster than 14 centimeters in 30 seconds at 20°C, as measured by a "Bostwick Consistometer." (See Fig. 4-12.) Any faster and it fails to meet the standard of identity for ketchup, making it a misbranded food under 21 U.S.C. § 343(h). Thus, while you may break your hand trying to get it out of the bottle, at least you can know your thick ketchup is legal.

For the offender who respects precision, federal law provides a detailed road map for measuring and perfecting the ideal level of ketchup runniness.

THE FEDERAL KETCHUP-TESTING PROTOCOL

The federal government's ketchup-testing protocol requires ketchup, a stopwatch, and a Bostwick consistometer. Note, however, that

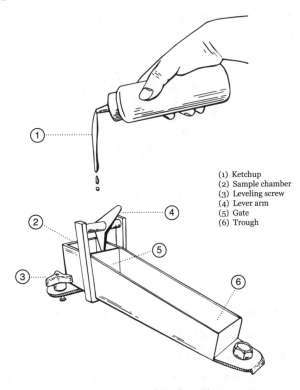

(1) Ketchup
(2) Sample chamber
(3) Leveling screw
(4) Lever arm
(5) Gate
(6) Trough

Fig. 4-12. Bostwick Consistometer.

the consistometer will probably set you back a few hundred dollars from a scientific supply company. Ketchup testing begins by filling the sample chamber "slightly more than level full, avoiding air bubbles as far as possible." Regulations instruct that any excess ketchup is to be scraped off with a straight edge.

Next comes the truly suspenseful part. The ketchup protocol instructs to release the gate of the consistometer by applying "gradual pressure on [the] lever, holding the instrument down at the same time to prevent its movement as the gate is released." (See Fig. 4-13.) Like a guillotine in reverse, the gate lifts up and ketchup starts to flow down the trough. When it does, it's imperative to "[i]mmediately start the stop watch or interval timer, and after 30 seconds read the maximum distance of flow to the nearest 0.1 centimeter." (See Fig. 4-14.)

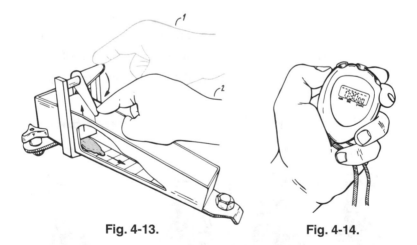

Fig. 4-13.   **Fig. 4-14.**

If the ketchup travels more than 14 centimeters, it's now potentially criminal ketchup. The only way to sell it legally is to conspicuously label it as "substandard" ketchup, with that warning appearing inside a rectangle and written in a twelve-point font (a fourteen-point font is required for batches of runny ketchup weighing more than a pound).

FEDERALLY COMPLIANT KETCHUP SPELLINGS

Federal law also specifies the ways that "ketchup" may be spelled on the bottle. Subsection (a)(3)(i) of the federal ketchup regulation allows for just three permissible spellings:

- Ketchup;
- Catsup; and
- Catchup.

That means federal prosecutors are powerless against the kind of monster who would spell it "catchup." Congress must act.

Thankfully, other spellings are not permitted. (See Fig. 4-15.) Under 21 U.S.C. § 343(g), foods are considered misbranded unless they bear the name specified in the standard. Section 343(i)(1) similarly provides that a food is misbranded "unless its label bears . . .

Fig. 4-15.

the common or usual name of the food, if any there be . . ." Thus, if you want to sell ketchup in America, you have just four choices: ketchup, catsup, catchup, or federal prison.

Sell Canned Pineapple with the Wrong Dimensions

Many provisions in the Code of Federal Regulations are the product of years of input from the scientific community. Some of the brightest minds in history have contributed to our health and safety by ensuring measurements, tolerances, and other critical specifications for things like medical devices, bicycle helmets, and children's toys.

Then there's Title 21, Section 145.180(b), which valiantly protects us from canned pineapple slices with outside arcs that are too short.

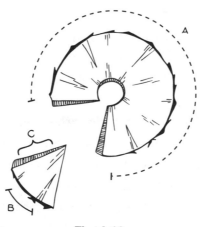

Fig. 4-16.

The federal canned pineapple regulation demands that a can of broken pineapple slices have no more than 10 percent of the drained weight made up of pieces with an arc of less than 90 degrees. And it doesn't stop there. Canned pineapple "chunks" must be predominantly more than 13 millimeters in thickness and width, pineapple "tidbits" are to be wedge-shaped sectors between 8 and 13 millimeters thick, and "fingers" have to be longer than 65 millimeters with no maximum dimension specified.

The regulation does allow canned pineapple to be sold in a style called "irregular pieces," but it can't include pineapple chunks. Perhaps most impressive is that the federal government sets its pineapple standards in the metric system.

As far as offenses go, selling out-of-spec canned pineapple in interstate commerce is fairly straightforward. With some pineapples, a few cans, a protractor, and a knife, an offender can easily churn out arc after 89-degree arc and sell them as "broken slices." That's enough for a misdemeanor under 21 U.S.C. § 333(a)(1).

FRUIT COCKTAIL

Canned pineapple also shows up in other regulated fruit products. The most famous is probably canned fruit cocktail. Under the federal fruit cocktail regulation, pineapples are allowed to make up between 6 percent and 16 percent of a can. They must, however, meet a different set of measurements than when sold on their own. No more than 20 percent of pineapple sectors can have an outside arc of more than three-fourths of an inch or less than three-eighths of an inch. (See Fig. 4-16[B].) No more than 20 percent of diced pineapples can be bigger than three-fourths of an inch in any dimension.

The most egregious federal crime that can be committed in a can of fruit cocktail, however, has absolutely nothing to do with pineapples. 21 C.F.R. § 145.135(a)(2)(v) requires fruit cocktail to contain at least 2 percent cherries. Any less and the can becomes a misbranded food item—that is, unless the cocktailer discloses on the label that the food is substandard fruit cocktail.

Regulation Facts

21 C.F.R. § 145.135

Amount Per Can

Peaches	**30–50%**
Pears	**25–45%**
Pineapples	**6–16%**
Grapes	**6–20%**
Cherries	**2–6%**

"Canned fruit cocktail, canned cocktail fruits, canned fruits for cocktail, is prepared from this mixture of fresh, frozen, or previously canned fruit ingredients of mature fruits."

Fig. 4-17.

Because the thought of under-cherried fruit cocktail is heart-breaking (think of the kids), this handbook won't go into any greater detail about it. It's fair to say, however, that there probably are cherry misers out there who are heartless enough to make it happen.

FOOD DEFECT ACTION LEVELS

The FDA is tasked with the awesome responsibility of keeping America's food supply safe. But eating a few bugs here and a little feces there never hurt anyone, right? At least, that's the FDA's position. In the agency's words, it's "economically impractical to grow, harvest, or process raw products that are totally free of nonhazardous, naturally occurring, unavoidable defects." By "unavoidable defects," though, the FDA means mold, bugs, rat hair, mammal feces, and parasites, among other things.

But relax, they're nonhazardous. Okay?

The FDA publishes a list of "defect action levels," which establishes just how much filth the FDA will let slide in raw food

Fig. 4-18.

products.[15] For example, canned or frozen asparagus can contain an average of forty thrips per 100 grams of asparagus before the FDA will consider it adulterated. What's a thrip? Just a tiny winged insect that you can apparently eat a ton of without noticing.

To put that into perspective, a typical can of asparagus contains around 500 grams of asparagus. Thus, a single can could have an acceptable allowance of around two hundred thrips. Although forty thrips may seem like a lot, it's that forty-first thrip per 100-gram sample where the FDA loses its patience. That's when it can become an adulterated food product and selling it becomes a federal crime.

Other examples of foods with high thrip tolerances are brussels sprouts, broccoli, and sauerkraut. If you've been looking for an excuse not to eat any of these, you're welcome. But thrips aren't the only bugs that are allowed in your food, nor are they the only kind of filth that federal regulations permit.

Bay Leaves

Aside from being an occasional surprise leaf-in-the-mouth during an otherwise enjoyable meal, bay leaves can have up to 1 milligram of mammal excreta (feces) per pound after processing.

Fig. 4-19.

Spinach

Canned or frozen spinach has its own surprises. Every 24 pounds of it can have a total of 12 millimeters of caterpillar. Thus, three 2-millimeter caterpillars are okay, but two 7-millimeter caterpillars are a little too much.

Fig. 4-20.

Cornmeal

Cornmeal is a real grab bag. The FDA wants it to have less than one whole insect per 50 grams, twenty-five insect fragments per 25 grams, and one rodent hair per 25 grams *or* one piece of rodent excrement per 50 grams.

Fig. 4-21.

These are just a few examples of the bugs, hair, and poop allowed in your food.

Fig. 4-22. Other Important Filth Limits

Peanut Butter – 1 rodent hair per 100 milligrams

Apple Butter – 4 or more rodent hairs per 100 milligrams

Cocoa Beans – 10 milligrams of mammal excrement per pound

Fig Paste – 13 or more insect heads per 100 grams

Ground Paprika – more than 75 insect fragments per 25 grams

Maraschino Cherries – 5 percent or more pieces are rejects due to maggots

Ginger – more than 3 milligrams of mammal excrement per pound

---

FEDERAL CHEESE LAW

According to government cheese statistics, Americans eat more than 35 pounds of cheese per person every year. That figure is up almost 10 pounds per person since 1995.[16] Needless to say, cheese is big business, and the government knows it. It's no surprise, then, that cheese is heavily regulated. There are federally prescribed standards of identity for more than fifty varieties and forms of cheese, from Asiago to Swiss.

Cheese is also one food product over which both the FDA and the USDA have oversight. When it comes to pasteurized process cheese, for example, the FDA takes a hard-nosed approach. Its standard of identity demands that the cheese not be too moist, that its fat content be just right, and that it be labeled properly when sold. Failure to comply, of course, renders the cheese misbranded and makes the cheesemaker a potential criminal.

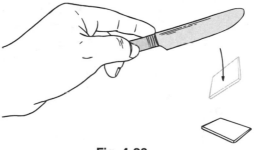

Fig. 4-23.

The USDA takes a slightly more elegant approach. It wants pasteurized process cheese to have a "pleasing and desirable taste." It shouldn't stick to the knife when cut into slices. (See Fig. 4-23.) And it should be "resilient and not tough, brittle, short, weak or sticky." It's okay if a cheese can't meet this standard. Many people can't. It's only when a cheesemaker falsely puts a USDA certification on their cheese product that they will be criminally liable under 7 U.S.C. § 1622. Otherwise, the cheese just has to live knowing it will never earn the coveted USDA badge of approval.

Sell Swiss Cheese Without Holes

Everyone knows that Swiss cheese is defined by its signature holes. What some may not know is that those holes are actually called "eyes" and that Swiss cheese without eyes is considered "blind."

Federal law places strict limits on when blind cheese can be sold without facing criminal charges. The FDA requires that Swiss cheese must have eyes and they must be "developed throughout the cheese," unless the cheese is being used for manufacturing purposes. And that makes some sense, because unevenly dispersed holes can make the cheesiness of a sandwich vary wildly from bite to bite.

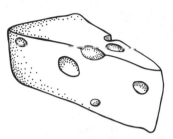

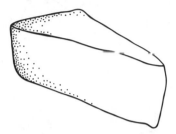

Fig. 4-24. Legal Swiss.   **Fig. 4-25. Criminal Swiss.**

The FDA isn't alone, though. The USDA is also concerned about blind cheese. If a cheesemaker wants to earn a coveted USDA rating of B or higher, his Swiss needs "well-developed round or slightly oval-shaped eyes which are relatively uniform in size and distribution" and the majority must be three-eighths to thirteen-sixteenths inch in diameter. For a USDA rating of C, eyes may be "collapsed," "irregular," "dull," "frog mouth," "uneven," "gassy," or "dead eyes," to name a few.[17] To be clear, these terms refer to the cheese, not the cheesemaker. The law permits cheesemakers to have dead eyes no matter what kind of cheese they are selling.

Sell Grated Cream Cheese

Grated cheese is "the class of foods prepared by grinding, grating, shredding, or otherwise comminuting [chopping up] cheese of one variety or a mixture of two or more varieties." However, 21 C.F.R. § 133.146(a) is clear that "cream cheese, neufchatel cheese, cottage cheese, creamed cottage cheese, cook cheese, and skim milk cheese for manufacturing *may not* be used" (emphasis added) to make grated cheese.

Fig. 4-26. Criminal Swiss

DON'T ADD HOLES

If beginning with a wedge of already-blind cheese, the cheese criminal must resist the urge to add holes manually. Keeping the cheese blind is essential to criminal liability.

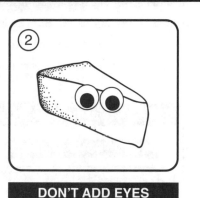

DON'T ADD EYES

Remember: "blind" cheese refers to the lack of naturally occurring holes, or "eyes," in the cheese. Adding other kinds of eyes to the cheese has no legal significance and isn't a defense.

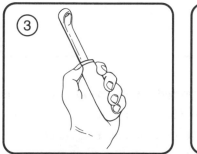

PLUG ANY EXISTING HOLES

If beginning with a wedge of cheese that already has holes, cheese offenders may attempt to plug them with appropriately sized cheese plugs. Using an apple corer is one way to make cheese plugs quickly and uniformly.

To be fair, this is actually pretty good advice nestled within a federal regulation. Grating cream cheese is a frustrating and mostly futile endeavor. But the law is the law: introducing a product called "grated cheese" into interstate commerce is a federal crime if it's made from cream cheese.

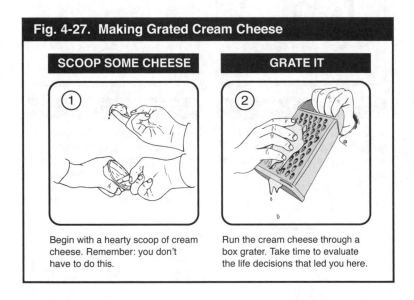

Fig. 4-27. Making Grated Cream Cheese

SCOOP SOME CHEESE

① Begin with a hearty scoop of cream cheese. Remember: you don't have to do this.

GRATE IT

② Run the cream cheese through a box grater. Take time to evaluate the life decisions that led you here.

Predictably, there are no reported cases of people being prosecuted for selling grated cream cheese. After all, it's punishment enough to have to clean a cheese grater full of cream cheese.

MEAT CRIMES

Ordering a steak well done, boiling a hot dog, and bologna just in general are all shockingly legal. At the same time, there are plenty of meat-related acts that are not only prohibited by law but that carry criminal penalties.

One of the very first comprehensive food laws passed by Congress was the Meat Inspection Act of 1906. It was enacted, at least in part, as a response to Upton Sinclair's novel *The Jungle*, which had just been published and turned stomachs everywhere.[18] In it, Sinclair purported to detail the less appetizing aspects of the early 1900s meat industry, including unsanitary conditions, sneaky methods for passing off rancid meat as fresh, and the stomach-turning secret recipes for popular canned meat products like deviled ham— or "de-vyled ham," as the meatpackers supposedly called it.

According to Sinclair, deviled ham was "made out of the waste ends of smoked beef that were too small to be sliced by the machines; and also tripe, dyed with chemicals so that it would not show white; and trimmings of hams and corned beef; and potatoes, skins and all; and finally the hard cartilaginous gullets of beef after the tongues had been cut out." It was then "ground up and flavored with spices to make it taste like something." And then there was "potted meat," which was made from pretty much anything that could be shoveled off the slaughterhouse floor.

By thoroughly nauseating America, Sinclair had hoped to shine a light on the evils of capitalism and spur a socialist revolt. What we got instead was the USDA and hundreds of meat regulations. But if Sinclair was hoping to end mystery meat products, he would be disappointed with our progress. Today, 9 C.F.R. § 319.760 requires deviled ham to be only slightly more appealing than he described it in *The Jungle*. It must be "a semiplastic cured meat food product made from finely comminuted ham and containing condiments." Federal regulations also ban the use of certain fillers in "potted meats," prevent overly moist "ham spreads," and outlaw America's worst nightmare: cheesefurters without enough cheese.

A meat product that doesn't conform to these regulations will be considered misbranded under 21 U.S.C. § 601(n)(7), and selling or transporting it "in commerce" is prohibited by 21 U.S.C. §

610(c). Under 21 U.S.C. § 676, selling prohibited meat is punishable by fines, imprisonment, or both.

The law also prohibits the sale of adulterated meat, including meat that has been made to look better than it is by adding certain ingredients. In *The Jungle*, Sinclair described the use of soda and chemicals to conceal the stench and color of rotten meat. Federal law now prohibits using paprika "in or on fresh meat, such as steaks, or comminuted fresh meat, such as chopped and formed steaks or patties; or in any other meat consisting of fresh meat (with or without seasoning)."[19] Even a sprinkle of the red stuff can make dull brown meat really pop, but also may result in criminal exposure.

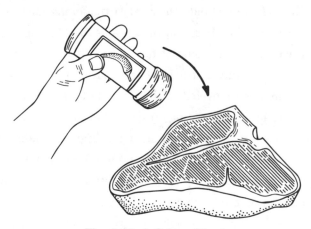

Fig. 4-28. A Crime Steak.

Of course, there are always exceptions. If the use of paprika is expected—as in chorizo, Italian sausage, or barbecued chicken— there is no prohibition on its use. Also, consumers are free to put paprika on steaks in the privacy of their own homes, because the prohibitions apply only to those selling or transporting meat in commerce. To become a federal criminal, a person has to put paprika on fresh meat (see Fig. 4-28) and sell or transport it in commerce.

Despite all these regulations, some completely legal meat products still sound oddly similar to the ones described in the very book that spurred the Meat Inspection Act. Links of head-cheese, scrapple, and a product called "turkey ham," for example, are all still legal as long as they comply with federal standards of identity. Here are a few examples:

TRIPE WITH MILK

According to 9 C.F.R. § 319.308, "tripe with milk" is a thing. It comes in a can. It has to be at least 65 percent tripe and not less than 10 percent milk. If you're doing the math, that leaves 25 percent of the product unaccounted for. But don't let that bother you. Focus instead on the 65 percent you already know is tripe.

HOT DOGS

It is often said that hot dogs are bad for you and you never really know what is in them. That's not entirely true. If you buy hot dogs compliant with 9 C.F.R. § 319.180(a), at least you can know they don't contain the sex glands of a chicken or other poultry. Prior to the rule, however, it's safe to assume some hot dogs totally did.

SPAGHETTI WITH MEATBALLS

Title 9, Section 319.306, of the C.F.R. requires that any product sold as "Spaghetti with Meatballs and Sauce," "Spaghetti with Meat and Sauce," or a similar name shall contain not less than 12 percent meat based on the weight of the fresh meat. "Spaghetti Sauce with Meat" is covered by a different section and has to be at least 6 percent meat. To recap, "Spaghetti with Meatballs and Sauce" and "Spaghetti with Meat and Sauce" are one thing, but "Spaghetti Sauce with Meat" is a totally different thing.

TURKEY HAM

"Turkey ham" is a meat product with a definition that reads like a menu at a fine restaurant: it is "fabricated from boneless, turkey thigh meat with skin and the surface fat attached to the skin removed."[20] If it's fabricated from meat cubes equal to or larger than one-half inch by one-half inch, then the turkey ham is legally required to be labeled "Chunked and Formed." (See Fig. 4-29.) Under no circumstances, however, may "turkey ham" contain ham. Is your mouth watering yet?

The federal turkey ham regulation also provides that "the product name on the label shall show the word 'Turkey' in the same size, style, color, and with the same background as the word 'Ham' and shall precede and be adjacent to it. Thus, using different fonts for the words "turkey" and "ham" may be enough to be found guilty of selling misbranded meat products. (See Fig. 4-29.) Likewise, because of the requirement that the word "turkey" precede the word "ham," selling "turkey ham" as "ham turkey" is probably also a crime.

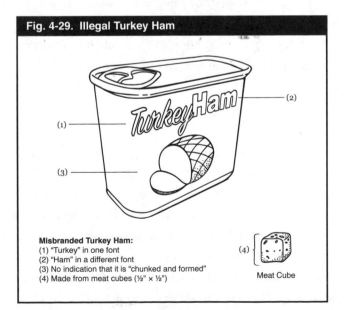

Fig. 4-29. Illegal Turkey Ham

(1)
(2)
(3)
(4)

Meat Cube

Misbranded Turkey Ham:
(1) "Turkey" in one font
(2) "Ham" in a different font
(3) No indication that it is "chunked and formed"
(4) Made from meat cubes (½" × ½")

Sell Pork from a Pig with a Pronounced Sexual Odor

American Meat producers are required to condemn any swine carcass that gives off a "pronounced sexual odor." In the meat business, that means no part of an affected pig carcass can be sold as food.

You're probably wondering what a sexual pig odor smells like. Or maybe you'd really rather not know. Either way, being able to detect a sexual odor is an important skill whether you're committing this crime or just going through life in general.

The sexual odor, better known as "boar taint," is caused by two chemicals, androstenone and skatole, and it's most common in older uncastrated male pigs. Aside from being a great metal band name, boar taint is said to smell like a mix of sweat, urine, and feces. Again, not unlike a metal band.

Some studies suggest that between 7.6 and 75 percent of pork consumers are unable to detect boar taint.[21] If true, that means as much as three-quarters of people could be eating sexual pork without knowing it. Scientists have tested several methods for

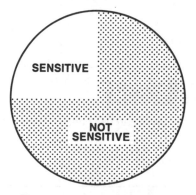

Fig. 4-30. Taint Sensitivity.

Fig. 4-31. Identifying Criminally Sexual Pork

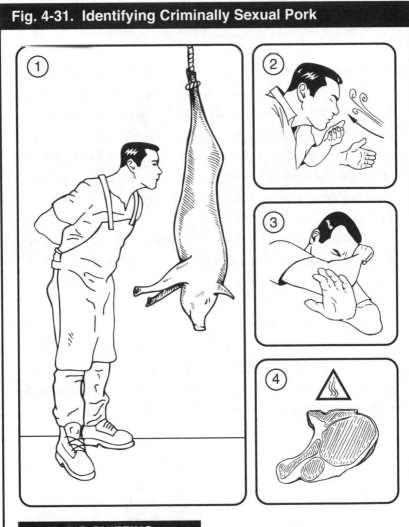

PIG SNIFFING

1. Identify a sniffable swine carcass (ideally uncastrated).
2. Gently waft the odor into your nostrils.
3. Avoid being overcome by particularly pronounced sexual odors.
4. Remember: even a moderately sexual pork chop is illegal to sell.

reliably detecting boar taint, including an electronic nose, lab tests, and even trained wasps. (Oh, by the way, you can train wasps.) Still, the most widely used method is the good old-fashioned human nose test.

Although 9 C.F.R. § 311.20 requires all pig carcasses with a *pronounced* sexual odor to be discarded, there is one important proviso. If the odor is "less than pronounced," then it's totally okay to chop the meat up, cook it, and sell it in a "comminuted cooked meat food product" or send it off to be rendered. Unfortunately, the law provides no guidance on when an odor is considered "pronounced" or "less than pronounced."

Even with a trained nose, however, boar taint is notoriously difficult to detect when meat is cold. To get the full effect, try to sniff only warm carcasses.

Sell a Dirty Egg

Title 21, Section 1033(g)(3), of the United States Code, also known as the Egg Products Inspection Act, defines a "dirty egg" as "an egg that has a shell that is unbroken and has adhering dirt or foreign

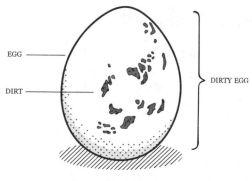

Fig. 4-32. A Dirty Egg.

material." In other words, Congress took great care to make clear that a "dirty egg" is an egg that is dirty. Laypeople may know it simply as an egg with dirt on it. In the business, though, they're known as "dirties."

For those who may still be confused by this sophisticated legal terminology, consult the following diagram in Fig. 4-32. If you're still confused after that, you probably can't be helped.

Federal egg law prohibits selling, buying, or transporting any "restricted egg," which includes dirty eggs. Violations are punishable

Fig. 4-33. Dirty Eggs

① APPLY DIRT

② ENSURE IT STICKS

NOTE: Gluing dirt to an egg isn't just the start of a federal crime, it's also a terrible arts and crafts project.

by a sentence of up to a year in prison. If, however, the offender commits egg fraud—perhaps by selling a bunch of dirties, claiming they're clean—the law authorizes an enhanced sentence of up to three years.

The crime of selling or transporting a dirty egg requires only two things: an egg and some dirt.

But dirties aren't the only kind of "restricted egg" that can give rise to criminal liability, either. Federal law also prohibits selling or transporting "checks," "incubator rejects," "inedibles," "leakers," and "losses."

In addition to selling and transporting restricted eggs, the Egg Products Inspection Act also makes criminal penalties available for other egg-related conduct.

ILLICIT EGG PLANTS

Egg plants (not to be confused with eggplants) are operations fraught with peril. Egg plant operators can get locked up if their facilities don't meet certain standards. For example, under 9 C.F.R. § 590.500, operators must take "every precaution" to exclude dogs, cats, and vermin. And while the vermin thing makes sense, it's not totally clear if egg plants used to have a problem with cats and dogs wandering in unannounced. Under the same section, egg plants must also be free of objectionable odors. Full compliance with the law may therefore mean some awkward conversations with certain employees. (You know who you are.)

UNCLEAN EGG HANDLERS

Egg handlers have their own strict set of rules. To be clear, "egg handler" isn't an insult; it's a technical term that refers to any

Fig. 4-34. Restricted Eggs

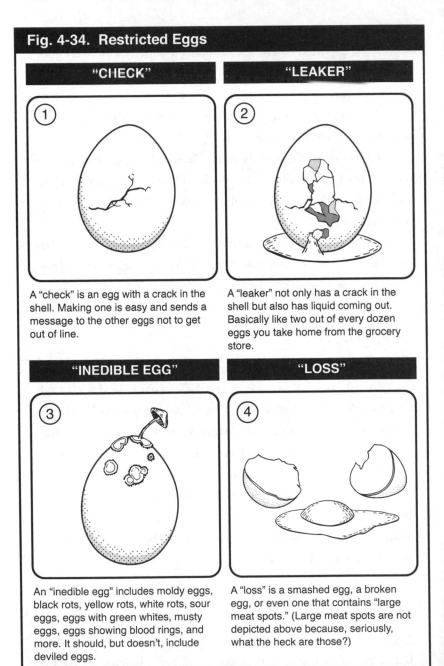

"CHECK"

① A "check" is an egg with a crack in the shell. Making one is easy and sends a message to the other eggs not to get out of line.

"LEAKER"

② A "leaker" not only has a crack in the shell but also has liquid coming out. Basically like two out of every dozen eggs you take home from the grocery store.

"INEDIBLE EGG"

③ An "inedible egg" includes moldy eggs, black rots, yellow rots, white rots, sour eggs, eggs with green whites, musty eggs, eggs showing blood rings, and more. It should, but doesn't, include deviled eggs.

"LOSS"

④ A "loss" is a smashed egg, a broken egg, or even one that contains "large meat spots." (Large meat spots are not depicted above because, seriously, what the heck are those?)

person who "engages in any business in commerce which involves buying or selling any eggs (as a poultry producer or otherwise), or processing any egg products, or otherwise using any eggs in the preparation of human food."

Under 9 C.F.R. § 590.560(c), egg handlers may not handle eggs if they have boils, sores, or infected wounds, or are wearing cloth bandages on their hands. Under subsection (g), they also aren't allowed to smoke or wear nail polish, jewelry, or perfume while handling eggs. It's not clear, but it certainly seems like the rule's author had a particular lunch lady in mind.

EGG-RELATED MURDERS

In drafting the Egg Products Inspection Act, lawmakers also foresaw a darker side to the egg business. 21 U.S.C. § 1041(b) extends the federal murder statute to America's egg inspectors, a law usually reserved for murders taking place at sea or in U.S. territories. In addition to killings, forcibly assaulting, interfering, or intimidating a federal egg inspector are also prohibited. Apparently, egg inspections can take quite a turn.

Sell Oversized (or Undersized) Noodles

America's love of carbohydrates is well documented. We consume pasta products at an average rate of almost 20 pounds per person, per year. Although this pales in comparison to Italy's per capita pasta consumption of more than 50 pounds per person annually, our country's noodle consumption steadily increases each year.[22] It has given us the Atkins diet, Olive Garden, and, of course, federal noodle law.

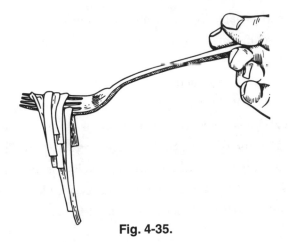

Fig. 4-35.

Title 21, Part 139, of the Code of Federal Regulations governs the manufacture and sale of macaroni products in general, and it sets rigid standards for the specifications of certain noodles in particular.

The FDA defines macaroni products as "the class of food each of which is prepared by drying formed units of dough made from semolina, durum flour, farina, flour, or any combination of two or

Fig. 4-36. Federal Noodle Specifications

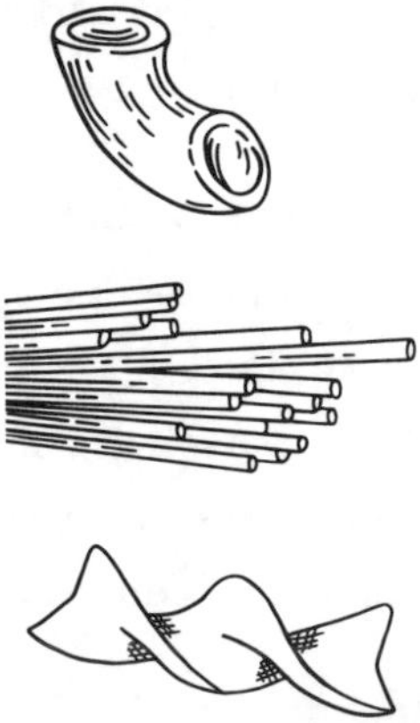

Macaroni
Must be tube-shaped.
Diameter is between 0.11 inch and 0.27 inch.

Spaghetti
Must be tube-shaped or cord-shaped.
Diameter is between 0.06 inch and 0.11 inch.

Vermicelli
Must be cord-shaped (not tubular).
Diameter is less than 0.06 inch.

Egg Noodles
Must be ribbon-shaped.
No federal size requirements.

more of these." And while there are hundreds of different pasta shapes, there are just three macaroni products with federally mandated shapes and dimensions: "macaroni," "spaghetti," and "vermicelli."

By contrast, federal law is woefully silent on countless other species of pasta. How many twists must a rotini have? Whose ears must orecchiette look like? Spaghettini, ziti, and even dinosaur pasta (pasta shaped like dinosaurs) are all wildly unregulated. Alphabet pasta can presumably be in any font, and there are no federal limits on the maximum diameter of a manicotti. Thus, a federal pasta conviction is unlikely for a person who unscrupulously sells wagon wheel pasta with five spokes instead of the traditional six.

Sell a Noncompliant Nut Mix

The federal rule governing "mixed nuts" isn't as concerned with nut size as it is nut variety. To avoid being misbranded, 21 C.F.R. § 164.110 requires a standard container of mixed nuts to contain at least four different kinds of nuts. The government will only tolerate a three-nut mix when the nuts are being sold in transparent containers of two ounces or less.

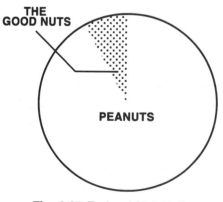

Fig. 4-37. Federal Nut Ratios.

The nuts eligible for inclusion in "mixed nuts" are almonds, black walnuts, Brazil nuts, cashews, English walnuts, filberts, pecans, and other tree nuts. And while peanuts may also be included, they do not count toward the mandatory three-nut or four-nut minimums.

MINIMUM NUT PROPORTIONS

Each tree nut ingredient need only make up 2 percent of the total nut weight. Applying the standard four-nut minimum, that means just 8 percent of the jar needs to be made up of good nuts, leaving a 92 percent allowance for peanuts.

This will come as no surprise to anyone who has purchased a container of these so-called mixed nuts based on the promising bounty of nuts shown on the label. In the future, pay close attention: there are rules for those nut lineup shots too.

Fig. 4-38.

MISLEADING NUT PICTURES

If a container of mixed nuts shows a pictorial representation of the mixture of nuts inside, it must accurately depict the relative proportions of the different nut varieties. If the label depicts only one of each kind of nut, the nuts must be shown in decreasing order of their predominance by weight.

For example, if a container were to depict a nut lineup like the one shown in Fig. 4-38, it would almost certainly be considered misbranded, because everyone knows that there is no way any jar of mixed nuts is ever going to be predominantly cashews.

And if there is one area where all Americans can agree there have been too few prosecutions, it's under-cashewing.

FEDERAL NUT FAQS

What's the minimum amount of cashews allowed in a jar of mixed nuts?
   There is no federal requirement that cashews be included, but if they are, the 2-percent minimum by weight applies. That's about ten cashews per 10-ounce jar.

Can I be indicted for picking all the cashews out of the jar, thereby making the jar of nuts noncompliant with the law?
   No. This federal crime can only be committed by introducing misbranded mixed nuts into interstate commerce or delivering them for introduction into interstate commerce. But that is a rude thing to do.

What the heck is a filbert?
   A hazelnut.

Then why didn't they just say that?
   I don't know.

Can I ask another question?
   Yes, unless it's about the hazelnut/filbert thing again.

I don't have any more questions.
   I knew it.

Chapter 5

HOW TO BECOME A FEDERAL CRIMINAL

WITH
ALCOHOL

A great American once declared that alcohol is "the cause of, and solution to, all of life's problems."[1] The federal government, on the other hand, has generally viewed more laws as the only real solution to all of life's problems. But even a quick read of some of the statutes they've passed makes one wonder if Congress has occasionally been trying both solutions at the same time.

This chapter discusses America's tumultuous love affair with alcohol, the messy breakup in the early 1900s, and the sweet, sweet reconciliation of the 1930s. It shows how a few fermented grapes or a little bit of malted grain, heat, and patience can yield something so delicious, intoxicating, and potentially criminal.

PROHIBITION, MOONSHINE, AND THE IRS

If there's one thing to be learned from our country's history with alcohol, it's that the only thing powerful enough to repeal a constitutional amendment is the American desire to get drunk.

From 1920 to 1933, the Eighteenth Amendment to the Constitution prohibited making, selling, or transporting liquor in the United States. Congress passed the Volstead Act to implement the constitutional ban on alcohol, making all sorts of liquor offenses into federal crimes—things like letting someone use your car to deliver moonshine.

During the thirteen years of Prohibition, however, evidence suggests that crime and corruption increased, liquor was made more dangerous by moonshiners, and any decrease in alcoholism was fleeting at best. In a major "we meant to do that" moment during the midst of Prohibition, President Hoover famously wrote: "Our country has deliberately undertaken a great social and economic experiment, noble in motive and far-reaching in purpose." The noble experiment was scuttled a few years later by the Twenty-first Amendment, which repealed the Eighteenth and Prohibition with it.

For the aspiring federal offender, Prohibition's lasting gifts are the countless criminally enforceable federal liquor laws that remain on the books or were passed in its wake. These laws make it a crime to do things like distill spirits without a permit, say something obscene on a beer bottle label, or build a secret pipeline of tax-free wine.

Of course, most of these laws aren't really designed to protect Americans from the ravages of alcohol at all. They're after something the government needs to feed its own bad habits: tax revenue.

For example, 26 U.S.C. §§ 5674 and 5053(e) make it a crime for a single person to brew more than one hundred gallons of tax-free beer for personal consumption in any given year. The limit is two hundred gallons for a household with two adults. The good news is that the law doesn't require cohabiting adults to marry before benefiting from the two-hundred-gallon limit. The bad news is that you don't get any increase in the beer limit when you have kids, no matter how badly you might need it.

The amount of tax-free beer that a person can legally brew at home with their roommates (platonic or romantic) is roughly five times the average annual per capita beer consumption in America. To visualize how much beer you'd need to brew to even be eligible for prosecution, Figs. 5-1 and 5-2 use a standard fifty-five gallon drum for scale.

>100 GAL.

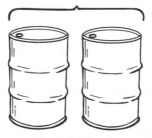

Fig. 5-1. Single.

>200 GAL.

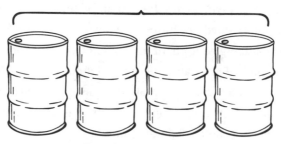

Fig. 5-2. Cohabitating.

These same limits apply to homemade wine. But as explained in the following section, federal liquor law isn't so permissive when it comes to distilled spirits.

Make Moonshine on a Boat

Long before Prohibition was even an idea, the commissioner of internal revenue told his tax enforcement agents that liquor was the government's "most important source of revenue." So, in 1879, the official *Internal Revenue Manual* instructed agents to surveil distilleries, to show up at random times of the night and day, and to prioritize surprise inspection visits over other duties.[2]

Lucky for those tax agents, the first comprehensive set of federal statutes published by Congress in 1874 had already given them the tools they needed to stop the worst kind of liquor offenses. They were authorized to break down the doors of distilleries, conduct nighttime stakeouts, and follow distillery customers home to see where the liquor was going. But those early federal liquor laws obviously would have been completely inadequate without Revised Statute § 3266, which made it a federal crime for anyone to make booze on a boat.

More than 140 years later, federal law still explicitly makes it a crime to distill liquor on a boat. Under Title 26, Section 5601(a)(6), of the U.S. Code, anyone who does "shall be fined not more than $10,000, or imprisoned not more than 5 years, or both." Even just possessing distilling equipment on a boat is a crime if you intend to use it to make liquor at some point. Of course, if you're on a boat with a still and you're not making liquor, you're basically just floating around with a big copper pot, which is an amazingly depressing way to become a federal criminal.

Fig. 5-3. Nautical Moonshinin'

① **GET A STILL**

② **PUT IT IN A BOAT**

To distill liquor, the offender will also need water, mash, and a heat source to operate the still. A fire extinguisher may also come in handy when the still, which operates at around 200°F, inevitably causes a boat fire.

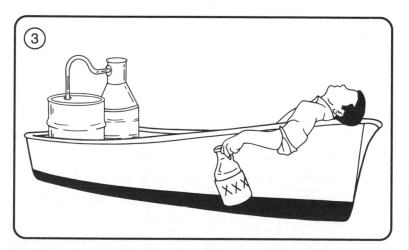

NOTE: The law doesn't explicitly require the boat to be in the water. For those offenders prone to motion sickness, distilling liquor in an old rowboat or canoe sitting in the backyard may be sufficient for criminal liability.

TRY A SHED INSTEAD

For boatless offenders, the law provides some alternatives. It's a crime to distill liquor on any other "prohibited premises," including a house, a shed, a yard, or any "inclosure" connected with a house. That means your humble toolshed and backyard are off-limits for distilling spirits. And, not that any self-respecting person would own one, but even a gazebo is arguably an "inclosure" within the meaning of the statute, making it a crime to manufacture boatshine, houseshine, shedshine, yardshine, or gazeboshine.

In reality, though, it's a federal crime for pretty much anyone in the United States to make their own beverage spirits no matter where they do it. Section 5601(a)(1) makes it a crime to possess a functional distilling apparatus (see Fig. 5-4) if it's not registered with the government. More broadly, subsection (a)(8) makes it a crime for anyone except a legally authorized distiller to produce spirits. And under 26 U.S.C. § 5686 a person can be charged for possessing bootleg spirits, part of a still, or any other "property" that the government thinks is going to be used to violate federal liquor law—including things you may have in your home right now.

POSSESSION WITH INTENT TO USE . . . SUGAR

Of all the white powdery substances that can get a person indicted, sugar is one that's both completely legal to buy and potentially criminal to possess. Whether you go to prison for sugar possession depends on whether the feds think you are a moonshiner.

In 1975 a man and woman in Georgia were indicted after ATF agents caught them driving around with a half ton of sugar in their car. Apparently the couple had spent the afternoon buying bulk sugar from at least seven different stores. When ATF searched the vehicle, they found approximately 1,035 pounds of

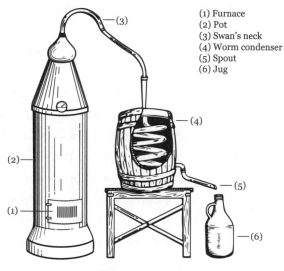

(1) Furnace
(2) Pot
(3) Swan's neck
(4) Worm condenser
(5) Spout
(6) Jug

Fig. 5-4. A Still.

sugar "in variously sized bags and bales in the trunk and on the back seat and front floorboard of the car."[3]

Even though there was no evidence the sugar was going to be used for nefarious purposes, the government believed the couple intended to use the sugar to make moonshine. If true, that would be a violation of 26 U.S.C. § 5686, punishable by up to a year in prison. But without any evidence that this particular half ton of sugar was destined to be distilled, the government would have to prove its case by other means. So what's a prosecutor to do when there isn't evidence that a crime has been committed, you might ask? Rely on improper evidence, of course.

For that, the prosecutors offered evidence that the man driving the car had been convicted of violating federal liquor laws on five earlier occasions, including for possession and transportation of bootleg whiskey. Put another way, the government argued that one of the defendants was the kind of guy who made illegal booze, so the defendants' sugar possession must have been criminal.

In closing arguments, the defense noted that the defendants had been arrested in the midst of a national sugar shortage, when prices were rising rapidly, grocery stores were rationing out sugar to customers, and people everywhere were hoarding it for use in canning. But having already heard the stuff about earlier convictions, the jury returned a guilty verdict for both defendants.

The defendants appealed their sugar convictions. They argued that the trial court had improperly allowed evidence of the driver's criminal record to be presented at trial and that there was insufficient admissible evidence to convict them on criminal sugar charges. The court of appeals agreed, pointing out that the defendants had been convicted of "an offense consisting of an essentially innocent act, the possession of sugar, which is converted into a criminal misdemeanor solely by their subjective intent in possessing the substance." The court reversed the convictions and instructed the trial court to dismiss the indictments.

Fig. 5-5.

Put a Smoke Screen Device on Your Car so You Can Get Away with Bootlegging

At the height of Prohibition, the November 1925 issue of *Popular Mechanics* reported that bootleggers had adapted a "weapon of war" to evade federal liquor agents. That weapon was a vehicle-mounted smoke screen device, capable of emitting "dense white clouds of vapor . . . from the rear of a speeding car, obscuring the vision of pursuers and giving the fugitives time to dart into side streets or lanes."[4]

By 1925, however, rumrunners had actually been using smoke screens for several years. But Congress started paying closer attention after one of their own was shot in the head during a shootout between rumrunners and revenue agents in the nation's capital. Senator Frank L. Greene of Vermont survived the shooting, but the rumrunners escaped in their car equipped with a smoke screen.[5]

Washington, D.C., officially had a smoke screen problem. During another incident a few years later, a police officer reportedly

suffered "near-blindness occasioned by smoke loosed from a rum car, which eluded him after a chase of many blocks." In response, a congressman from Washington proposed changing the law so that anytime police killed a rumrunner in a car with a smoke screen, it would automatically be labeled a "justifiable homicide."[6]

Congress never enacted a blanket authorization to kill rumrunners. It did, however, eventually make it a federal crime for anyone to have "in his possession or in his control any device capable of causing emission of gas, smoke, or fumes, and which may be used for the purpose of hindering, delaying, or preventing pursuit or capture" while violating federal liquor laws. The law, which remains on the books, provides for a fine of up to $5,000 or up to ten years in prison.

Several states enacted their own laws against putting smoke screen devices on vehicles as well. A South Carolina statute provides for a mandatory minimum sentence of six months for anyone caught driving with a smoke screen device, whether the device is attached to the car or not. Even having a "substantial part" of a smoke screen device in a car is enough for a conviction.[7]

Vermont, North Carolina, and Virginia also still ban vehicle-mounted smoke screen devices whether there is liquor in the car or not. In fact, in Virginia it's not only a crime to have a smoke screen device on your own car; it's a crime for any person in charge of a repair shop to not tell police if they discover a smoke screen device on a car that comes in for service.[8]

SMOKE SCREEN TECHNOLOGY

If history has taught us anything, it's that crime pays and is ultimately good for society. At least, that's true when it comes to the history of smoke screen devices, a technology perfected by a Prohibition-era rumrunner from New Orleans named Alonzo Patterson.

Patterson designed a vehicle-mounted device that would inject a mixture of mineral oil and paint pigment directly into a car's exhaust manifold at the flip of a switch. When the mixture hit the hot manifold, it would atomize instantly, releasing a notoriously effective smoke screen from the car's tailpipe.

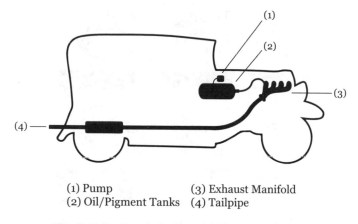

(1) Pump   (3) Exhaust Manifold
(2) Oil/Pigment Tanks   (4) Tailpipe

Fig. 5-6. Patterson's Smoke Screen Device.

Although Patterson successfully used the device to elude revenue agents for years, he later got a job with the federal government and donated the technology to the U.S. Navy, which used it to conceal troop movements during World War II. On October 1, 1946, Patterson's smoke screen device was awarded U.S. patent number 2,408,429.

DEVICES NOT EXPRESSLY PROHIBITED

When it comes to evading federal liquor agents, 26 U.S.C. § 5685(a) only prohibits devices that emit gas, smoke, or fumes. While that clearly outlaws the use of smoke screens, it dangerously underestimates the ingenuity of rumrunners.

Sure enough, in 1960 the FBI reported that a local sheriff had seized a bootlegger's car equipped with both a smoke screen sys-

tem and "a device for spraying carpet tacks in the path of a pursuing vehicle." Both devices could be activated by a switch panel
on the car's dashboard.[9] And while the smoke screen device clearly
would be prohibited by Section 5685(a), the tack sprayer would not.
So, what other evasion devices might Congress have overlooked?

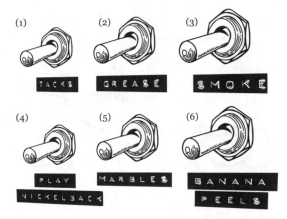

Fig. 5-7. Common Evasion Devices (Probably).

Because of its limitation to gases, smoke, or fumes, the law
doesn't address solids or liquids designed to slip up a pursing car.
(See Fig. 5-7 [1], [2], [5], and [6].) Likewise, offensive sounds used
to overwhelm a rumrunner's pursuers would also be outside the
scope of the law. (See Fig. 5-7 [4].)

Sell "Pre-War Strength" Malt Liquor

During Prohibition, Congress enacted the Volstead Act to implement the Eighteenth Amendment's nationwide ban on liquor.
When Prohibition ended, the Volstead Act was rendered void and
Congress enacted the Federal Alcohol Administration Act to replace it. The FAAA's purpose was to regulate the once-again legal
distribution of liquor in America.

Fig. 5-8.

Among its many prohibitions, the FAAA makes it illegal to distribute alcoholic beverages bottled, packaged, or labeled in violation of federal liquor regulations. One of those regulations, 27 C.F.R. § 7.29(f), prohibits malt liquor producers from labeling their bottles with enticing terms like "strong," "high-test," "full old-time alcoholic strength," and "pre-war strength." (See Fig. 5-8.) The law forces brewers to choose between complying with federal law and appealing to customers looking for a beer with that familiar "pre-war" kick. Under 27 U.S.C. § 207, such violations carry criminal penalties.

Of course, this raises some important questions. Can the government really make it a crime to call a beer "strong"? What if it actually *is* strong? Also, which war are we even talking about, anyway? After all, the text of the federal ban on "pre-war strength" beer doesn't identify any one war in particular. Could brewers become criminals for claiming their beer has pre–*Civil* War strength? What about pre–Cold War strength? *All* beer is pre–World War III strength—at least so far.

The ban was actually intended to address promises of beer with the strength it had prior to the First World War. That's when President Woodrow Wilson issued a proclamation banning the production of malt liquor containing more than 2.75 percent alcohol by weight. And although Wilson's proclamation was billed as a necessary measure to conserve grain for the war effort, it was really just one of several steps toward complete Prohibition, which came the following year.

When Prohibition was finally repealed in 1933, those dark days of weak, low-alcohol "war" beer were still fresh in the minds of Americans. Their livers yearned for a beer stronger than the measly 2.75 percent alcohol beer they had been forced to drink during World War I.

Around that same time, the bill that would ultimately become the FAAA was working its way through Congress. In its favorable report on the bill, the House Ways and Means Committee made a point of saying that selling beer on the basis of alcoholic content was nothing more than an attempt to "take advantage of the ignorance of the consumer and the psychology created by prohibition experiences." So even though the committee acknowledged the psychological trauma caused by Prohibition, it nonetheless found that

> legitimate members of the [beer] industry have suffered seriously from unfair competition resulting from labeling and advertising that uses such terms as "strong," "extra strength," "high test," "high proof," "pre-war strength," [and] "14 percent original extract" ... Usually such representations of excess alcoholic content are false, but irrespective of their falsity, their abuse has grown to such an extent since repeal that the prohibition of all such statements is in the interest of the consumer and the promotion of fair competition.

When the bill became law in 1935, its restrictions went even further: it banned *any* statement of alcohol content on a malt liquor label—even if completely accurate.

Decades later, in 1994, the Coors Brewing Company asked the Supreme Court to declare that restriction unconstitutional. Coors had been denied permission to truthfully disclose the alcohol content of its beer on its product labels because 27 U.S.C. § 205(e)(2) expressly prohibited it. Coors sued the government, claiming that the ban violated the First Amendment.

In response, the government argued that the statutory ban on alcohol content labeling was necessary to prevent "strength wars" between competitors in the malt liquor market. Some manufacturers were already claiming their product had "power" or "strong character" or was "dynamite." The government was apparently of the belief that if the percentage of alcohol by volume was allowed to appear on beer bottles, the malt liquor business would inevitably devolve into a market-wide slugfest, with the alcohol content of malt liquor increasing again and again until everyone was either drunk or dead.

The Supreme Court wasn't convinced. Although the justices acknowledged the possibility of strength wars, the empirical evidence showed that beer drinkers cared far less about alcohol content and much more about taste and calories. With respect to Coors specifically, the court was bothered that law had prevented its disclosure of "truthful, verifiable, and non-misleading factual information concerning alcohol content." The court believed that federal regulation should favor greater disclosure, not less.

At oral argument, Justice Ruth Bader Ginsburg pointedly asked the government's lawyer: "Has Congress said . . . for any other food or drug, 'thou shalt not tell the public what's in this commodity'?"

The answer, of course, was no.

More fundamentally, the court found that the labeling law

was woefully inconsistent with its supposed goal of preventing strength wars. For example, Section 205(e) categorically prohibited statements of alcohol content on malt liquor labels, but *required* it to appear on high-alcohol wine labels. Similarly, the law prohibited statements of alcohol content on all beer *labels* but allowed that information to appear in beer *advertisements* throughout most of the country. (See Fig. 5-9.)

As the unanimous decision stated succinctly: "There is little chance that § 205(e)(2) can directly and materially advance its aim, while other provisions of the same Act directly undermine and counteract its effects." The court held the ban on truthful disclosures of alcohol content to be an unconstitutional limitation of free speech.[10] So, after *Rubin v. Coors*, can a brewer still be criminally charged for discussing alcohol content on its beer labels? Certainly not for a "truthful and accurate statement" of alcohol content, which federal liquor regulations now expressly allow. But what about more

Fig. 5-9.

suggestive terms like "strong," "high-test," and "pre-war strength" on malt liquor labels or advertisements? Coors didn't challenge the prohibition on those kinds of statements, and they remain prohibited by 27 C.F.R. §§ 7.29(f) and 7.54(c)(1).

To become a federal criminal, and maybe spark a strength war in the process, a brewer need only label his product as "strong," "extra-strength," or something that might be similarly tempting to a no-nonsense alcoholic. For an extra dose of illegality, however, malt liquor labels also violate federal law if they "imply that a physical or psychological sensation results from consuming the malt beverage." (See Fig. 5-9.) Because, after all, the government can't have people thinking that malt liquor might make them feel a certain way.

Imagine if word got out.

Sell Wine with a Label That Insults a Competing Wine

Like beer and liquor, wine is also subject to strict federal labeling requirements. One rule exposes winemakers to criminal penalties if they say mean-spirited things about other winemakers. Specifically, 27 C.F.R. § 4.39(a)(2) prohibits any statement on a wine label that is "disparaging of a competitor's products." Under 27 U.S.C. § 205(e), doing so is a prohibited practice and Section 207 makes it a federal misdemeanor. A related rule prohibits winemakers from saying or depicting obscene things on their wine labels.

For the foulmouthed, highly competitive vintner, these rules are intolerable. Study after study has proved that most people buy wine based solely on the label. And nothing moves merlot like a profanity-laden, competitor-disparaging label battle. But until these rules are declared unconstitutional, winemakers will just have to play nice.

Fig. 5-10.

OTHER THINGS YOU CAN'T SAY ON A WINE LABEL

Title 27, Section 4.39, of the Code of Federal Regulations goes well beyond labels that disparage competing wines. The regulation prohibits saying a number of other things on wine labels. Things like:

It Will Get You Drunk

27 C.F.R. § 4.39(a)(7)(iii) prohibits labeling wine in a way that "tends to create the impression that a wine . . . has intoxicating qualities." After all, we wouldn't want folks getting that impression.

It's "Zombie" Wine

Wine-labeling regulations prohibit the use of certain words in a wine's brand name. If a word happens to also be the name of a distilled liquor product, Section 4.39(a)(9) says it can't be used in naming a wine. Examples of words prohibited by the regulation include "Manhattan," "Cuba Libre," and, yes, "Zombie."

Although the regulation is intended to prevent confusion of

wines with liquor products, the text of the rule doesn't actually require that the use of a cocktail name be misleading to be prohibited. Because of that, even winemakers selling fermented juice made from the brains of the living to their undead customers should exercise caution when naming their wines.

It Will Cure You

Like many products, winemakers are federally prohibited from making untrue statements about the effects of their wine on consumer health. That includes unfounded claims that drinking wine will be curative or therapeutic. But even if winemakers can't legally say it's therapeutic, they can't stop you from believing it.

It Has Bubbles (if It Doesn't)

Another statute, 26 U.S.C. § 5662, makes it a crime to represent "any still wine to be an effervescent wine or a substitute for an effervescent wine." Unlike the much snootier labeling rules that prohibit calling wine "champagne" if it's not actually from the Champagne district of France, this statute addresses what really matters: it makes it a federal crime for a wine seller to lie about whether their wine has bubbles.

Subliminally Advertise Alcohol

In 1976, the Senate Subcommittee on Alcoholism and Narcotics held two days of hearings on the effects of liquor advertising on public health. The goal was to figure out what, if anything, the government could do to prevent alcoholism by regulating liquor ads. The committee heard testimony from psychologists, federal officials, and even former L.A. Dodgers pitcher Don "Newk" Newcombe.

But then there was Wilson Bryan Key. Dr. Key had recently authored *Subliminal Seduction*, a book that sought to reveal how

advertisers had been secretly manipulating consumers and pol-
luting their minds with hidden images of sex acts, sex organs, and
even the word "sex" itself. All of this, Key claimed, was to subconsciously seduce consumers into buying things like liquor and cigarettes by appealing to their sexual desires.

To prove it, Key put on a slide show for the senators. He explained to them how a photo of a bottle neck was actually a penis, a
pair of fingers were really testicles, and if you looked close enough,
you could see the word "S-E-X" hidden in ice cubes, even if you had
to squint a little. But it wasn't all sexual. Key also insisted that scenes
of male castration and death were being hidden in ads, not to turn
people on, but to subconsciously terrify them into purchasing liquor.

The problem with Key's testimony was that even after an entire slideshow of death and genitalia, the senators still didn't see
the things he saw:

SENATOR WILLIAMS: Quite frankly, in the ice cube I consciously
found no assault upon my conscious perception.

Undeterred, Dr. Key pleaded with Senator Williams:

DR. KEY: Did you see the first one? I would be delighted to run
again for you the Johnny [sic] Walker Black Label ad that included the castrated penis and the skulls.

But Senator Williams had seen enough castrated penises for
one day. He responded:

SENATOR WILLIAMS: Yes. I did see it, and I saw the other ads. I
never, however, saw this content, but that again is something
you are suggesting we do not consciously see.

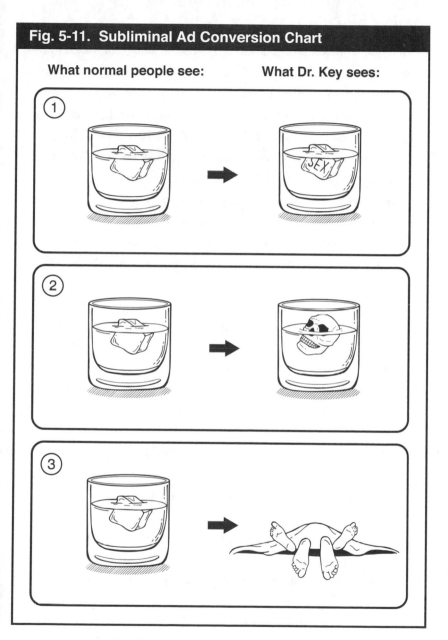

Fig. 5-11. Subliminal Ad Conversion Chart

Dr. Key left Capitol Hill without convincing lawmakers that hidden images of sex and death were pervasive enough to warrant action. His work was widely dismissed as a wild conspiracy theory. But imagine how frustrating it must have been to be in Dr. Key's shoes, being the only one who could see genitalia everywhere. (See Fig. 5-11.)

Even if Congress didn't buy it, Dr. Key wasn't totally alone in his suspicions of subliminal advertising. Just before Christmas 1973, a few years before the subcommittee hearings, regulators received complaints about a television commercial for the board game Hūsker Dū? In the commercial, the words "Get it" flashed on the screen for a few moments, and some people complained it was an attempt to manipulate them into buying the game through the insidious practice of subliminal messaging.

In response to the Hūsker Dū? incident, the FCC announced its official position that advertisements using subliminal messages were "contrary to the public interest" and "clearly intended to be deceptive." But is there any proof that subliminal advertising even works? Is anyone actually using it? And how about all of those penises that Dr. Key found lurking in the shadows of advertisements? Was any of it really there at all?

Liquor advertisers bristled at the accusation. In 1981, a representative of the American Association of Advertising Agencies submitted testimony to the ATF slamming Dr. Key, remarking:

> *I suggest that we should not take too seriously anyone who can sense an insinuation in every advertising statement, and for whom a phallic symbol is anything longer than it is wide.*

Despite this protest, the ATF officially banned subliminal liquor advertising in 1984. Today, 27 C.F.R. §§ 7.54(h), 4.64(k), and 5.65(h) prohibit the technique in ads for beer, wine, and spirits. Under 27 U.S.C. §§ 205(f) and 207, doing so is a federal crime and punishable by a fine of up to $1,000 per offense.

Be Annoyingly Drunk on a Wildlife Refuge

Being drunk isn't usually a federal crime. With the exception of drunk pilots, drunk bus drivers, drunk train conductors, and drunk ship captains, most people have to stumble onto federal property before they can be federally charged for their drunkenness. Even then, just being drunk may not be enough. Sometimes the law requires that a person be disruptively, dangerously, or annoyingly drunk before they can be charged.

As one example, 50 C.F.R. § 27.81 prohibits entering or remaining on a national wildlife refuge while intoxicated to a degree that may "unreasonably annoy persons in the vicinity." Under 16

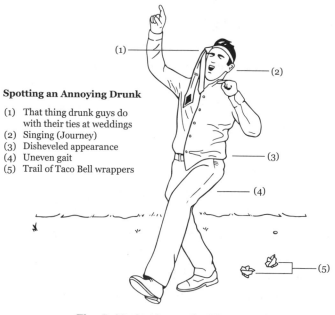

Spotting an Annoying Drunk

(1) That thing drunk guys do
      with their ties at weddings
(2) Singing (Journey)
(3) Disheveled appearance
(4) Uneven gait
(5) Trail of Taco Bell wrappers

Fig. 5-12. An Annoying Drunk.

U.S.C. § 668dd, unreasonably annoying drunks can be sentenced to a term of imprisonment, a fine, or both.

Unfortunately, there's no clear federal criteria for determining when a person has graduated from being just an annoying drunk to being an *unreasonably* annoying one. Also unclear is how drunk a person needs to be to violate the related prohibition on being so drunk that they pose a danger to himself or others.

In fact, in 2011 a man was acquitted of a charge brought under Section 27.81, even though it was alleged that he left a party at 3:00 a.m., hopped a fence into a wildlife refuge, drank some seawater, got dehydrated, and was found "screaming and yelling and dancing around" by federal agents. He was, however, found guilty of trespassing, so there's always that.[11]

OTHER PLACES THE GOVERNMENT WON'T LET YOU GET DRUNK

In addition to national wildlife refuges, national forests, and national parks, federal law makes it a crime to drink, get drunk, or be drunk in lots of other places. Some of them include:

- the National Arboretum;
- the Treasury Building;
- the U.S. Mint;
- the post office;
- all property administered by the NSA;
- the National Archives; and
- the Federal Law Enforcement Training Center.

As the next chapter explains, however, there are countless other things that can send a person to prison if done on federal properties like the ones above, whether or not alcohol is involved.

Fig. 5-13. Federal Drunkenness

THE FEDERAL LAW ENFORCEMENT TRAINING CENTER

According to the FLETC, it's the largest provider of law enforcement training in the country. It offers training in firearms and tactical driving, among other things.

For some reason, they don't want people drinking alcohol there.

UNITED STATES POST OFFICE

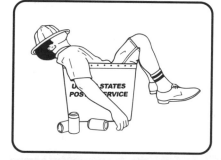

For aspiring offenders, the post office is the gift that keeps on giving. Federal law prohibits going to the post office drunk. Drinking alcohol while at the post office is also prohibited, unless you get permission from the postmaster general.

Misusing mail bins is also a crime, but that can be done sober.

UNITED STATES TREASURY BUILDING

The U.S. Treasury Building is one of Washington, D.C.'s most recognizable landmarks. It's featured on the ten-dollar bill and boasts massive granite columns and an impressive set of front steps.

Going there or being there under the influence of intoxating beverages is also a federal crime.

Chapter 6

HOW TO BECOME A FEDERAL CRIMINAL

ON FEDERAL PROPERTY

I t's hardly surprising that a Congress made up of mostly grumpy old men would pass a law telling you to get off their lawn. Sure enough, Title 40, Section 5104(d), of the U.S. Code prohibits stepping on the turf at the United States Capitol, and Section 5109(b) makes it punishable as a federal crime. That, however, is just one of many crimes a person can commit on federal property.

169

The government's criminal jurisdiction extends to acts performed in national parks, on military bases, in government buildings, and even on certain islands that contain enough bat feces to get the president's attention. Many of the places discussed in this chapter are already premier destinations for recreation and tourism. They may also be potential hotbeds of criminal activity.

FEDERAL LAND

The federal government owns or administers roughly 650 million acres of land in the United States. That's about 30 percent of all land in the country. This includes national parks, national forests, federal wildlife refuges, military bases, and fisheries, among other places. In the contiguous forty-eight states, most of this federal land is located west of the Mississippi River. (See Fig. 6-1.)[1] Farther north, more than 60 percent of Alaska is under federal control.

Fig. 6-1.

The government's authority to own and regulate all this land comes mainly from the "Property Clause" in Article IV, Section 3, of the United States Constitution, which provides that "the Congress shall have Power to dispose of and make all needful Rules and Regulations respecting the Territory or other Property belonging to the United States . . ."

Pursuant to that power, Congress has not only enacted lots of criminal statutes, it has authorized agencies like the National Park Service, Bureau of Land Management, and the Forest Service to make criminally enforceable regulations for the lands they administer. Because of that, there are now thousands of things a person can do on federal property that are federal crimes.

FEDERAL BAT POOP JURISDICTION

Congress has also asserted criminal jurisdiction over some pretty strange places not identified in the Property Clause. For example, in 1856, the United States decided it wanted to start laying claim to unoccupied islands with significant amounts of bat or bird poop, more technically known as guano. Under the appropriately named Guano Islands Act, Congress declared that

> *whenever any citizen of the United States discovers a deposit of guano on any island, rock, or key, not within the lawful jurisdiction of any other Government, and not occupied by the citizens of any other Government, and takes peaceable possession thereof, and occupies the same, such island, rock, or key may, at the discretion of the President, be considered as appertaining to the United States.*

In other words, if a U.S. citizen happened to be wandering around on an unoccupied island somewhere in the world and discovered a literal shitload of bat poop, the president could call dibs on the whole place, send in troops, and enforce criminal law. Yes, guano was once a very valuable fertilizer and source for materials used in making gunpowder. But technology has come a long way since the mid-1800s, and it's been a while since America has seized an island just for the poop. Nonetheless, the law still permits crimes on guano islands to be punished under federal law as if they had occurred on the high seas.

FEDERAL PRISON FOR STATE CRIMES

As broad as the government's authority to make crimes may be, there isn't always a federal crime on the books to cover something that happens on federal property. To fix that, Congress enacted the Assimilative Crimes Act, which gives the government authority to "assimilate," or adopt by reference, any state crime from the state where the federal property is located and charge it as a federal crime.

The only catch is that the Assimilative Crimes Act doesn't apply if there is already a federal law that covers the conduct. That means the government can't just choose to charge a state crime—say, one with a stiffer penalty—when a federal statute punishes the same offending behavior. As just one example, in 1996 an Oregon man was federally charged for sleeping in a post office that was open to the public twenty-four hours a day. The case wasn't only remarkable because it involved a post office that was open for more than fifteen minutes in the middle of the day, but it also involved federal prosecutors charging a person in federal court for violating a state trespass statute.

On appeal to the United States Court of Appeals for the Ninth Circuit, the homeless defendant argued that he'd been improperly charged under the Assimilative Crimes Act because there were federal postal crimes he could have been charged with—namely, causing a disturbance and disobeying a sign. The key question for the court was whether those similar federal offenses precluded the application of the state law. In holding that they did, the Ninth Circuit Court quoted the Supreme Court's decision in *Lewis v. United States*, which explained:

> *There are too many different state and federal criminal laws, applicable in too many different kinds of circumstances, bearing too many different relations to other laws, to common-law tradition, and to each other, for a touchstone to provide an automatic general answer to this . . . question. Still, it seems fairly obvious that the Act will not apply where both state and federal statutes seek to punish approximately the same wrongful behavior—where, for example, differences among elements of the crimes reflect jurisdictional, or other technical, considerations, or where differences amount only to those of name, definitional language, or punishment.*

In other words, there are tons of state and federal crimes. There are so many, in fact, that it's often impossible to know whether a particular act is a federal crime, a state crime, both, or neither. Even so, the Assimilative Crimes Act remains one of many tools in the government's arsenal, and yet another reason it's not terribly hard to become a federal criminal on government property.

GETTING AWAY WITH MURDER

Surprisingly, however, there may actually be one place where would-be federal felons actually can act with impunity. In his article entitled "The Perfect Crime," law professor Brian C. Kalt argues that there is a fifty-square-mile section of land at the perimeter of Yellowstone National Park in Idaho where federal crimes can be committed but not brought to trial.

In Kalt's hypothetical case, an offender carries out a federal crime spree in the Idaho portion of Yellowstone, during which the offender makes moonshine, poaches wildlife, strangles people, and steals their picnic baskets. Ordinarily, the offender would be looking at several federal felony charges and facing prison. But the government has a problem: the offender has a right to trial by jury.

As Kalt explains, Article III, Section 2, of the United States Constitution requires a federal criminal trial to be held in the state in which the crime was committed, and the Sixth Amendment requires that the jury be drawn from both the state *and* the federal district in which the crime was committed. Because the Idaho portion of Yellowstone is technically in the federal district of Wyoming, the Constitution would require a jury to be made up of people living in the Idaho portion of Yellowstone National Park—the only place located in both the state and the district of the offense. At last count, the population of that tract of land is exactly zero.

Of course, this so-called zone of death isn't an invitation by the federal government. Rather, it's what Kalt describes as an example of Congress doing a bad job of drawing its district lines. But without a jury a person can't be tried for a felony, and the "Yellowstone Strangler" would walk free.[2]

However, the same might not be true of other hardened criminals, like, say, the Yellowstone Off-Leash Cat Walker. Although off-leash cat walking is prohibited by 36 C.F.R. § 7.13(h) and made criminal by 18 U.S.C. § 1865, the offense may be punished only by up to six months in federal prison. Under 18 U.S.C.

§ 3559, that makes it a Class B misdemeanor and allows it to be tried without a jury. These lesser offenses may enable federal prosecutors to nab an offender in the "zone of death" who would otherwise skate.

With the exception of a possible fifty-square-mile loophole, however, there remain around 649,968,000 acres of federal land where a person can be tried and convicted of federal crimes. So, what other things can send an aspiring offender to federal prison if done in a national park? Those crimes are discussed in Part I of this chapter. What about a national forest? Part II covers those. Or how about all of the crimes a person can commit in federal buildings and the nation's capital? Yes, there are plenty of those too. A few are discussed in Part III.

PART I: National Parks

The National Park System, which began with establishment of Yellowstone National Park in 1872, has since grown to include superlative natural, historic, and recreation areas in every major region of the United States and its territories and possessions; these areas, though distinct in character, are united through their interrelated purposes and resources into one National Park System as cumulative expressions of a single national heritage; individually and collectively, these areas derive increased national dignity and recognition of their superb environmental quality through their inclusion jointly with each other in one System preserved and managed for the benefit and inspiration of all the people of the United States . . .

—54 U.S.C. § 100101(b)

THE NATIONAL PARK SYSTEM

The National Park System is an expansive network of federally protected land. It spans millions of acres and includes properties like the White House, monuments like Mount Rushmore, and each of the fifty-nine officially designated national parks.

Congress has given the secretary of the interior broad power to make rules for the management and use of park areas. Under 18 U.S.C. § 1865, violations of these rules are punishable as federal crimes. Examples include:

- scattering human ashes without a permit;
- snowshoeing or tobogganing in a parking lot;
- using a hovercraft;
- delivering someone by parachute;
- gambling;
- hitchhiking;
- using drugs, poison, explosives, or electricity to catch fish;
- teasing animals; and
- towing a water-skier from a hang glider without a permit.

For each of these offenses, the maximum punishment is only six months' imprisonment and a fine. But because they're considered "public welfare offenses," prosecutors don't need to prove a violator acted with any criminal intent, and the accused has no right to a jury. So even though a person caught electrocuting fish might not get locked up for a long time, or at all, unintentionally zapping a federal trout is still enough for a guilty verdict.

If you happen to be a person with a mostly functional cerebrum, a few of these rules may strike you as unnecessary. Why would anyone need a rule telling them not to tease wild animals?

How much fun is tobogganing in a parking lot, anyway? Who drove the Park Service to think these were problems in the first place? Was it you, Greg?

Sadly, time has shown that the crimes people will commit in the national parks are as limitless as human stupidity itself. Park visitors have been arrested for taunting bison, taking selfies with bears, and urinating into Old Faithful. This section discusses a few others.

Make an Unreasonable Gesture to a Passing Horse

Some regulations are drafted with an unsettling degree of specificity. Others are hopelessly vague. Then there are the ones that are both vague and specific at the same time, like the federal prohibition on making unreasonable noises or gestures while horses or pack animals are passing by in a national park.

The most straightforward element of this offense is that it must be committed on National Park Service land. Flipping off a horse on private land, or really any place outside the control of the Park Service, isn't enough for federal criminal liability. Of course, if

Fig. 6-2.

you *do* get caught making obscene gestures to someone's horse on private land, state and local police may have some questions for you.

To be a federal crime, the prohibited gesture must also be made while a horse or pack animal is "passing." The law doesn't differentiate between gestures made *to* passing horses and those that are merely made in their presence. What is clear, however, is that the regulation was drafted with a total disregard for stationary horses. They just have to stand there and deal with your noises and gestures without legal recourse.

Where things get murky, however, is the gesture itself. The rule has always prohibited making an "unreasonable" gesture to a passing horse, but in 1983, when the Park Service was considering amendments to its rules, a member of the public expressed concern that the gesture rule was "too vague to be enforceable." So the Park Service amended the regulation to prohibit only gestures that are unreasonable "considering the nature and purpose of the actor's conduct, and other factors that would govern the conduct of a reasonably prudent person," which totally cleared up everything.[3]

At a minimum, before making any gesture to a passing horse, it's important to ask yourself, "Would a reasonably prudent person do this?" If the answer is no, then making the gesture could be a crime. The law's consideration of "other factors" may include any personal beef you have with the particular horse and whether he was asking for it.

GESTURES TO CONSIDER

Without meaningful guidance on which particular gestures are considered "unreasonable," a determined offender may try a variety. One popular gesture that could be considered unreasonable is the forearm jerk, also known as the *bras d'honneur* or "arm of honor." It is commonly understood to mean "Up yours."[4]

Fig. 6-3. The *Bras d'Honneur*.

The gesture is performed by bending one arm into an L-shape and thrusting it upward while driving the opposite hand downward to slap the biceps. (See Fig. 6-3.)

Another potentially unreasonable gesture is the so-called chin flick. (See Fig. 6-4.) But be advised: one well-known jurist has publicly said the gesture shouldn't be considered anything more than dismissive. In 2006 a reporter for the *Boston Herald* approached the late Justice Antonin Scalia as he left church and asked how he would respond to his critics' claims that his religious beliefs undermined his impartiality. His response? A chin flick.

Fig. 6-4. The Chin Flick.

The *Herald* ran a story calling Scalia's gesture obscene, a claim to which Scalia took great offense. The Supreme Court justice responded with a fiery letter to the editor, even citing an excerpt from Luigi Barzini's book *The Italians* to support his position.

Fig. 6-5. The Full Moon.

Although the nature of the chin flick remains a matter of dispute, a gesture with no ambiguity is the full moon. (See Fig. 6-5.) In performing the moon, the mooner's bare buttocks are displayed to the gesture's target. Notably, of all the gestures discussed so far, mooning has likely resulted in the most arrests, thanks to public decency laws. Still, there are no reported federal convictions for moonings directed to horses, whether in a national park or elsewhere.

Interestingly, however, the rumored history of mooning suggests it may not have always been understood as a wholly "unreasonable" display. In his book *The Naked Man*, author Desmond Morris claims it was once believed that exposing one's buttocks could ward off evil forces. Specifically, Morris says, superstitious people—including Martin Luther—believed that the devil had no buttocks and that by exposing one's own buttocks in his general direction, the devil would be so envious at the mere sight of a rear end that he would avert his gaze and leave the mooner alone. Morris even claims that during thunderstorms "some men would rush to their front doors and thrust their naked buttocks in the direction of the storm in an attempt to drive it away."[5] Sounds like a nice neighborhood.

Although these tales of superstitious moonings may be pure lore, defense lawyers faced with a tough horse-mooning case should consider looking into the superstitions of their client. If the mooning was an effort to ward off a horse believed to be an evil spirit, an insanity defense should also be evaluated.

GESTURES NOT MADE TO HORSES

If you drop your pants in the forest and there's no horse around to see it, did you commit a crime? Maybe. 36 C.F.R. § 2.34(a)(2) prohibits making an obscene gesture on public land without any requirement that pack animals be present.

In fact, Section 2.34 prohibits a whole range of "disorderly conduct" in national parks and forests. Parkgoers have been charged under that section for things like saying "Fuck you" to a park ranger, masturbating in a restroom while a park police officer watched "for about a minute," and even leaving a love note for a member of a girls' high school cross-country team.[6] Depending on the circumstances, it is conceivable that a garden-variety mooning, chin flick, or *bras d'honneur* could also be charged as a crime.

Because of its breadth, though, the obscene gesture rule is vague and sometimes convictions don't stick. Take, for example the case of a man arrested during a 2009 wilderness sex sting jointly conducted by the National Park Service and Forest Service.

In that case, an undercover park ranger was walking along a scenic trail in a national park when he encountered another man out for a stroll. Rather than wave as he passed, the man grabbed his own crotch and kept walking. Intrigued, the park ranger caught up with him down the trail and tried to test the waters by remarking that they were in "an open community." Smooth.

In response, the man asked the park ranger if he'd like to have sex and the park ranger said "Okay." According to the park ranger's testimony in the trial that followed, "About twenty seconds later, [the man] walked over to [the ranger] with his left hand extended and grabbed the ranger's genitals." The ranger also testified that, "[b]ased on the firmness of the grasp, [the ranger] did not believe this was an accidental touching." The grab lasted "very briefly" and only until he "could get the words out: 'Police officer, you're under arrest.'" Of course, that really depends how slow you say it.

The man was found guilty, but the Fourth Circuit Court of Appeals reversed his conviction. In the court's view, the crotch grab—no matter how firm—was invited by the park ranger's flirtatious chitchat and therefore not obscene under the circumstances. On those facts, the court held Section 2.34(a)(2)'s use of the term "obscene" was unconstitutionally vague as applied and the court of appeals ordered the trial court to enter a judgment of acquittal.[7]

Roll Something Down a Hill

36 C.F.R. § 2.1(a)(3) prohibits "tossing, throwing or rolling rocks or other items inside caves or caverns, into valleys, canyons, or caverns, down hillsides or mountainsides, or into thermal features." Because the rule treats tossing, throwing, and rolling equally, the manner of propulsion is a matter of personal preference for the offender.

Fig. 6-6. Tossing Something Down a Hill.

Although it may seem broad, Section 2.1(a)(3) is not a blanket ban on all object tossing. The rule only prohibits tossing, throwing, and rolling things in or on seven specific natural features. Most of them—like valleys, caves, and caverns—are easily identified. "Hillsides," however, aren't defined, making the line between a slight grade and a hill dangerously unclear. Park visitors hoping to avoid arrest may be wise to consult topographical maps, carry bubble levels, and avoid tossing anything, even on gentle slopes.

It's fair to assume that the anti-tossing rule was intended to prevent injuries to park visitors. Its drafters were probably also hopeful that it would deter the countless idiots who keep throwing things into geysers and thermal pools. Had the rule been issued sooner, it might have even prevented people from plugging up Yellowstone's Handkerchief Pool with coins, broken bottles, rocks, hairpins, and a small horseshoe.[8]

But then again, maybe not. Tourists have a long tradition of throwing stuff into other stuff. In 1927, a Yellowstone park ranger named George Marler documented the extent of the problem when he attempted to clean out a thermal spring and took an inventory of what he found. Among many, many other things, Marler found a frying pan, a rubber boot, seventeen cans, a pitchfork, a forty-gallon drum, a whole tree, a bottle of Vaseline, and a guidebook to Yellowstone Park from 1913,[9] In 2018, Yellowstone's Ear Spring barfed out "a cement block, cans, dozens of coins and a baby's pacifier, dating back to the 1930s."[10] No sign of the baby, though.

Today, throwing any of these items into a thermal feature would certainly constitute a criminal offense. Rolling any of them down a hill would also violate the law. But even though it's clear rolling some*thing* down a hill is prohibited, the rule is silent on the legality of rolling some*one.*

Fig. 6-7. Rolling Down a Hill (Legally Ambiguous).

The rule also contains what could be called "the Sisyphus loophole." Because it only prohibits rolling things *down* hillsides, rolling things *up* hillsides may be entirely lawful.

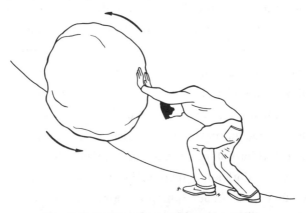

Fig. 6-8. Rolling Something Up a Hill.

Of course, the feds can still charge you once the rock inevitably comes rolling back down.

Drink a Beer on a Bicycle

Under most circumstances, riding a bicycle in a national park is perfectly lawful. There are, however, a few forbidden bike-related activities punishable as crimes under federal law. Title 36, Section 4.30(h)(5), of the C.F.R. is one example. It prohibits "operating a bicycle while consuming an alcoholic beverage or carrying in hand an open container of an alcoholic beverage." (See Fig. 6-9.)

Even if one abstains from drinking alcohol completely, just carrying an open beer is enough for a bicyclist to commit this offense.

Fig. 6-9.

It should be noted, however, that bike selection is critical. On the one hand, drinking atop a penny-farthing bicycle has a certain undeniable aesthetic appeal. (See Fig. 6-9.) On the other hand, this kind of bicycle typically has a seat height of over 50 inches, making drunken falls particularly risky for the offender. Couple that with the challenging terrain of a national park, and the risk of injury only increases.

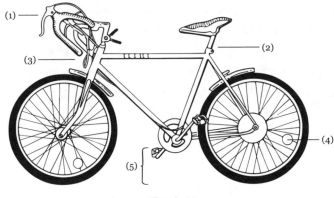

Fig. 6-10.

Bike selection can actually have legal significance too. Riding a noncompliant bike in a national park is itself a federal crime. Section 4.30(h)(3) prohibits riding a bicycle at night, through a tunnel, or in low visibility if the bike isn't equipped with "a white light or reflector that is visible from a distance of at least 500 feet to the front and with a red light or reflector that is visible from at least 200 feet to the rear." The only exception is if the bike rider straps the required lights or reflectors to his own body.

Thus, if ridden under the right circumstances, the bicycle depicted in Fig. 6-10 could result in criminal charges because it doesn't have lights or reflectors visible from the front or rear. (See Fig. 6-10 [2]-[3]).

The bike's pedal height (5), its braking system (1), and its complete lack of a horn or bell can also make it a crime to ride on other non-park properties. For example, at the National Institutes of Health Federal Enclave in Montgomery County, Maryland, riding a bike without a horn or other warning device is prohibited by 45 C.F.R. § 3.27 and punishable as a crime under 40 U.S.C. § 1315. On the Fort Stewart Army Base in Georgia, bicycles are prohibited "if the pedal, in its lowermost position, is more than 12 inches above the ground," and all bikes on the base must have working brakes.

Even with a fully compliant bike, the National Park System prohibits something as simple as riding a bike next to another bike. Section 4.30(h)(4) prohibits "operating a bicycle abreast of another bicycle except where authorized by the superintendent." In other words, unless you have permission from a park superintendent, even sober bike riding with appropriate lights and reflectors is a federal crime once you get alongside another bike.

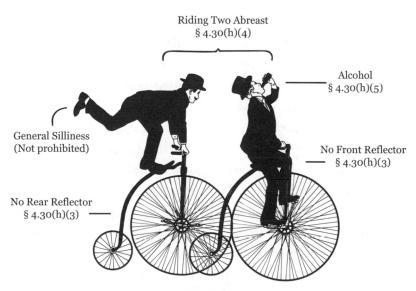

Fig. 6-11.

As shown in Fig. 6-11, Section 4.30(h)(4) makes it possible to commit multiple federal crimes with minimal additional effort.

NIGHT BIKING AND THE FOURTH AMENDMENT

Violations of these bicycle regulations aren't just crimes, they may also serve as effective ways to get a free pat-down from a man in uniform.

As a general matter, the Fourth Amendment to the United States Constitution doesn't allow law enforcement officers to just stop and frisk someone unless the officer has first observed some "objective manifestation that the person stopped is, or is about to be, engaged in criminal activity." Put differently, police are supposed to have reasonable suspicion to believe that a person is engaged in criminal activity before detaining them.[11]

In 2010, a federal district court in California held that this constitutional requirement was at least initially met when a park ranger stopped and frisked a bicyclist he spotted riding through Yosemite National Park at 2:00 a.m. without a light. The ranger detained the bicyclist on suspicion of violating 36 C.F.R. § 4.30(h)(3)—the prohibition on lightless night biking—and patted him down for weapons.

During the frisk, however, the ranger found a small "stash box" in the bicyclist's pocket, which contained a white powdery substance. The bicyclist admitted it was the street drug MDMA, so the ranger placed him under arrest and continued his search. When the ranger searched the bicyclist's backpack, he found more drugs. When all was said and done, the bicyclist was charged with possession of MDMA, LSD, hashish, and marijuana, as well as one super serious count of "operating a bicycle at night without a light."

Prior to trial, however, the court ruled that the drugs and any statements the bicyclist made to the ranger had been illegally obtained. The court noted that "biking without a light is anything but an inherently dangerous crime" and determined that the officer's extended search of a small box was not justified in the case of a suspected night biker. Based on these findings, the court granted the bicyclist's motion to suppress, resulting in the dismissal of his case.[12]

Don't Clean Up Your Dog's Poop

36 C.F.R. § 2.15(a)(5) requires all national park visitors to comply with "pet excrement disposal conditions." In most parks, that means that failing to throw away your dog's poop is a federal

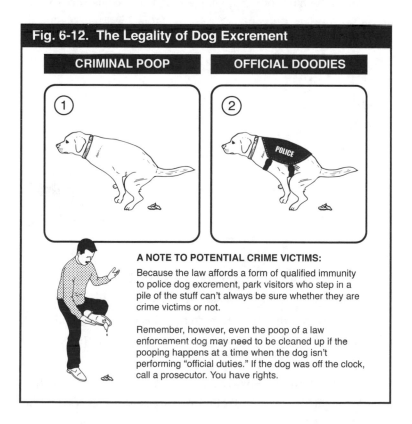

Fig. 6-12. The Legality of Dog Excrement

CRIMINAL POOP

OFFICIAL DOODIES

① ②

POLICE

A NOTE TO POTENTIAL CRIME VICTIMS:

Because the law affords a form of qualified immunity to police dog excrement, park visitors who step in a pile of the stuff can't always be sure whether they are crime victims or not.

Remember, however, even the poop of a law enforcement dog may need to be cleaned up if the pooping happens at a time when the dog isn't performing "official duties." If the dog was off the clock, call a prosecutor. You have rights.

crime. However, Section 2.15(f) contains one notable exception: the otherwise strict requirement that park visitors throw away their dogs' poop "does not apply to dogs used by authorized Federal, State and local law enforcement officers in the performance of their official duties."

Okay, but what if you aren't a complete sociopath? What if letting other people step in your dog's poop is a bridge too far? Can you still become a federal criminal in a national park with your dog? Absolutely. Subsection (a)(2) of the same regulation requires all dogs in national parks to be properly restrained in a crate, cage, or a "leash which shall not exceed six feet in length." An offender need only attach her dog to an extra-long leash, or use no leash at all, to be guilty of this offense. In fact, the law applies to all pets (meaning any animal that has been domesticated), so walking a ferret on an extra-long leash could be a crime too.

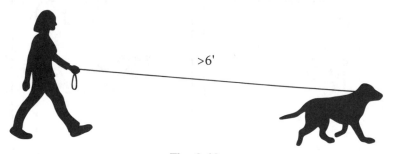

>6'

Fig. 6-13.

But be careful when it comes to federal leash regulations; a violation might just get you tased. That's what happened to a California dog owner in 2012 when he took his dogs for an off-leash jog in an area that had just recently become part of the National Park System.

On that fateful day—which happened to be the first day that a park ranger had ever patrolled the area—the dog owner was approached by a park ranger and warned about the federal leash rules. When the ranger asked the dog owner for his name, he was nervous that he would be put on an "offending dog walker" list, so he gave the ranger a fake last name and said he was going to leave. The park ranger responded by grabbing his arm and telling him that he wasn't free to go. She then called for backup.

The dog owner asked if he was under arrest, but the park ranger didn't respond. When he started to leave once again, the park ranger drew her Taser and pointed it at his chest. The dog owner then asked the ranger what gave her the authority to detain him, to which she replied, "The Constitution." The dog owner responded, "That is no kind of answer. Come on, dogs, we're leaving." Three steps later, he was on the ground with a dart in his buttock and electricity pulsing through his body. He was awarded $50,000 in damages.[13]

Use a Metal Detector just for Fun

For some people, crimes that require a friend to ride alongside them on a bicycle or a dog to walk with them are impossible. They don't have friends and their dogs keep running away. We're talking about strange, lonely, and unapproachable people. These aren't just any outcasts. These are the type of people deranged enough to own something that can just as easily get them arrested in a national park: a metal detector.

36 C.F.R. § 2.1(a)(7) prohibits anyone in a national park from "using a mineral or metal detector, magnetometer, side scan sonar, other metal detecting device, or sub-bottom profiler." Even just *possessing* a metal detector in a national park is enough to violate this regulation and can expose the possessor to the criminal penalties available by statute.

Because this crime concerns a very specific and sophisticated audience—"detectorists," as they call themselves—this section will speak in highly technical terms that only the metal detecting community will understand.

Click, click, click-click, beep, beee—

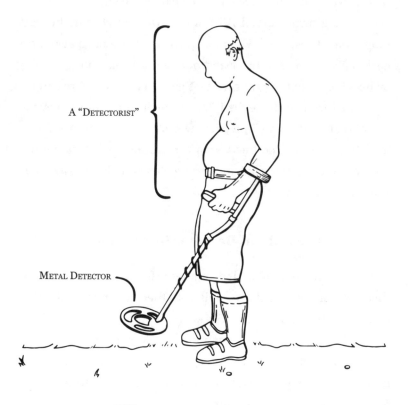

A "Detectorist"

Metal Detector

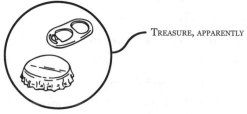

Treasure, apparently

Fig. 6-14.

Just kidding. But seriously, metal detectors are permitted in national parks only if they are being used for "authorized scientific, mining, or administrative activities." For that reason, recreational treasure seekers face up to six months in federal prison if they get caught metal detecting on federal land or even if they just happen to have their metal detector in the trunk of their car while visiting a national park.

Where things get really serious, though, is when a detectorist actually finds buried treasure. No, not the typical haul of bottle caps and pull tabs they find on a normal hunt while the rest of us are trying to enjoy our vacations, but actual treasure. The Archaeological Resources Protection Act (ARPA) provides for even stiffer prison sentences than the national parks' metal detector ban. If a person finds and digs up a buried artifact that turns out to be more than one hundred years old, 16 U.S.C. § 470ee provides for a sentence of up to a year. The sentence can be as much as five years in prison for a repeat offender.

Camp Within 25 Feet of a Hydrant

Camping in national parks is a heavily regulated activity. Not only is each park subject to the rules that govern the National Park System as a whole, but national park superintendents are also authorized to issue their own camping rules specifically for the individual parks they oversee. Because of that, the rules for campers can vary greatly from park to park, and violations of those rules are punishable as federal crimes under 18 U.S.C. § 1865.

For example, in California's Joshua Tree National Park, camping in a cave is strictly off-limits. In Utah's Zion National Park, campers can't put up a clothesline more than fifteen feet long or attach more than two hammocks to a tree. In 2008 a Maryland

Fig. 6-15. Criminal Camping

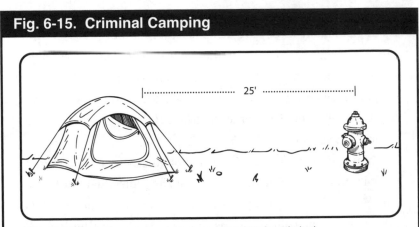

A standard criminal campsite. Just close enough to be criminal.

A more flagrant example. Requires two hydrants and a lot of chutzpah.

Criminal glamping. In the absence of a hydrant, a stream or road will do.

man was sentenced to two years of federal probation after he was tried and convicted of "unauthorized camping" on the Cape Hatteras National Seashore. In reality, he was just sleeping in his pickup truck with his family.[14]

But some federal camping rules apply no matter what national park a person is in. One of those rules prohibits "camping within 25 feet of a water hydrant or main road, or within 100 feet of a flowing stream, river or body of water, except as designated."[15]

As far as federal crimes go, camping too close to a hydrant is only slightly more involved than falling asleep in your truck at the beach, but it's every bit as much of a crime.

For the minimalist, this crime can be committed in a carefully placed tent. Plus, rules issued by the superintendent of Zion National Park classify hammocks as a "camping style," so even just lying in a hammock too close to a hydrant may be enough for a criminal charge in that park. For high-maintenance criminals, it's also one of the countless crimes that can be committed in an RV.

Break the Rules in Specific National Parks

Aside from the general prohibitions applicable to all national parks, the secretary of the interior has issued regulations specific to certain parks.

Mount Rushmore, for example, has just one rule: Don't climb it. But people haven't always complied. In 2009, three Greenpeace activists were arrested after they rappelled down Lincoln's forehead and unfurled a banner. In 2012 a man was arrested for trying to climb the landmark for no reason in particular.

The temptation to climb Mount Rushmore, and the government's sour attitude about it, may be traceable back to 1959, when Cary Grant and Eva Marie Saint scuffled with James Mason's henchmen

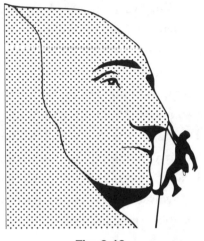

Fig. 6-16.

on the presidents' faces in Alfred Hitchcock's *North by Northwest*. What many may not know is that the Department of the Interior revoked Hitchcock's permit to film on Mount Rushmore just before filming when the feds caught wind that he was planning a violent chase scene across the faces. In fact, Hitchcock later confessed in an interview that he had "wanted Cary Grant to slide down Lincoln's nose and then hide in the nostril and get a sneezing fit."[16]

After assurances from Hitchcock that he would be respectful of the memorial, the Department of the Interior reluctantly reissued his permit, but only allowed him to use a mock-up of Mount Rushmore and prohibited him from having characters climb on the presidents' faces—even in scenes shot on a soundstage.

Hitchcock didn't keep his word, though. The characters are climbing all over the presidents' faces in the film. When the movie was released, audiences were so convinced by the mock-up used by Hitchcock that the Department of the Interior demanded he remove a credit thanking them so the public wouldn't think they had actually allowed it.[17]

Mount Rushmore is just one of many examples. Title 36, Part 7, of the C.F.R. contains special regulations for almost one hundred individual areas in the national park system.

THE GRAND CANYON

The Grand Canyon became a national park in 1919 and is one of the most-visited national parks in the country. 36 C.F.R. § 7.4 regulates certain activities within the park, including white-water boating trips. Anyone leading a white-water boating trip through the Grand Canyon must have a permit. All people boating through the canyon must bring their human waste with them when they leave. But the regulation likely to upset the most people is found in subsection (b)(5), which prohibits cats, dogs, or any other pet from coming along for the ride.

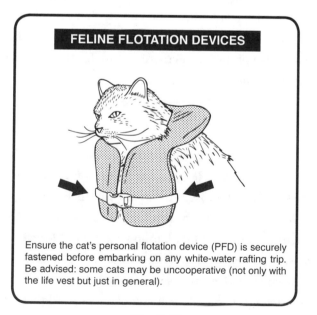

FELINE FLOTATION DEVICES

Ensure the cat's personal flotation device (PFD) is securely fastened before embarking on any white-water rafting trip. Be advised: some cats may be uncooperative (not only with the life vest but just in general).

Fig. 6-17.

The sad part about this rule is that it bars cats from doing the thing they are known to love most: white-water rafting.[18] If a cat person does choose to break this law, however, there's no reason to be reckless. Personal flotation devices should be provided to all passengers, whether feline, canine, or human. (See Fig. 6-17.)

YELLOWSTONE

Yellowstone was the first U.S. national park. It features some of the most recognizable natural features in the world, like Old Faithful and the Grand Prismatic Spring. It can also be dangerous. Truman C. Everts famously spent "Thirty-Seven Days of Peril" lost and alone in the Yellowstone wilderness after being separated from an expedition party in 1870. I mean, the guy ate a raw bird to stay alive.[19]

As wild as it may be, it's not a total free-for-all. Swimming in a thermal feature is off-limits (not to mention probably deadly). Dogsledding and skijoring (being pulled on skis by a dog, horse, or vehicle) are also prohibited activities. And, for the last time: *stop throwing things into the damn geysers.*

YOSEMITE

The National Park Service actually has a long tradition of stamping out fun. In 1968, the NPS put an end to a longstanding nightly tradition known as the Yosemite Firefall, in which burning embers were spilled over the edge of Glacier Point, creating the appearance of a three-thousand-foot flaming waterfall. 'Merica.

Since that time, the NPS has also issued regulations banning other majestic practices in Yosemite, like fishing from horseback and gathering grubs from logs if you can be seen doing it from a road.

HOT SPRINGS, ARKANSAS

Hot Springs, Arkansas, is known for its natural hot springs, once believed to possess therapeutic properties. The springs are so good, in fact, that in 1832 Congress decided to get into the bathhouse business and opened a free bathhouse in Hot Springs for indigent bathers. Congress also designated some of the springs as a national park. Not long after, they made it a federal crime to lie in order to get a free bath.

Eventually, however, the area was overrun with crime, including mobsters and illegal gambling, and, in 1950, Bill Clinton moved into town (unrelated). The government ultimately closed its free bathhouse, but Title 16, Chapter 1, Subchapter XL, of the U.S. Code still makes it a federal crime to try to bathe in a bathhouse without a doctor's note or to bathe in violation of bathhouse regulations. That includes using thermal water for unapproved purposes and bathing if you don't have complete control of your bodily functions.

ALASKA

About 60 percent of the National Park System is located in Alaska. That's more than 54 million acres of space to get into trouble with wolves, grizzlies, wolverines, and the federal government.[20] In Katmai National Park, for example, one criminally enforceable regulation makes clear that "continuing to engage in fishing within 50 yards of a bear is prohibited." Of course, the bear may enforce this prohibition before the feds get a chance.

Other Alaskan park regulations prohibit things like collecting occupied seashells, feeding an unskinned wolverine to your dog, and violating the "same-day airborne rule," which makes it a crime to fly to an Alaskan park unit and kill a wolf or wolverine with a

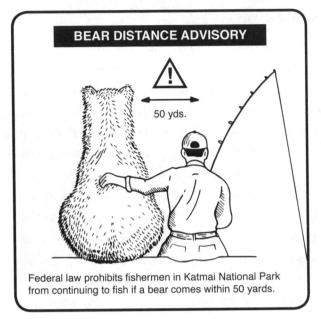

BEAR DISTANCE ADVISORY

50 yds.

Federal law prohibits fishermen in Katmai National Park from continuing to fish if a bear comes within 50 yards.

Fig. 6-18.

weapon before 3:00 a.m. the following day. And while the same-day airborne rule doesn't apply if you fly in on a regularly scheduled commercial airline, it does apply to more weapons than you might expect. Slingshots and blowguns are included.[21] For what it's worth, though, the law says nothing about killing a wolverine with your bare hands before 3:00 a.m.

PART II: National Forests

It is the policy of the Congress that the national forests are established and shall be administered for outdoor recreation, range, timber, watershed, and wildlife and fish purposes.

—16 U.S.C. § 528

Clog a Toilet in a National Forest

Fig. 6-19. Clogging a Toilet.

36 C.F.R. § 261.11(a) prohibits any person in a national forest from "depositing in any toilet, toilet vault, or plumbing fixture any substance which could damage or interfere with the operation or maintenance of the fixture." Toilet-clogging offenses are punishable by fines, imprisonment, and unrelenting ridicule from friends and family.

To be guilty of this offense, the law requires only that the offender put "a substance" into the toilet that is capable of clogging or damaging the toilet. Prior to 1981, the regulation specifically identified bottles, cans, cloths, rags, metal, wood, stones, and flammable liquids as prohibited toilet deposits, but the rule was later amended to refer more broadly to "substances." Thus, there are currently no legal limits on the types of clog-inducing substances that an offender might use to commit this offense. (See, for example, Fig. 6-19.)

Fig. 6-19.

Obviously, clogging a toilet on purpose is a heinous offense, particularly when the toilet is the only one for miles in the forest. But without getting into too much detail, there are ways to clog a toilet that may be entirely accidental. (See Fig. 6-20.)

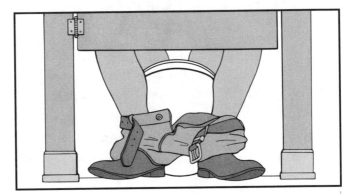

Fig. 6-20. Alternative Methods.

In fact, the government expressly reserves its right to prosecute you for even accidental cloggings. Title 36, Section 261.1(c) clarifies that, unless otherwise stated, "intent is *not* an element of any offense under [Part 261]," which includes toilet clogs.

As a further complicating factor, the law doesn't leave many alternatives for forest visitors who are fearful they may run afoul of the toilet-clogging ban, however inadvertently. A separate subsection of Section 261.11 provides that failing to dispose of sewage "either by removal from the site or area, or by depositing it into receptacles or at places provided for such purposes," is also a prohibited act.

As a result, accidentally clogging a toilet can be charged as a federal crime, but so can avoiding a toilet altogether and disposing of waste elsewhere in the forest. The only sure bet is to hang on to it and take it with you when you go. The kids are going to love this vacation.

Shoot a Gun into a Cave

Under 36 C.F.R. § 261.10(d)(3), visitors to national forests are prohibited from "discharging a firearm ... [i]nto or within any cave." That means it's not only a federal crime to shoot a gun *into* a cave but also while you're inside one. It's not just guns either. Discharging any "implement capable of taking human life, causing injury, or damaging property" is unlawful. (See Fig. 6-21.)

Now, you might be asking, "What's left of the Second Amendment if it doesn't even protect my right to defend myself against disgusting, disgusting bats?" And that's a weird thing to ask, even to your therapist. But if the federal ban on shooting guns in a cave has you upset, you're really not going to like the fact that setting off fireworks—a right so basic that the framers didn't even bother putting it in the Constitution—is also unlawful. Specifically, 36 C.F.R. § 261.10(o) prohibits "discharging or igniting a firecracker, rocket or other firework, or explosive into or within any cave" in a national forest.

But note: if you find yourself in federal prison for lighting a sparkler in a cave, you will want to come up with a better story for why you're in there. Everyone knows sparklers are the least intimidating firework of all. Luckily, there are plenty of other federal cave crimes.

Fig. 6-21. Cave Shooting

CAVE POOPING

36 C.F.R. § 261.58(ee) prohibits "depositing any body waste in caves except into receptacles provided for that purpose." It's the government's way of telling people to stop pooping in caves unless the Forest Service puts out a barrel.

CAVE SMOKING

National Park regulations explicitly prohibit smoking in caves and caverns. In the National Forest System, forest supervisors have prohibited smoking in certain caves, so it's best to always ask if a cave in a forest is a nonsmoking cave before lighting up.

REVEALING SECRET CAVE LOCATIONS

There's also a kind of cave so special that it's a federal crime for certain government employees to even disclose the location of one unless specifically authorized. It's called a "significant cave." The idea of the disclosure ban is to protect caves with important cultural, scientific, or other value. But we all know which well-heeled superhero is behind the rule.

CAVE THEFT

If you manage to find a significant cave, it's a federal crime to take home a souvenir—you know, like a thousands-of-years-old stalactite hanging from the ceiling. The Federal Cave Resources Protection Act of 1988 makes it a crime to take, buy, or sell any "cave resource," including stalagmites, stalactites, and other cave features. If you owned one before November 18, 1988, however, you get a pass.

Move a Table

The United States Bureau of Land Management (BLM) oversees millions of acres of public land, including picnic and camping areas open to the public. As fun as that may sound, 43 U.S.C. § 1733(a) makes it a federal crime to violate any rule issued by the secretary of the interior governing the occupancy and use of those areas. One of those rules, 43 C.F.R. § 8365.2–3(f), strictly prohibits moving a table.

This offense is probably committed by some variation of the approach depicted in Fig. 6-22. Once the table has been located and moved, there's really nothing more for the offender to do. Whether he moves the table an inch or a foot, the text of the law makes no distinction. The regulation also prohibits moving a stove, litter receptacle, and a couple other things. Doing any of those things exposes the mover to a fine of as much as $1,000 and up to a year in prison.

However, purely accidental table moving is probably not a crime. 43 U.S.C. § 1733(a) requires prosecutors to prove that the table mover acted "knowingly and willfully." In this case, that means the offender must have moved a table on purpose and knowing it was illegal to engage in table moving.

According to some courts, it's important to prove that a person intended to do something illegal before convicting them, because it's not always obvious whether doing a particular thing can subject a person to criminal liability. That's particularly true when conduct is prohibited by an obscure administrative regulation and not a statute. In such circumstances, courts have said that "Congress would have wanted to require a voluntary, intentional violation of a known legal duty" before imposing criminal liability.[22] Apparently those courts don't think it's obvious that things like moving picnic tables without authorization are federal crimes. The same could probably be said of BLM's ban on chasing people, playing a radio too loud, gutting a fish in a bathroom sink, or searching for buried treasure on lands administered by the BLM.

Lucky for you, you have this handbook, and nobody can ever say you didn't know these things were illegal.

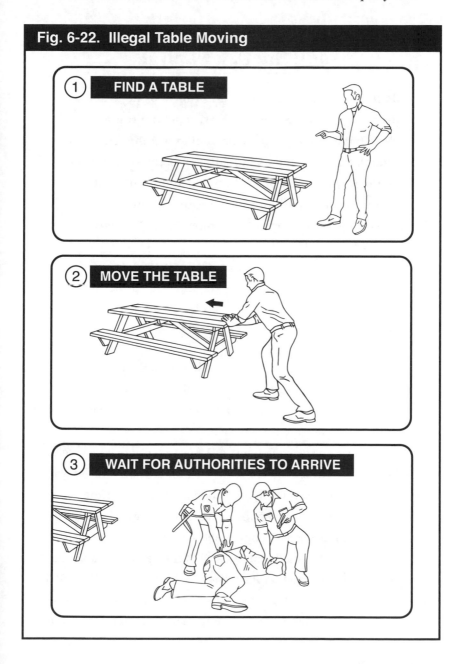

Fig. 6-22. Illegal Table Moving

PART III: Federal Buildings and the U.S. Capital

Be it enacted by the Senate and House of Representatives of the United States of America in Congress assembled, that a district of territory, not exceeding ten miles square, to be located as hereafter directed on the river Potomack, at some place between the mouths of the Eastern-Branch and Connogochegue be, and the same is hereby accepted for the permanent seat of the government of the United States.

—Act of July 16, 1790, 1 Stat. 130

THE CRIME CAPITAL: WASHINGTON, D.C.

Since the year 1800, Washington, D.C., has been the United States' capital city. It's home to the iconic Capitol Building, the White House, the Supreme Court, and dozens of other government buildings, national parks, and monuments.

For the aspiring federal offender, D.C. is Graceland. It's a mecca. It's the only place where a person can become a three-time federal offender by abandoning a fish in the National Arboretum, taking a nap at the Smithsonian, and posting an unauthorized flyer on a bulletin board at the Government Accountability Office—all before lunch.

If that weren't enough, large parts of the capital area are administered by the National Park Service. Under 18 U.S.C. § 1865 and 36 C.F.R. § 7.96, that means it's a crime to do things like speak from an oversized soapbox in Lafayette Park, play croquet without a permit, or harass a golfer in any park area within the national capital region.

Obviously, Congress has an interest in protecting federal property. If they don't, nobody will. But the government also knows not to underestimate the destructive force of American tourists. In fact, one particularly destructive day at the U.S. Capitol even inspired its own federal anti-fun statute.

The Dormant Capitol Sledding Ban

The day was Easter Monday 1876. The destructive force was a horde of kids—ten thousand of them, to be exact—and they had come to the Capitol lawn to roll Easter eggs down its sloping landscape. What they left in their wake was total destruction. Well, destruction of the grass, anyway. Still, the sight of damaged turf was enough to spur action in Congress, and lawmakers promptly introduced a bill to make sure it could never happen again.

The proposed law, more formally known as "an act to protect the public property, turf, and grass of the Capitol Grounds from injury," was written to require the Capitol Police "to prevent any portion of the Capitol Grounds and terraces from being used as playgrounds or otherwise, so far as may be necessary to protect the public property, turf and grass from destruction or injury." And although the bill's sponsor cited the utter destruction caused by the egg rollers as the principal reason for the legislation, he explained that it was also necessary to protect the grounds from cattle, which apparently wandered through the Capitol grounds with some frequency in 1876.

Robert Withers, a member of the Senate committee reviewing the bill, had concerns. The Virginia senator was still new enough to Washington to have a beating heart and feelings. He viewed the egg roll as "almost a prescriptive right acquired by custom." He thought it would be a shame to "debar these children from an enjoyment which they enter into with so much zest and which it affords us all pleasure to witness."[23] For the rest of the Senate, the idea of kids having fun didn't compute. This was precious government grass. It warranted the most stringent protections. The committee reported the bill to the Senate and it was passed into law a short time later.

Unfortunately, nobody told the kids. The following Easter, children arrived for the egg roll but were turned away, eggs in hand. And for the next 140 years the law served another, more controversial purpose: it functioned as a statutory ban on sledding at the U.S. Capitol.

In 2015, however, Americans took back their God-given right to sled at the U.S. Capitol in a coordinated act of civil disobedience. During a particularly snowy March, protesters flocked to the Capitol grounds to stage a "sled-in," urging the Capitol Police to not enforce the 140-year-old sledding ban.

Sure enough, the police caved and let the sledders do their thing. Later that year, Congress even snuck language into the Legislative Branch Appropriations Bill providing that:

> *The Committee understands the need to maintain safety and order on the Capitol grounds and commends the Capitol Police for their efforts. Given the family-style neighborhood that the Capitol shares with the surrounding community the Committee would urge the Capitol Police to forebear enforcement of 2 U.S.C. 1963 ("An act to protect the public property, turf, and grass of the Capitol Grounds from injury") and the Traffic Regulations for the United States Capitol Grounds when encountering snow sledders on the grounds.*

The same instruction has been included in the Appropriations Bill each year since. Thus, at least for the time being, the sledding ban won't be enforced.

Bring Stilettos over Three Inches to the Capitol

Other Capitol offenses can be found in Title 40, Section 5104, of the U.S. Code. Stepping on the turf, climbing a tree, and injuring a shrub are just a few examples.

But it's not all about the landscaping. Subsection (e)(2) prohibits bringing "stilettos" over three inches to the Capitol. The law isn't concerned with high heels, though. It refers to knives and other bladed weapons.

Fig. 6-23. The Capitol Stiletto Policy

LEGAL	ILLEGAL	
A stiletto.	Also a stiletto.	A stiletto stiletto.

In addition to "stilettos," Section 5104 also prohibits carrying "daggers" and "dirks" in the Capitol or on its grounds. What's a dirk? It's pretty much a dagger. What's a dagger? It's basically just a knife. The use of these somewhat antiquated terms is likely due to the statute's old age: it was passed in the early 1930s. But that shouldn't be a surprise to anyone. After all, imagine trying to get a dirk-control bill passed today.

It's also unsurprising that Congress would want to ban dangerous weapons from the Capitol in the first place. Lawmakers have had their fair share of close calls with armed members of the public.

In 1989 a reporter pulled out a gun and a bullet while interviewing former Senator Bob Dole. He did it in an effort to make a point about how lax Capitol security was. The reporter, Pulitzer Prize–winner Jack Anderson, supposedly snuck the gun into the Capitol with his camera crew's equipment.

Anderson was never charged for the stunt. To his credit, though, he turned out to be right about Capitol security. A few years after Anderson's incident with Senator Dole, another man made it through security with a gun. This time it was a fully loaded .357 Magnum. Unlike Anderson, however, this guy wasn't there just to prove a point.

According to letters found in the man's briefcase, he had come to the Capitol in his capacity as "world president." He was on a mission to investigate a conspiracy he called "Watergate 2," which involved President Bush, Vice President Dan Quayle, Ronald Reagan, Candice Bergen (Murphy Brown), Jimmy Smits, and Jack Nicholson, among others.[24] You see, back in 1991, allegations of a vast celebrity-president conspiracy were still strange enough to be considered suspicious.

The world president was arrested and charged with carrying a dangerous weapon on the Capitol grounds. He was also ordered to undergo a competency evaluation. Jimmy Smits, however, still runs free.

Unarmed visitors to the Capitol can also be charged. Subsection (e)(2)(D) of Section 5104 prohibits using "loud, threatening, or abusive language, or engag[ing] in disorderly or disruptive conduct" in order to disrupt a hearing or session of Congress.

Of course, when you write the law, you can also exempt yourself from it. So lawmakers created an exception for themselves and their employees for "any act performed in the lawful discharge of [their] official duties." Although the Constitution's Speech or Debate clause would arguably exempt them anyway, lawmakers wanted to be extra sure that they and their staff could be just as loud, threatening, and abusive at work as they needed to be (only for official business, of course).

Make a Bold Statement at the Supreme Court

A stone's throw east of the Capitol, the Supreme Court has its own set of rules. Visitors aren't allowed to walk their dogs on leashes longer than four feet, carry signs with supports made of anything but wood, or hold vigils. Visitors can't sell things, climb on the statues, or—in many cases—engage in the very kind of expressive activity that the Supreme Court itself has protected elsewhere.

For example, 40 U.S.C. § 6135 makes it a federal crime to "display in the Building and grounds a flag, banner, or device designed or adapted to bring into public notice a party, organization, or movement." Under that statute, visitors to the Supreme Court have even been arrested for the messages on their clothing. (See Fig. 6-24.)

Another statute, 40 U.S.C. § 6134, makes it a crime to "make a harangue or oration, or utter loud, threatening, or abusive language in the Supreme Court Building or grounds." That should make any freedom-loving American wonder: *What the hell is a harangue and why can't I make one?*

In 2017, the U.S. Court of Appeals for the D.C. Circuit admitted that the word "harangue" didn't necessarily "roll off the average person's tongue," but that didn't make the statute unconstitutionally vague. The case was *United States v. Bronstein* and the defendants had been charged with interrupting an oral argument in the Supreme Court, demanding that the justices overturn their controversial campaign finance decision in *Citizens United v. Federal Election Commission*.

In *Bronstein*, the trial court ruled that although the defendants could be prosecuted for uttering "loud" language, the words

Fig. 6-24. Protest Jackets

COHEN v. CALIFORNIA

In 1968, 19-year-old Paul Cohen went to the Los Angeles County Courthouse wearing a jacket that said "Fuck the Draft." He was arrested and charged with disturbing the peace—a state crime in California.

The U.S. Supreme Court reversed Cohen's conviction, holding that a state couldn't criminalize the mere display of the word "fuck." He also got the Supreme Court to write "fuck" twice in an opinion. Nice.

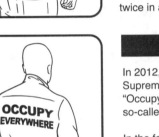

SCOTT v. U.S.

In 2012, a protester was arrested at the U.S. Supreme Court for wearing a jacket that said "Occupy Everywhere," in reference to the so-called Occupy movement.

In the false-arrest case that followed, the district court held that the decision in *Cohen* didn't make Scott's arrest illegal because Section 6135 applied only to certain types of displays, regardless of their content. The court also said "fuck" once.

A "MOVEMENT"

NOTE: Although you might be able to wear a "Fuck the Draft" jacket in the Los Angeles County Courthouse but not at the Supreme Court, Section 6135 only prohibits bringing attention to "a party, organization, or movement."

A jacket that simply states an irrefutable fact might not be considered part of a "movement," even if it's something everyone believes deep down or knows to be true but is too afraid to admit. (See image at left.)

"harangue" and "oration" were too vague to permit a prosecution. Sure, the dictionary said a harangue really was just a tirade and an oration was just a formal speech, but words are hard. The court thought the defendants could only be expected to understand words like "loud." A harangue-based prosecution wouldn't be allowed.

The judges of the appeals court disagreed. As they explained, the meaning of the statute was clear: "making disruptive public speeches is clearly proscribed behavior—even in staccato bursts, seriatim." (Great, now I have to go look up those words too). The harangue prosecution went forward and the defendants were sentenced to a year of probation.

Disrupt Official Business at the White House

When Thomas Jefferson was president, the general public was free to enter the White House pretty much anytime. Eventually, though, certain events would ruin that level of open government for everyone—like the time Andrew Jackson invited the public to come help him eat a 1,400-pound wheel of cheese in the entrance hall of the presidential mansion. The cheese disappeared quickly, but a stubborn cheese stain reportedly remained on the White House floor for quite some time.[26] This is why we can't have nice things.

Today, only authorized individuals are allowed to enter the White House, cheese or no cheese. 18 U.S.C. § 1752(a)(1) makes it a federal crime to go inside or to enter the grounds without permission. The penalty is up to ten years in prison.

Despite the prospect of these stiff penalties, unauthorized entry to the White House grounds is like lots of things the government prohibits: people still seem to do it an awful lot.

Fig. 6-25. Disrupting Presidential Business

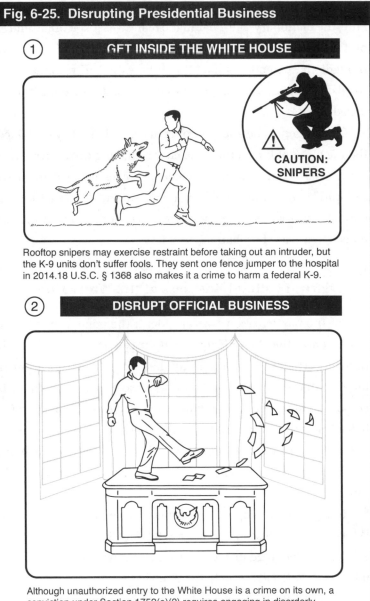

① **GET INSIDE THE WHITE HOUSE**

⚠️ CAUTION: SNIPERS

Rooftop snipers may exercise restraint before taking out an intruder, but the K-9 units don't suffer fools. They sent one fence jumper to the hospital in 2014.18 U.S.C. § 1368 also makes it a crime to harm a federal K-9.

② **DISRUPT OFFICIAL BUSINESS**

Although unauthorized entry to the White House is a crime on its own, a conviction under Section 1752(a)(2) requires engaging in disorderly conduct with the intent to disrupt "government business"—important stuff, like executive orders and presidential tweets.

On Thanksgiving Day 2015, for example, a man jumped the White House fence while wearing the American flag as a cape. When he moved to dismiss his indictment, he argued that his fence jumping was protected under the First Amendment because he did it with the "noble purpose" of "call[ing] attention to various deficiencies in the Constitution." He also claimed the statute was unconstitutionally overbroad because it "would prevent all fence jumping protests seeking to illustrate that the fence was inadequate ... [e]ven a jump that has nothing to do with endangering the President."

Shockingly, the court wasn't convinced that fence adequacy protests were actually a thing.

A year earlier, another fence jumper made it all the way across the North Lawn and through the front doors of the White House, which *someone* left unlocked. When you have snipers on the roof, who needs to lock up, right? But aside from the occasional assassination attempt, most White House fence jumpers don't seem to have a clear plan for what they'll do if they manage to make it inside. If they want to commit another crime, however, Section 1752(a)(2) says all they need to do is "disrupt the orderly conduct of Government business or official functions" once they're in there.

Have Disruptively Bad Hygiene in the Library of Congress

The Library of Congress is a high-class place. It's home to a rough draft of the Declaration of Independence, hundreds of miles of bookshelves, and the largest publicly available collection of comic books in the United States. Understandably, there are strict rules of conduct that library visitors must follow.

Breaking library rules with the intent to disturb other people is a criminal offense under 40 U.S.C. § 5104(e)(2)(C) and punishable by up to six months in prison. One rule expressly prohibits having such "offensive personal hygiene" that it interferes with the use of a reading room.

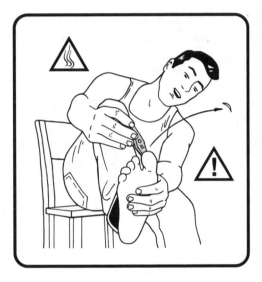

Fig. 6-26.

Unfortunately, the law provides no guidance on what constitutes sufficiently offensive personal hygiene. In fact, it's the only time "offensive personal hygiene" appears in the Code of Federal Regulations. Also unclear is whether offensive *acts* of personal hygiene can also constitute crimes under § 5104. (See Fig. 6-26.)

The rules also prohibit bathing in a fountain at the Library of Congress. Thus, if a library visitor attempts to fix his criminally offensive hygiene with a quick fountain bath, he may be committing yet another offense under 36 C.F.R. 702.2(b)(9). It's a classic catch-22.

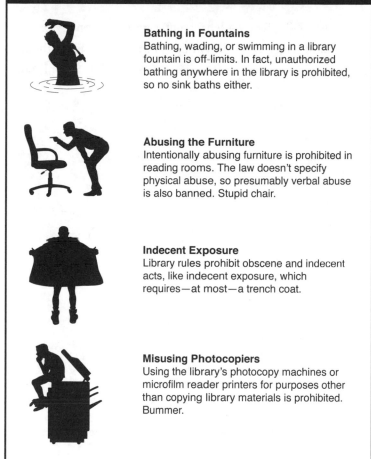

Fig. 6-27. Library Crimes

Bathing in Fountains
Bathing, wading, or swimming in a library fountain is off-limits. In fact, unauthorized bathing anywhere in the library is prohibited, so no sink baths either.

Abusing the Furniture
Intentionally abusing furniture is prohibited in reading rooms. The law doesn't specify physical abuse, so presumably verbal abuse is also banned. Stupid chair.

Indecent Exposure
Library rules prohibit obscene and indecent acts, like indecent exposure, which requires—at most—a trench coat.

Misusing Photocopiers
Using the library's photocopy machines or microfilm reader printers for purposes other than copying library materials is prohibited. Bummer.

The hygiene rule and the bathing ban are just a few of the many criminal offenses that can be committed at the Library of Congress.

The Library of Congress also has an express prohibition on urinating or defecating in a reading room, which is not shown in Fig. 6-27. You're welcome.

Injure a Government Lamp

40 U.S.C. § 8103(b)(4) makes it a federal crime to injure a government-owned lamp. Fig. 6-28 (below) depicts the punching method. Of course, there are many ways to injure a lamp, and this is only one.

Fig. 6-28.

Importantly, the law provides that this particular crime can only be committed in Washington, D.C. True, injuring a lamp elsewhere may still get you into trouble. To earn a federal conviction under this statute, however, the victim lamp must be both property of the government and located in the nation's capital.

If an offender has trouble finding an innocent lamp to target, they may take comfort in knowing that Section 8103(b) isn't only concerned with lamps. It also protects government sinks, shrubs, pipes, and hydrants, among other things. Accordingly, Fig. 6-29 shows another way this offense could presumably be committed.

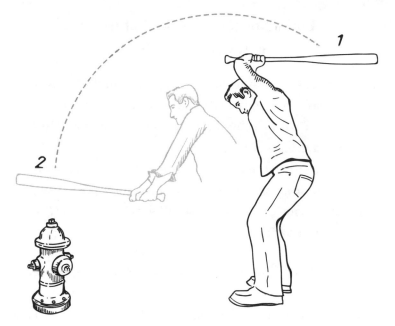

Fig. 6-29.

As a final note, this crime requires that the government property actually be injured. Merely threating to injure a government lamp is likely not sufficient to become a federal criminal under this statute.

Fig. 6-30. Threatening a Lamp (Weird, but Not a Crime).

Take a Stroller into the Bathroom
at the National Zoo

The National Zoo in Washington, D.C., has African elephants, tigers, chimpanzees, and pandas. Admission is free and it's open year-round. Because it's part of the Smithsonian Institution, though, there are rules. Federal rules.

Title 36, Part 520, of the C.F.R. serves as the zoo's code of conduct. For purposes of this section, we'll call it the "Zoo Code," because that's more fun to say. Among other things, Section 520.4 of the Zoo Code prohibits:

- catching or attempting to catch any free-roaming animals at the zoo;
- holding children over guardrails, fences, moats, walls, or other safety barriers;
- bringing strollers, baby carriages, or other conveyances, except wheelchairs, into exhibit buildings and public restrooms;
- engaging in ball games, or any athletic activity, except in places as may be officially designated for such purposes; and
- damaging, defacing, picking, or removing any herb, shrub, bush, tree, or turf at the zoo.

Some readers may see the ban on strollers in bathrooms as an unfair attack on parents. Some parents may learn of the ban on holding children over moats or guardrails and think: *Listen, buster, I didn't come all the way to this free zoo and pay zero dollars for my kid to not get a good look at the Sumatran tigers.* But under 40 U.S.C. § 6307, both are equally punishable by up to sixty days in prison (or five years if the offender finds a way to cause over $100 of damage in the process).

Fig. 6-31. Zoo Crimes

Take a Stroller into a Bathroom
A ban on bringing baby carriages into bathrooms may seem like a great excuse for parents to grab a little "me time," but the law still allows people to bring the babies themselves into the bathrooms, so it's not as good as it might seem.

Try to Capture a Zoo Animal
The federal prohibition on catching or trying to catch free-roaming zoo animals applies no matter how hungry you are.

Pick Herbs
Shrubs, bushes, trees, and turf are also protected from removal at the National Zoo, thus putting an end to senseless shrub-nappings.

Hold a Child over a Moat
In the category of worst ideas ever, this one is right near the top of the list. But, hey, here we are with a federal rule reminding us not to do it.

Play Ball Games
In addition to ball games, the Zoo Code prohibits any athletic activity except in officially designated areas. It's a shame, too, because where else can you play an authentic game of Monkey in the Middle?

Draw the Pentagon

Title 32, Part 234, of the Code of Federal Regulations establishes a code of conduct for all people at the Pentagon in Arlington, Virginia. One of its provisions, Section 234.15(b), provides that it's "unlawful to make any photograph, sketch, picture, drawing, map or graphical representation of the Pentagon Reservation" without getting permission first.

Fig. 6-32.

Violations of the Pentagon-sketching rule, like all other sections in the Pentagon's code of conduct, are made criminal by 10 U.S.C. § 2674, which authorizes the secretary of defense to make criminally enforceable rules regarding conduct at the Pentagon. Specifically, "any person who willfully violates any rule or regulation prescribed pursuant to [10 U.S.C. § 2674(c)] commits a Class B misdemeanor," and can be sentenced to up to six months in prison.

Although one might presume that the prohibition on sketching the Pentagon applies only to people who are actually present at the Pentagon when sketching it, the text of the regulation and statute aren't entirely clear. For example, subsection (a) of the anti-sketching regulation provides that "the use of cameras or other visual recording devices *on the Pentagon Reservation* is prohibited" (emphasis added), but subsection (b) simply prohibits making a "photograph, sketch, picture, drawing, map or graphical representation *of the Pentagon Reservation*" (emphasis added).

Fig. 6-33. Other Pentagon Crimes

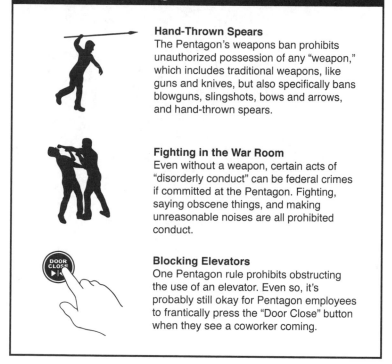

Hand-Thrown Spears
The Pentagon's weapons ban prohibits unauthorized possession of any "weapon," which includes traditional weapons, like guns and knives, but also specifically bans blowguns, slingshots, bows and arrows, and hand-thrown spears.

Fighting in the War Room
Even without a weapon, certain acts of "disorderly conduct" can be federal crimes if committed at the Pentagon. Fighting, saying obscene things, and making unreasonable noises are all prohibited conduct.

Blocking Elevators
One Pentagon rule prohibits obstructing the use of an elevator. Even so, it's probably still okay for Pentagon employees to frantically press the "Door Close" button when they see a coworker coming.

As a result, artists drawing Pentagons in the privacy of their own homes may be left wondering whether they, too, should seek permission from the Department of Defense to avoid criminal charges. But another section in the Pentagon code of conduct suggests that physical presence at the Pentagon is probably required. Section 234.2 provides that the Pentagon conduct regulations "apply to all areas, lands, and waters on or adjoining the Pentagon Reservation and under the jurisdiction of the United States, and to all persons entering in or on the property." Thus, private Pentagon drawing is probably allowed.

Chapter 7

HOW TO BECOME A FEDERAL CRIMINAL

ON THE HIGH SEAS

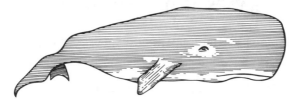

Article I, Section 8, of the Constitution gave Congress the power "to define and punish Piracies and Felonies committed on the high Seas . . ." Not long after getting that power, Congress got right down to making all sorts of piratical things illegal. Of the thirty-three paragraphs in the Crimes Act of 1790, five addressed pirates and pirate sympathizers. These original pirate crimes even included a three-year prison sentence for anyone who would dare "entertain" a pirate.

A few hundred years later, it's still a federal crime to do classic pirate stuff like plunder a ship or tie up the master in the hold. But there are also lots of non-pirate crimes that can be committed on the high seas, on ships, or with a sailor's underwear.

PIRATES AND THE HIGH SEAS

In 1696, an English Admiralty judge explained that piracy is simply "a sea-term for robbery." Others described pirates as nothing more than sea thieves.

Dismissive as that may sound, Congress has long viewed piracy as a particularly serious criminal offense, imposing the stiffest penalties allowed by law for convicted pirates and privateers. As one early example, the Crimes Act of 1790 required a mandatory death sentence for pirates and accessories to piracy. Even before the United States was a country, dozens of pirates were tried, convicted, and hanged in South Carolina.

Although there are presently very few pirate convictions, Title 18, Chapter 81, of the U.S. Code still sets forth the full range of piratical acts prohibited by federal law. To this day, 18 U.S.C. § 1651 requires life imprisonment for anyone who commits piracy on the high seas. Section 1652 carries the same punishment and classifies any U.S. citizen as a pirate when he commits a robbery, murder, or act of hostility against the United States on the high seas. And then there's Section 1653, titled "Aliens as Pirates." Sadly, it's not nearly as exciting as its title suggests.

Federal pirate law also punishes what could be called "white-collar" pirate offenses. One clause in Section 1654 prohibits investing in a pirate ship in order to share in its illicit proceeds. Another section of the federal pirate code prohibits knowingly receiving pirate booty (stolen goods, not the other thing). Each of those is punishable by a sentence of up to ten years in federal prison.

But even traditional piracy need not occur on the water to be prohibited by federal law. When sea thieves get off their boats and commit robberies onshore, Section 1661 provides for a life sentence just as if it had occurred on the high seas. And, to keep up with the times, 49 U.S.C. § 46502 makes it a crime to commit any act of "aircraft piracy" (better known as hijacking), making it totally appropriate to consider "D. B. Cooper" one of America's most infamous sky pirates.

Still, most people would probably agree that piracy in its purest form belongs on the high seas. But what are the "high seas," exactly? For many years, English and American courts held that the term referred exclusively to the unenclosed ocean. Robbers on rivers, lakes, and streams were just robbers and couldn't legitimately call themselves pirates.

In 1893, however, the Supreme Court held that the "high seas" weren't limited to seas and oceans. In the court's view, the Great Lakes were "high seas," too, because:

the Great Lakes possess every essential characteristic of seas. They are of large extent in length and breadth; they are navigable the whole distance, in either direction, by the largest vessels known to commerce; objects are not distinguishable from the opposite shores; they separate, in many instances, states, and in some instances constitute the boundary between independent nations; and their waters, after passing long distances, debouch into the ocean.

Just like that, lake pirates were born.

In the early 1900s, Lake Michigan got its very own lake pirate named Dan Seavey. According to the lore, Seavey got entire ship crews drunk and stole their vessels. He set up fake beacon lamps in a trick called "moon-cussing," causing ships to crash against rocks so he could steal their cargo. In 1908, he even got some ink in the *New York Times* when he led federal revenue agents on a seven-day chase across Lake Michigan, which ended with a literal shot across his bow.

Despite all this, it's not clear whether Seavey was ever actually charged with piracy, though federal pirate law certainly would have allowed it.

Correspond with a Pirate

A person can be sentenced to a term of up to three years in prison for corresponding with someone they know is a pirate. Millennial offenders can take comfort in knowing that law doesn't require any particular method of correspondence, so it's entirely possible that those late-night texts you've been sending may one day earn you a criminal conviction after all.

But when can you really *know* if someone is a pirate as the law requires? Is it enough if they're just giving off a strong pirate-y vibe? That would make it almost impossible to legally date in Brooklyn. And what if you don't even talk about pirate stuff? Can you still be found guilty then?

Fig. 7-1. Corresponding with a Pirate

NOTE: Although texting probably counts as "correspondence," at least one federal court has held that "perfectly innocent" correspondence with a pirate is not a criminal offense and at least some level of criminal intent is required. Sending booty pictures to a pirate may, however, be evidence of other crimes.

In 1818, the fate of two men depended on the answers to those very questions. The case was *United States v. Howard* and the defendants were two branch pilots who made a living by guiding ships through the Delaware River.[1] Their indictment alleged that on July 10, 1817, while sailing about twenty miles off the Cape of Delaware, the defendants encountered a black schooner full of suspicious characters who claimed they were headed to New

York. At first, the defendants and the schooner's crew exchanged the usual pleasantries, trading some fresh fish for gin, as was customary at the time.

But then things got weird.

The commander of the black schooner offered the defendants $5,000 if they would help land the schooner and its cargo somewhere along the Delaware River. That would be roughly $80,000 today. Tempting as it was, the defendants understandably found the whole thing a little too suspicious and refused the offer. They decided to part ways with the schooner and head back into the bay.

When the defendants set sail, however, the black schooner followed them all the way to Cape May. As branch pilots, the defendants would ordinarily have charged to guide a ship into the bay, so they dropped anchor and went aboard the schooner to demand their usual fee. But the commander of the black schooner had a counteroffer that went something like this: "No, but I'll give you $60 for your skiff, or we're going to take it from you by force." The defendants refused and promptly lost their skiff as promised.

A little while later, as the crew of the schooner was using their brand-new skiff to unload five trunks and a bag of money, the defendants overheard them planning to sink their ship and its remaining cargo. Having just missed out on $5,000, then $60, and then their own skiff, the defendants suggested that it would be a pity to destroy the boat and offered to take it.

Ultimately, the crew abandoned the schooner they came in on and the defendants took it to a port in Lewistown, Pennsylvania, along with their bruised egos. When they arrived, they reported the whole ordeal to a customs officer, who in turn told the district attorney. Rather than commend them for their integrity, the prosecutor indicted the two branch pilots for getting too chummy with suspected pirates.

Of course, nobody knew who the men on the black schooner were, where they were from, what was in the trunks they unloaded, or whether they were pirates at all. Still, that didn't keep the government from bringing the case to trial and urging the jury to presume that the mystery men must have been pirates and that the defendants knew it.

At the end of trial, the judge instructed the jury on the three essential findings it would have to make to return a guilty verdict. As to the first element—whether the men on board the schooner were in fact pirates—the judge instructed the jury that although their conduct was certainly "mysterious, and highly suspicious," there wasn't any actual proof they were pirates. As the judge told the jury:

> *They might have acquired the property which they were so anxious to preserve, as well by robbery on land, by capture from Spanish subjects on the high seas, under a commission from the revolutionary government of South America, (which would not amount to acts of piracy,) as by unauthorized robbery on the high seas. The master of this vessel may have run away with the cargo committed to his care, to transport from one place to another, which would be no offence within the 8th section of the act of congress, if the vessel was foreign, nor within the general law. Or, he may merely have intended a breach of the revenue laws of the United States, by smuggling his cargo on shore.*

In other words, the men had almost certainly committed *some* crime, but the judge believed "it would be carrying the doctrine of presumption to an alarming extent" for the jury to presume that their crime was piracy specifically.

The same was true of the crime's second essential element, which required a finding that the defendants knew they were dealing with actual pirates at the time they spoke. On that point, the judge told the jury that just because the defendants thought they were "very suspicious characters," that wasn't enough for a conviction. The defendants had no way to know whether the men were pirates, some other kind of criminal, or just strange altogether.

Clearly, the judge didn't think a person could be guilty of corresponding or confederating with pirates if they had nothing more than a suspicion about someone's pirate status. But what about the nature of the correspondence? Even if you do know someone is a pirate, are all kinds of conversations with them categorically barred by federal law?

According to the judge in *Howard*, the answer is no. Even correspondence with a known pirate must be intended to advance a piratical cause. That is, "there must be something of criminal intention, in the person who confederates and corresponds with the pirates." As the court explained to the jury, a person can't be criminally convicted for having "perfectly innocent" conversations with pirates, which might include conversations intended to bring a pirate to justice, or to try and get them to leave the pirate life behind entirely. Instead, only true confederates of pirates can be convicted.

The jury returned a verdict of "not guilty."

CORRESPONDING WITH PIRATES TODAY

In the two hundred years since *Howard*, there have been no major developments in the law of pirate correspondence. To be found guilty, a person still probably needs to:

- find someone who seems like they might be a pirate;
- learn enough about them to be confident they have actually committed acts of piracy and aren't just going through a Johnny Depp phase;
- strike up a conversation and get their number; and
- discuss pirate stuff in an affirming (not discouraging) way.

As *Howard* demonstrated, however, even a questionable case may be enough to get charged by an eager prosecutor. For those looking to avoid criminal charges, it may be best to cut ties with all of the potential pirates in their life. On the plus side, concerns of federal pirate charges can also make for a great excuse to get out of an unhealthy relationship or refuse to give out your number in the first place.

Give Your Boat to a Pirate

As the old saying goes, the two happiest days in a boat owner's life are the day he buys his boat and the day he sells it. A strong contender for the *third* happiest day in a boat owner's life is the day he gives his boat to a pirate.

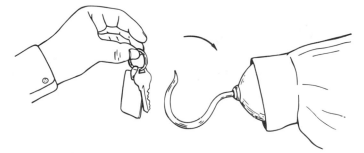

Fig. 7-2. Hand/Hook Over the Keys.

18 U.S.C. § 1656 makes it a federal crime for any person to voluntarily "yield up" a vessel on the high seas to a pirate. The text of the statute suggests that a person can be guilty of this federal crime for nothing more than giving a boat to a person who happens to be a pirate, even if the boat giver has no knowledge of their piratical ways.

Unlike the federal prohibition on corresponding with a pirate, Section 1656 contains no explicit requirement that the offender know they're dealing with an actual pirate. The absence of such language may be significant, because the Supreme Court has held that statutes should be read together with related statutes and in a way that doesn't render other statutory language superfluous or unnecessary. Thus, a person on trial for accidentally giving his boat to a pirate should expect prosecutors to argue that Congress intentionally chose to leave out any requirement that a person know the recipient of his boat is a pirate, thereby imposing criminal liability even without knowledge that the boat recipient was a pirate.

Fig 7-3. Say Goodbye.

Without clear guidance from the courts or Congress, all boat owners should assume that anyone they give their boat to might be a pirate. If confronted with the obvious signs, like a peg leg, hook hand, and a weird accent, it's too risky to assume they're just from Louisiana. As with the ban on corresponding with pirates, this statute also serves as an airtight excuse not to let your brother-in-law borrow your boat anymore. Tell him you simply can't take the risk that he might be a pirate.

Shanghai a Sailor

Some nautical crimes don't involve pirates at all. 18 U.S.C. § 2194 is one of them. It prohibits "shanghaiing sailors." For those unfamiliar with the term, it refers to the practice of kidnapping a person to work on a ship through the use of force, threats, lies, or while the person is drunk or on drugs. Historically, a combination of all of these tactics was the preferred method of those doing the shanghaiing.

The federal ban on shanghaiing was introduced in Congress in 1906 with the strong support of people who had seen men disappear for months at a time while held prisoner aboard ships that they boarded when drunk. Many of these men had been unsuccessful in bringing their captors to justice. Some disappeared entirely. One congressional witness—the district attorney for Baltimore—explained that the "crimps" and "runners" responsible for tricking these men into servitude would typically be paid $10 or $12 for every man delivered to the ship, which the captain would then deduct from each man's wages.[2] He testified: "They engage any or all sorts of men who can stand on two legs, and they sometimes engage them when they are in a condition when they can not stand on their legs. [Laughter.]"

That was certainly true in the 1911 case of *United States v. Domingos*, in which Joe Domingos was criminally charged for shanghaiing a Florida man named William Mitchell. Domingos was the proprietor of a boardinghouse for sailors in Pensacola and worked as a professional crimp, meaning he made a living by providing the masters of shorthanded vessels with seamen to work aboard their ships on foreign voyages.[3]

William Mitchell was one of the unlucky seamen staying at Domingos's boardinghouse while home from his last voyage. One day, Domingos took Mitchell to the consul of Uruguay, where Mitchell was asked to sign shipping articles committing him to work aboard the Uruguayan steamship *Oriental* just before it departed on a foreign voyage. The only problem? Mitchell was drunk. Really, *really* drunk.

Fig. 7-4. William Mitchell.

Mitchell was so drunk, in fact, that when Domingos brought him down to the boat landing to board the ship, Mitchell had to be "hoisted aboard the ship by combined efforts of [Domingos], a boatman, and the ship's tackle." (See Fig. 7-4.) Once aboard, they put him in the sailors' living quarters to sleep off the booze.

When Mitchell woke up and realized where he was, he went to the ship's master, who didn't speak English, and "objected to remaining on board and continuing the voyage, for which he had signed articles." Mitchell was eventually brought back ashore and reported the debacle to authorities.

Aside from Mitchell having experienced what might be the worst hangover of the twentieth century, United States attorney Frank Cubberly argued that Mitchell was also the victim of a crime. After all, the new anti-shanghaiing law seemed clear enough. It read:

> *Whoever with intent that any person shall perform service or labor of any kind on board of any vessel engaged in trade and commerce among the several states or with foreign nations . . . shall procure or induce, or attempt to procure or induce, another by force or threats or by representations which he knows or believes to be untrue, or while the person so procured or induced is intoxicated or under the influence of any drug, to go on board of any such vessel to perform service or labor thereon, shall be fined.*

But the Circuit Court for the Northern District of Florida ruled that the government improperly charged Domingos with shanghaiing Mitchell because prosecutors hadn't alleged that Mitchell was forced. In the court's view, the text of the law only prohibited taking a person aboard a ship to do work if the person had been "procured or induced by force or threats or by false representations." Even if intoxicated, a person still had to have been "so procured or induced" to be considered a victim of shanghaiing.

The court explained:

> However reprehensible may be the practice of inveigling drunken seamen aboard ship for the purpose of signing them in contracts which they are incapable of comprehending, and whatever may have been the intention of Congress by this legislation to protect the unwary seamen from falling hapless victims to the ingenious snares of hospitable runners, if the legislative purpose was to prohibit the mere inducing of drunken seamen aboard ship for the purpose of shipping them in the service of the vessel, the statute falls lamentably short of the mark.

The court dismissed the charges and Domingos was set free to inveigle sailors another day.

Since the failed *Domingos* prosecution, there have been no reported shanghaiing convictions. Even so, the law is not yet a dead letter. In 2003 the attorney general issued a regulation specifically identifying forcible shanghaiing as an offense for which a DNA sample must be collected from the defendant upon conviction. The Department of Justice will be ready with a swab next time a crimp slips up.

SHANGHAIING: SAN FRANCISCO–STYLE

For a purist looking to shanghai someone in a historically accurate way, tales from the seedy underbelly of nineteenth-century San Francisco provide guidance on how it was done. In his book

The Barbary Coast, Herbert Asbury described the methods used by Bay Area crimps to inveigle sailors and sell them off to ship captains.[4]

Fig. 7-5. Bung-starter.

Fig 7-6. Slung shot.

One infamous technique was devised by "Miss Piggott," a San Francisco bar owner who used a combination of seduction, intoxication, a trapdoor, and some good old-fashioned blunt-force head trauma. According to Asbury, Piggott would begin by having her trusted runner, Nikko, lure an unsuspecting sailor into her bar, where the mark would be strategically positioned over a trapdoor installed in the floor. Piggott would then give him a drink called the "Miss Piggott Special," which was "equal parts of whisky, brandy, and gin, with a goodly lacing of laudanum or opium."

Then came the coup de grâce. As the liquor and opium took hold of the sailor's faculties, "Miss Piggot leaned across the bar and tapped him on the head with a bung-starter, while Nikko made matters certain with a blow from a slung shot." (See Figs. 7-5 and 7-6.) Piggott would then pull a lever to open the trapdoor, dropping the unconscious victim onto a mattress below. He'd be sold to a shipping company thereafter and the inveiglement would be complete.

Sailors tricked into service this way were said to be "sent to Shanghai," though not in the literal sense. In common parlance, a "Shanghai voyage" was any long and dangerous trip on the high seas, and being duped into one—or "shanghaied"—was enough of a problem that Congress had to get involved.

Board a Ship That's About to Arrive but Hasn't Yet

If you get your life advice from desk calendars, you've been told not to wait for your ship to come in but to swim out to it. It's not just a good way to live; it's also a pretty effective way to become a federal criminal.

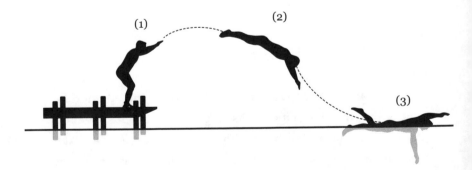

Fig. 7-7.

18 U.S.C. § 2279 provides that "whoever, not being in the United States service, and not being duly authorized by law for the purpose, goes on board any vessel about to arrive at the place of her destination, before her actual arrival, and before she has been completely moored, shall be fined under this title or imprisoned not more than six months, or both." In plain English, that means it's a federal crime for civilians to get on a boat that's about to arrive but hasn't quite yet.

By its text, the law doesn't really care *why* a person boards a boat before it arrives. It doesn't require that the early boarder intend to commit a crime on the boat or try to get a free ride. The law only requires that the person isn't in the United States service and isn't otherwise "authorized" by law to get on the boat early. In fact, in 1872, a federal court held that the government doesn't

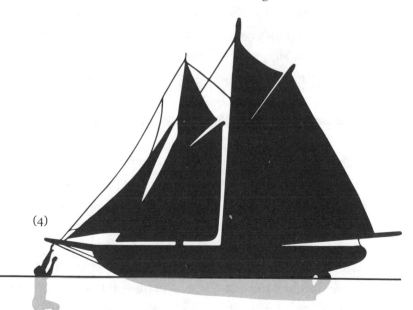

(4)

even need to prove either of those two things in a prosecution for early boarding.[5] Getting on a ship too early is enough.

But *why*? Is it a federal ban on impatience? As it turns out, there was a time when the purpose of the law was quite clear to everyone—at least those living in coastal cities—and it just so happens that it's related to the federal prohibition on shanghaiing sailors.

As a federal judge in Oregon explained in 1890:

> *The evil which this section is intended to prevent and remedy is apparent, and in this district notorious. For instance, lawless persons, in the interest or employ of what may be called "sailor-mongers," get on board vessels bound for Portland as soon as they get in the Columbia river, and by the help of intoxicants, and the use of other means, often savoring of violence, get the crews ashore, and leave the vessel without help to manage or care for her. The sailor thereby loses the wages of the voyage, and is dependent on the boarding-house for the necessaries of life, where he is kept, until sold by his captors to an outgoing vessel, at an enormous price.[6]*

That's right. When ships came in, runners and crimps would swarm the vessels with promises of liquor and women to lure the crew into servitude. As Asbury describes in *The Barbary Coast*, the scene was actually pretty horrifying. "It was not uncommon for two opposing runners to seize a sailor's ear between their teeth and hang on, biting hard, until the bewildered and frightened seaman cried out the name of the boarding-house master which had been most forcibly impressed upon his mind." The runners even carried a standard set of tools for luring or kidnapping the arriving sailors: "a revolver, a knife, a blackjack or slungshot, a pair of brass knuckles, a flask of liquid soap, obscene pictures, and as many bottles of rum and whisky, all liberally dosed with Spanish fly, as could be crowded into their pockets."

Fig. 7-8. Sailor Runner Tools.

Armed with booze, weapons, and smut, you might be wondering, *What's with the soap?* Well, if the runners wanted to be really clever, they would sneak aboard a ship and put some soap into the crew's soup, causing a revolt among the disgusted sailors when they sat down for mealtime. The runners would then lure away the disgruntled sailors.

These invasions also raised other concerns. An annual report of the New York Commissioners of Quarantine published in 1874 complained that the gangs of runners were invading ships on a daily basis. Because they boarded the ships illegally and without permits, they also frequently stumbled into ships infested with disease. In addition to their violence, the runners ended up becoming vectors of disease. The quarantine report advocated for a new law making it a crime to board any vessel without a permit from the health department. After all, if there was one thing the violent, sometimes murderous sailor runners were truly worried about, it was getting caught without a proper permit.

A RECENT PROSECUTION

Antiquated as it may seem, it's still a federal crime to board a ship too early, whether you're planning on sinking your teeth into a sailor's ear or not. For the entire twentieth century, the government kept this statute on a shelf and focused on other law-enforcement priorities. About 130 years later, however, prosecutors finally dusted off the early boarding statute to prosecute a true modern-day scourge: environmental activists.

In 2004, Greenpeace and several activists were criminally charged under the early boarding statute when they climbed aboard a cargo ship a few miles off the coast of Florida.[7] Greenpeace had intel that the ship was bringing illegally logged mahogany from Brazil into the United States (a federal crime of its own). The activists planned to get on board and unfurl a banner that read "President Bush, Stop Illegal Logging," but they were apprehended before the unfurling could occur.

The individual activists each pleaded guilty. They were sentenced to receive fines ranging from $100 to $500 and were forever branded federal criminals for their premature boat boarding. Greenpeace, on the other hand, fought its charges, arguing that the boat-boarding statute was unconstitutionally vague and that the indictment should be dismissed. Greenpeace lost that argument but called the government's bluff and demanded a trial by jury.

After several days of trial, the judge found that the government had presented insufficient evidence to send the case to the jury. In the end, Greenpeace was acquitted, though its members remained convicts.

Detain a Seaman's Clothes

Federal law provides that "a person detaining a seaman's clothing shall be fined not more than $500, imprisoned for not more than 6 months, or both." Yes, the statute means what it says: if you have a seaman's clothes and you refuse to give them back, you're a federal criminal.

The law doesn't specify any particular articles of clothing, so it's safe to assume that everything from a seaman's sou'wester (hat) to his skivvies (underwear) benefits from federal protection.

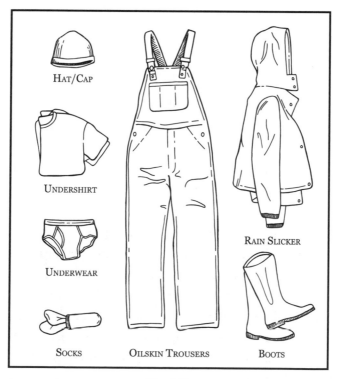

Fig. 7-9.

Note, however, only the clothes of current seamen are protected. As recently as 1987, a federal court held that the seaman's clothing statute had not been violated when the owner of a mobile home park detained the clothes of an out-of-work seaman. According to the court, a person must be actively engaged or employed on a vessel for his clothes to earn federal protection. That's because federal law defines a "seaman" as "an individual (except scientific personnel, a sailing school instructor, or a sailing school student) engaged or employed in any capacity on board a vessel." So remember: stealing a sailor's underwear may be a federal crime, but stealing a sailing student's underwear will probably be handled at the state or principal's-office level.

EARLY CLOTHESNAPPINGS

Historically, this particular offense was most often committed on dry land by the crimps and boardinghouse keepers trying to keep their resident sailors on a short leash. But this offense also has a notorious history at sea. Masters of ships would sometimes lock away their seamen's clothes while the vessel was in port so that the crew wouldn't run away. Other times, sailors had their clothes detained as punishment.

It was that practice which spurred two nineteenth-century seamen to file a lawsuit against their ship's master.[8] In 1851, Robert Williams and Samuel Gates were crewmembers of the bark *Gibraltar*, a ship docked in the Cuban harbor of Matanzas. Early one morning, the ship's mate called for all hands to report for duty, but nobody responded. When the mate yelled out for the crew a second time, Samuel Gates (not a morning person) responded: "You need not kick up such a noise, for you were answered the second time." For the mid-1800s, that was quite a burn.

Having none of it, the ship's mate started hurling insults at Gates, and Gates returned the favor. Then things really got out of hand. When Gates's fellow crewmember, Robert Williams, intervened, the ship's mate punched him. Williams punched back but was grabbed by the hair and dragged to the ground by none other than Harvey Jordan, the ship's master and the guy who was supposed to be everyone's levelheaded boss. While Williams was being held down on the deck by Jordan, the mate kicked him in the head a few times for good measure. Gates tried to break it up, but the mate punched him in the face twice for it.

When the dust settled, and after the men had returned to their work, the ship's mate approached Williams and Gates. Instead of apologizing, however, the mate stated simply and eloquently: "I will knock your brains out with a handspike." Williams complained to his master: "Captain Jordan, do you hear that?" Not one to defuse a good encore fracas, the master replied, "I do hear it."

Gates and Williams refused to do any more work until they could have their grievances heard. The master responded by having the men dragged off the ship and thrown in the local prison at Matanzas without any clothing or bedding, where they allegedly slept on flagstones and used their boots for pillows. The master detained their clothes on board the ship and later sold them after sailing away.

Back onshore, the men successfully sued Jordan, in part because he had detained their clothes. The Circuit Court of Massachusetts found that Jordan was wrong "to detain all their clothing from them during eight days, and then sail away and finally deprive them of it." They were each awarded $48 (about $1,500 in today's dollars).

But was it a *crime* to detain the clothes of a seaman? Not yet, apparently. Even after amendment in 1895, the law only provided that "the clothing of any seaman shall be exempt from attachment and that any person who shall detain such clothing when demanded by the owner shall be liable to a penalty of not exceeding $100." There were no explicit criminal penalties in the law.

Of course, the fact that it wasn't a crime didn't stop federal prosecutors from charging people for it. In 1903, one particularly frustrated prosecutor wrote to the attorney general to complain:

> *I am continually having trouble with the boarding-house keepers who detain seamen's clothing...*
>
> *It has been the custom of this office for years to have such boarding-house keeper arrested, when he or she detained such seaman's clothing, and acting under instructions from your Department, I procured some time ago a complaint to be made against a boarding-house keeper, and took it before Mr. Commissioner Benedict and applied for a warrant. He came to the conclusion, after examining the law, that a warrant could not issue, as the law provided for an action for a penalty and not for a crime. I then took the matter to Judge Thomas, and after reading the law over, he, too, decided that it was an action for a penalty and not a criminal action.*

The prosecutor proposed an amendment to the statute that would provide "that any person detaining a seaman's clothing shall be deemed guilty of a misdemeanor." Congress agreed and it has been a federal crime to detain a seaman's clothing ever since.

By its terms, the law is expressly concerned with attachments and liens being placed on seamen's clothes. But the text permits a conviction for anyone who detains a seaman's clothes, no matter the circumstances.

Fig. 7-10. Detaining a Seaman's Clothes

TAKE THE CLOTHES

The law specifies no particular means by which an offender must obtain a seaman's clothes in the first place.

Illicit methods of obtaining clothes may include:

- swiping unattended laundry;

- stealing clothes from a seaman's bedroom in the middle of the night (shown); or

- taking clothes directly off a seaman.

REFUSE TO GIVE THEM BACK

Once the clothes have been obtained, the offender need only "detain" them to be guilty of a federal crime.

CAUTION: Stealing a seaman's clothes may create a higher-than-normal risk of being chased by a naked sailor. Offenders should always keep a safe distance from angry, naked seamen, unless they're into that sort of thing.

Be a Stowaway

18 U.S.C. § 2199 makes it a federal crime to hide aboard a vessel without the master's permission for the purpose of obtaining transportation. Naturally, any attempt to become a stowaway on

a vessel requires a bulletproof ruse for getting onto the ship in the first place and remaining undetected until the ship has left port.

A method frequently employed by the stowaways of the early 1900s was to hide in the cargo hold of their target vessel, whether

Fig. 7-11. Stowing Away on a Vessel

① **GET IN A BARREL**

If using the Balboa technique, the stowaway must locate a barrel of sufficient size to conceal himself. Although the dog is optional, it will make the trip less lonely.

②

ENLIST AN ACCOMPLICE

The stowaway may require outside help to ensure he's properly sealed into the barrel.

NOTE: The accomplice may face criminal liability for aiding and abetting a stowaway.

③ **SNEAK ABOARD**

Stowaways must get on board a vessel undetected. Balboa is said to have sold several barrels of grain (he himself among them) to a departing vessel.

with the help of the ship's crew or by simply sneaking aboard. But even centuries before that, stowaways were already perfecting the art of concealing themselves among the cargo of ships destined for the Americas. In 1510, one early pioneer of stowing away named Vasco Núñez de Balboa snuck aboard an expedition to South America by hiding in a barrel with his dog. Balboa wasn't just looking for free travel, though; he was trying to escape his creditors back in Spain. And while it's not clear how much debt he had, he was desperate enough to be sealed in a barrel with a mastiff-greyhound mix, so he must have had student loans.

In 1939, when Congress finally got around to considering a criminal statute prohibiting stowaways, an American ship captain testified in support of the law. He described how some stowaways had only been discovered when they started fires in the ship's cargo hold. And then there were the stowaways who just wanted the thrill of a free ride.

In the hearings before Congress, Ralph Emerson of the Maritime Unions of the CIO testified:

I know one professional stowaway who is a skylarker. She is known as "Stowaway Mary." She has stowed away, I guess, on every passenger ship we've ever had. I caught up with her once, in Bermuda where she had even gone to the extent— she has done it so often that she knew just what to do and she came aboard the ship well dressed. She was a psychopathic case coming from a nice family on Long Island. After she got out to sea she got in conversation with girls in the salon of the ship and walked down to the dining room with them and in the rush, of course, when the steward was placing people at the tables, she just walked by him and never said anything, and sat down and then later in the evening she told one of

them "I have a cabin by myself and I do not like it down there;
can I come over and sleep in your room?" The result was that
one of the girls told her "All right," and they let her come in
with them. She did that for 2 nights, but when morning came
and the ship was getting into Bermuda, evidently her psycho-
pathic ego got the best of her and, when the girls came back
to their stateroom they found missing all sorts of things, and
she had taken all the jewels.

As Stowaway Mary demonstrated, dressing the part, acting the part, and possessing a general sneakiness are key attributes of a successful stowaway.

STOWAWAYS: "THE SCUM OF THE COUNTRY FROM WHICH THEY COME"

Believe it or not, there was a time in the United States when immigration was a contentious issue. Even before the tales of Stowaway Mary led to the enactment of the stowaway statute, federal law had prohibited stowaways in one form or another for over one hundred years, whether by denying them entry to the United States entirely or by punishing them criminally when they arrived.

These laws were largely written in response to the influx of European immigrants in the late 1800s and early 1900s and the complaints of customs and immigration officials. One of them, the deputy collector of customs for the Port of New York, Chas McLelland, wrote to the Speaker of the United States House in 1888 to express that he was "embarrassed by reason of the numerous 'stowaways' lately coming into [the] port [of New York]." McLelland complained that this made it necessary to hire more customs inspectors in order to see that the stowaways were "properly disposed of" and asked Congress to enact a law punishing shipmasters who failed to prevent stowaways aboard their ships.

With few exceptions, the law at that time was basically silent on what to do with stowaways arriving in the United States. One judge took the bold step of declaring that "the master of a ship at sea has no right to take a stowaway found on his vessel, and heave hi[m] overboard in mid-ocean." Another reportedly held that it was wrong for the master of a ship to shave a stowaway's head just to put a mark on him.[9] So stowaways clearly had *some* rights.

But even when Congress enacted the Immigration Act of 1907, it provided no guidance on what to do with stowaway immigrants arriving at the ports of the United States. Instead, the act focused on banning all sorts of other people, including:

> *All idiots, imbeciles, feeble-minded persons, epileptics, insane persons, and persons who have been insane within five years previous; persons who have had two or more attacks of insanity at any time previously; ... polygamists, or persons who admit their belief in the practice of polygamy; ... prostitutes ... [and a number of other prohibited people].*

It wasn't until ten years later that Congress amended the Immigration Act to expressly ban stowaways. In doing so, however, Congress wrote an important exception into the law, providing that "any such stowaway, if otherwise admissible, may be admitted in the discretion of the Secretary of Labor ..."

In other words, so long as a stowaway wasn't an idiot, an imbecile, a feebleminded polygamist, an epileptic prostitute, or some other kind of prohibited immigrant, the secretary of labor could choose to permit the stowaway to stay in the United States. Even with this ban, however, anti-stowaway sentiment still ran high.

In 1921, Frederick A. Wallis, the commissioner of immigration for the state of New York, authored an article entitled "Treating Incoming Aliens as Human Beings," which addressed the massive influx of immigrants continuing to occur at Ellis Island. His thesis was simple: America should be able to pick only the best immigrants to come to the country and turn away the rest.

Wallis decried stowaways in particular as a "menace that threatens the safety of the country." He explained that

> the stowaways, as a class, are made up of the scum of the country from which they come. They are, with but few exceptions, ex-convicts, criminals and degenerates. We are told that they are frequently assisted in going aboard vessels by the police officials of these countries. However, sometimes we find among the stowaways a worthy case, but to determine the admission of any of the stowaways is an exceedingly difficult undertaking.

Put differently, Wallis was saying that he believed other countries were sending stowaways to the United States, but when they sent them, they weren't sending their best. They were sending criminals, ex-convicts, and degenerates, and some of them, he assumed, were good people.

About twenty years later, in 1940, Congress finally enacted a federal criminal statute authorizing the prosecution of stowaways found aboard any "vessel" destined for the United States. Just a few years later, a case came before a federal court in California that would test the limits of the new law.

In *United States v. Lloyd Keith Peoples*, the government alleged that the defendant hid himself aboard a navy seaplane that was departing from Honolulu. Sometime after takeoff, he was found

Fig. 7-12. Stowing Away on an Airplane

WHEEL WELL

The FAA has recorded more than one hundred attempts at stowing away inside an airplane's wheel bay. According to FAA statistics, more than 75% of the stowaways died by freezing or falling.

CARGO HOLD

Unlike the wheel bay, cargo holds are pressurized and protect the stowaway from falling. A couple of baggage handlers have survived domestic flights after being accidentally trapped in the hold.

ON BOARD

Though difficult to get past security and the gate agent, stowaways have successfully hidden aboard flights in the bathrooms or by getting lucky with an extra seat.

and apprehended before the plane landed in California. He was later charged in federal court with violating the federal stowaway statute.

Peoples moved to dismiss his charges on the grounds that a seaplane was not a "vessel" within the meaning of the stowaway statute. Quoting Supreme Court Justice Oliver Wendell Holmes Jr., the court agreed, explaining:

> *Although it is not likely that a criminal will carefully consider the text of the law before he murders or steals, it is reasonable that a fair warning should be given to the world in language that the common world will understand, of what the law intends to do if a certain line is passed. To make the warning fair, so far as possible the line should be clear.*

In dismissing the charges against Peoples, the court also sent a message to lawmakers in Washington: "If Congress wishes to make stowing away on a seaplane a crime, it can so provide, but that is a matter for the legislators and not the court."

Congress listened. It amended the stowaway statute to include airplanes the following year, thereby giving rise to a whole new class of criminal stowaways. In the decades since, airborne stowaways have hidden themselves in airplane bathrooms, cargo holds, and even the landing gear compartment on a number of jetliners. With a few exceptions, however, the results have largely been tragic. The majority of wheel-well stowaways have fallen or frozen to death midflight.

One notable exception is the person who likely holds the title of most successful airborne stowaway—a Chicago woman who has repeatedly evaded airport security and flown aboard airline flights even without a boarding pass.[10]

Chapter 8

HOW TO BECOME A FEDERAL CRIMINAL

IN OTHER WAYS

In 1957, *West Side Story* made its Broadway debut. One year later, and for supposedly unrelated reasons, Congress enacted the Switchblade Knife Act, prohibiting the manufacture, sale, and transportation of switchblade knives in "interstate commerce." It certainly wasn't because Congress was scared of dancing street gangs with switchblades. No way.

The new law allowed people with only one arm or members of the military to carry switchblades from state to state. Two-armed civilians could still be charged.

It's not just switchblades, though. Lots of other things are subject to federal criminal law simply because they move in "interstate commerce." Fireworks, toys, and even your own internal organs can each be the instruments of federal crime. Things like government-created cartoon characters and certain wardrobe choices can also land you in federal prison.

LAWN DARTS, CLACKER BALLS, AND EVERYTHING ELSE IN INTERSTATE COMMERCE

In the 1970s, the so-called greatest generation thought it was a good idea to let their kids play with things like metal lawn darts and "clacker balls." If you're not familiar with these toys, that's probably because you were lucky enough to be born in an era when both were already banned. If you are familiar with them, I'm sure nobody notices the scars and you look fine.

Today, these toys aren't just illegal; they're *criminal* to sell. Though to be fair, who could have guessed that three-pound, foot-long darts with metal points, which were made to be thrown in the general vicinity of little kids, would end up being dangerous? From 1980 to 1988, lawn darts sent 6,100 people to the emergency room. They even claimed lives.

Another toy called "clacker balls" also sent plenty of kids to the hospital. Clackers were made of two hard plastic balls at the end of a cord with a ring in the middle. They were meant to be "operated in a rhythmic manner by an upward and downward motion of the hand so that the two balls will meet forcefully at the top and bottom of two semi-circles thus causing a 'clacking' sound." In addition to being strikingly similar to an Argentinian throwing weapon called "bolas," clackers had a tendency to break apart and cause shrapnel-like injuries to kids.

Luckily for the soft skulls and precious little eyes of generations to come, Congress enacted the Federal Hazardous Products Act in 1972, which gave the Consumer Product Safety Commission the authority to ban or regulate consumer products that present unreasonable risks of injury. In passing the law, Congress expressed its view that state and local government couldn't be trusted to adequately protect the public from these kinds of dangerous products. So, through its constitutional power to regulate interstate and foreign commerce, Congress gave the CPSC the authority to make family picnics and playgrounds a little less fun everywhere.

As a result, 16 C.F.R. § 1500.18(a)(7) now bans the sale or manufacture of clacker balls unless they've passed rigorous impact testing. Subsection (a)(4) completely bans metal lawn darts. Under 15 U.S.C. § 1264, delivering either prohibited toy "into interstate commerce" is a federal crime.

But what is all this business about "interstate commerce," anyway? We know that Article I, Section 8, of the Constitution gives Congress the power to regulate it, but what *is* it? And what kinds of things does it let the federal government put you in prison for? Here are some quick FAQs:

FREQUENTLY ASKED QUESTIONS ABOUT INTERSTATE COMMERCE

Congress can "regulate" interstate commerce by statute, but can I go to prison for violating regulations?

Only if Congress believes it's "necessary and proper" to do so. (Heads-up: they totally do.)

Does something have to cross state lines to be "in interstate commerce"?

Good question, but no. In 1942, the Supreme Court held that Congress's power to regulate interstate commerce "extends to those *intrastate* activities which in a substantial way interfere with or obstruct the exercise" of that power.

Right, but if I do something in the privacy of my own home or on my own land, that isn't interstate commerce, is it?

Where did you get that idea? It might be. For example, in *Wickard v. Filburn,* the Supreme Court held that the federal government could restrict the amount of wheat a person grows at home for his own personal use, because if enough people grew wheat at home, it might affect national wheat prices.

Okay, but what if—

It's commerce. All right? It's all commerce.

Even if—

Yes.

With that part settled, let's now discuss a few of the countless other ways to become a federal criminal both in and out of interstate commerce.

Sell Children's Pajamas with a Warning Label Written in the Wrong Font

Believe it or not, there actually are times when using Comic Sans can be a crime. Obviously it will always be the preferred choice for passive-aggressive notes around the office, but some federal labeling requirements are simply too strict when it comes to typeface to allow the world's most hated font.

Take children's pajamas, for example. Under 16 C.F.R. § 1615.1, tight-fitting pajamas must have a warning label explaining that they're more flammable when worn loose (even though that's how

Fig. 8-1.

all the cool babies wear them). (See Fig. 8-1.) For pajamas sold in a package, the warning label must be written in an 11-point Arial or Helvetica font. If sold on hangers, however, the warning tag must be written in 18-point type. Either way, no Comic Sans.

Toys and other children's products, including pajamas, are considered "misbranded hazardous substances" if they aren't labeled as required by federal regulations. Under the Federal Hazardous Substances Act, introducing mislabeled pajamas into interstate commerce is a prohibited act and selling pajamas labeled in the wrong font could get you ninety days in federal prison.

THE COMIC SANS LOOPHOLE

In addition to the labels discussed above, all tight-fitting pajamas must also have a tag advising kids to wear their PJ's in a "snug-fitting" fashion. Notably, this second label doesn't have to be in Arial or Helvetica; the law requires only that a "sans-serif font" be used. Sadly, Comic Sans meets this requirement.

```
WEAR SNUG-FITTING
NOT FLAME RESISTANT
```

Example in 10-pt-Arial font

Fig. 8-2.

Pajama labels are just one example of the government's disdain for serifs and undying love of Arial and Helvetica. Other federal regulations require the labels on things like ear plugs, tobacco products, and, of course, mattresses to use fonts without the criminal flourish of a serif.

OTHER WARNING LABEL REQUIREMENTS

Other children's products, like toy balls and marbles, are less concerned about fonts and more focused on a painful level of clarity. For example, 16 C.F.R. § 1500.19(b)(4)(i) requires that a toy marble be labeled with a warning that includes the phrase "This toy is a marble." Similarly, subsection (b)(3)(i) explains that a small toy ball must explain that "this toy is a small ball."

True, these warnings are primarily anti-choking measures, which is a good thing. But there are other mandatory warning labels, the necessity of which suggest a grimmer outlook for humankind.

Consider the modern marvel that is food in self-pressurized containers. (Think spray cheese.) 21 C.F.R. § 101.17(a)(1) requires that it be sold with a clear warning that the user should "avoid spraying in eyes."

No, the regulation doesn't make it a crime to actually *spray* the food into your eyes. It is a free country, after all. It's only a crime to manufacture or sell spray food without the warning. A similar

Fig. 8-3.

regulation, 21 C.F.R. § 501.17(a), requires the same warning be put on spray food for pets. (Think spray cheese, only this time for dogs.) But remember: the warning isn't there for the benefit of your dog. It's there for you. You're the one who can't be trusted to resist spraying dog food in your eyes.

In fact, if federal regulations prove anything, it's that the government is extremely concerned about your eyes. The Code of Federal Regulations prescribes an uncomfortably great number of mandatory warnings that manufacturers must put on their products, all in an effort to finally get Americans to stop putting things in their eyes already.

Following is a list of things the government wants you to keep out of your eyes so badly that it's willing to put someone in prison if they don't tell you not to. The chart also highlights other key information that Americans have apparently proven they need to be told.

Fig. 8-4. Things to Not Put in Your Eyes		
Product	**What else you need to know**	**Regulation**
Athlete's foot cream	Change your socks daily.	21 C.F.R. § 333.250
Ear-drying drops	The drops are flammable.	21 C.F.R. § 344.52
Male genital desensitizer	Put it only on your penis.	21 C.F.R. § 348.50
Sunscreen	You can get it out of your eyes with water.	21 C.F.R. § 352.52
Dandruff shampoo	It's for external use only. (Don't eat it.)	21 C.F.R. § 358.750
Lasers	Don't stare directly into the beam.	21 C.F.R. § 1040.10

Yes, it may be troubling to learn that civilization has reached a point where things like over-the-counter jock itch cream must warn customers not to put the product in their eyes, especially when there is no reason anyone should ever be applying jock itch cream anywhere near their eyes. Heck, athlete's foot cream is required to direct its users to "pay special attention to spaces between the toes" when applying it. And while it's hard to imagine that a person could know they need to buy the cream but be totally lost in figuring out where to put it to stop the burning, here we are, America.

If there's any glimmer of hope in all of this, it's that these rules have largely been put into place because of unscrupulous manufacturers and not raw human stupidity alone. What's even better is that the government sometimes chooses to make defendants out of the misbranded products themselves, resulting in some of the greatest case names in American jurisprudence.

Take, for example, the 1964 case of *United States v. 2000 Plastic Tubular Cases, More or Less, Each Containing 2 Toothbrushes . . .* There, the government successfully sought the forfeiture of roughly two thousand toothbrushes that the seller had dubbed the "Conqueror" and that he promised would eradicate "trench mouth."

The toothbrush seller, who called himself a "Medical-Dental Researchist," advertised his brushes as "a must for engaged couples as the best aid for prevention of cancer, heart disease, and defective birth of their offspring." Although it sounded like one hell of a toothbrush, it was, in reality, just a toothbrush. The government prevailed and the two thousand toothbrushes were condemned.[1]

Other great lawsuits brought against misbranded, mislabeled, hazardous, or other products that managed to run afoul of federal law include:

- *United States v. Seventy-Five Boxes of Alleged Pepper*;
- *United States v. Eleven Gross Packages of Dr. Williams' Pink Pills*;
- *United States v. 267 Boxes of Macaroni*;
- *United States v. Twenty-Five Packages of Panama Hats*;
- *United States v. 11¼ Dozen Packages of Article Labeled in Part Mrs. Moffat's Shoo Fly Powders for Drunkenness*;
- *United States v. 76,552 Pounds of Frog Legs*; and
- *United States v. Thirty-Dozen Packages of Roach Food*.

And, of course, there was the 1974 case of *United States v. An Article Consisting of Boxes of Clacker Balls*, in which the government prevailed in obtaining the condemnation and destruction of roughly fifty thousand sets of clacker balls. Just think of all the resources our federal government has committed to plastic balls attached to a cord.

Distribute Matchbooks with an Unclinched Staple

Some products are considered hazardous not because of how they're labeled but because of how they're made. Matchbooks, for example, have been regulated in excruciating detail since the mid-1970s. Back then, hospital records suggested that Americans were sustaining nearly ten thousand matchbook-related injuries each year, because of course they were.

These injuries and accidents weren't only caused by people playing with matches. They included match heads breaking apart and lodging in people's eyes, spontaneous combustion, and entire matchbooks going up in flames with the strike of a single match.

In response to that fiery mini epidemic, the Consumer Product Safety Commission stepped in with what would become Title 16, Part 1202, of the Code of Federal Regulations. The proposed rules would require all matchbooks delivered into interstate commerce to meet minimum safety standards. The rules addressed everything from the location of the friction strip to how well the cover needed to say closed, right down to the tiny little staple that holds everything together. (See Fig. 8-5.)

Matchbook makers weren't thrilled with the new regulations. The estimated capital investment for a manufacturer to comply with the new rules was more than $800,000. But the CPSC had nothing to lose, particularly since consumers wouldn't feel a difference. After all, data showed that roughly 80 to 90 percent of all matchbooks were given away for free. Of course, that raises an even bigger question: Who exactly was out there *buying* matchbooks?

Unfortunately, the regulation was no match for the combination of people and fire. Even after the rules were put in place, matchbook-related injuries decreased only slightly. Still, it remains a federal crime for a matchbook maker to distribute matchbooks that fail to comply with the standards set forth in 16 C.F.R. § 1202.4. (See Fig. 8-5.) When compared with others in the fire-starting business, however, matchbook makers actually have it pretty easy.

Fig. 8-5. Illegal Matchbooks

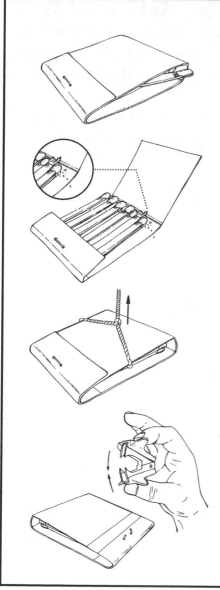

PROTRUDING HEADS

If any portion of a match head sticks outside the cover while the cover is closed, the matchbook is considered hazardous. That's what a match gets for being curious.

CRUMBLED HEADS

The federal matchbook regulations were written at a time when roughly one-third of matchbook-related injuries were caused by match head fragments becoming lodged in people's eyes. Crumbled, cracked, or split heads are now banned.

DEFECTIVE COVERS

In 1976, regulators proposed a rule that all matchbook covers remain closed when a force of up to five pounds was applied in any direction. The final rule only requires covers to remain closed without external force.

UNCLINCHED STAPLES

16 C.F.R. § 1202.4(a)(h) requires that "a staple used as an assembly device for securing the cover and combs shall be fully clinched so that the ends are flattened or turned into the cover." Anything less than a full clinch exposes the matchbook maker to criminal liability.

LETTING KIDS PLAY WITH CIGARETTE LIGHTERS

Unlike matchbooks, cigarette lighters are required to undergo highly detailed testing procedures before being sold. What that really means is that manufacturers are required to give their lighters to a bunch of little kids to play with before they can be sold in the market.

Unfortunately for the kids involved, the whole thing is a total sham. The test lighters they get are duds. The law requires that they have no fuel in them and that they be incapable of making a flame.

Fig. 8-6.

Worse, the federally mandated testing protocol is a strange, Machiavellian, *Lord of the Flies*–type exercise in which the weak are separated from the herd, children are scolded for helping one another, and success is rewarded with punishment.

The Testing Protocol

To begin with, 16 C.F.R. § 1210.4 requires cigarette lighter testers to round up at least one hundred kids between three and a half and four and a quarter years old to play with their lighters. Subsection (b) encourages them to catch kids where they feel most comfortable: their nursery schools and day cares.

Once the testers have a pool of little kids assembled, the trickery starts. Adult testers are told to "talk to the children in a normal and friendly tone to make them feel at ease and to gain their confidence." In lulling the kids into this sense of safety, though, the testers are expressly prohibited from claiming the test will be fun. It won't be.

The testers start by convincing the kids that their help is needed for a "special job," but the testers can't discuss the dangers of lighters or matches. If a kid tries to do the right thing and tells the tester that their parents told them to never touch a lighter, the testers have to feed them a government script, saying: "That's right—never touch a real lighter—but your [parent, etc.] said it was OK for you to try to make a noise with this special lighter because it can't hurt you."

And just like that, months of good parenting go right out the window.

Next, the testers are required to teach the kids how to use a lighter, telling them that it won't make a flame, only a noise. They then place a lighter in each child's hand, saying: "Now you try to make a noise with your lighter. Keep trying until I tell you to stop."

What the testers don't tell the kids is that the lighters actually can create a spark. If a kid manages to create one, the tester is supposed to say, "That's a spark—it won't hurt you," and encourage them to continue playing with the lighter. If the kid is successful, the tester snatches the lighter away and makes them sit and watch the other kids who haven't succeeded yet.

The federal lighter testing protocol also includes the unforgiving requirements that:

- if one kid tries to operate another kid's lighter, the tester has to say: "No. Ho(ohc) has to try to do it himself(herself)";
- "if a child becomes upset or afraid, and cannot be reassured before the test starts," they are eliminated; and
- "if a child disrupts the participation of another child for more than one minute during the test, the test is stopped and both children are eliminated."

In this context, "eliminated" just means excluded from the test results, so relax. In the end, though, what does all this accomplish? Sure, the lighter makers learn how effective their childproofing is. But what about the kids? Does anyone stop to ask whether they're left more confused than ever about when it's okay to play with a lighter? Nobody cares.

Whatever the costs, it's a federal crime for a lighter maker to sell lighters that don't pass the tests. If a few preschoolers have to endure the rigors of federally mandated testing, America is up for the task.

Lose a Stick of Dynamite and Fail to Report Its Length and Diameter

Dynamite has an amazing history. In 1867 it was invented by Alfred Nobel (as in "Nobel Prize"). By 1927 it was used to carve 90 percent of Mount Rushmore (that's the one with the faces). And, in 1949, Wile E. Coyote began educating America's youth about how to use it to murder a federally protected migratory bird (*Geococcyx californianus*).

One of the tricky things about dynamite, however, is that it can become fairly volatile as it ages. That's one reason why the federal Safe Explosives Act requires it to be handled and stored with care.

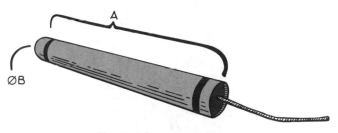

Fig. 8-7. Dynamite Stick.

If you're like most responsible dynamite owners, you know that the law requires you to store it in a legally compliant "magazine." By definition, a "magazine" is really just a room where you store explosives. By law, however, you're required to sweep the floor regularly, ensure your dynamite room has proper lighting, and refrain from smoking around your stock of explosives, though the latter is what might be referred to as a "self-enforcing" law.

But say you've done all that. You keep your dynamite stored in a clean, well-lit room and you've even stopped keeping a stick under your pillow just in case of late-night intruders. You're doing everything right. Then one day you notice your stock is a stick short. You've looked everywhere it could be: in your trunk, in the kids' rooms, and even your secret hiding place at the local playground. No luck. You now have an important decision to make: properly report your missing dynamite, or become a federal criminal for failing to do so.

As an initial matter, losing the explosives can be completely accidental and still be a crime. Under 18 U.S.C. § 842(k), there is no requirement that a person lose a stick of dynamite on purpose to be guilty. In fact, the loss itself isn't necessarily the crime; the offense occurs when the owner fails to properly report the lost dynamite to ATF within twenty-four hours of discovering it's missing.

Fig. 8-8.

Take the gentleman in Fig. 8-8, for example. Even though his dynamite is "lost" the second it leaves his pocket, the twenty-four-hour window for reporting it probably won't start until he gets home and realizes it's missing. And, honestly, who among us hasn't had that experience? But loss is just one of the perils of concealed-carry dynamite. 18 U.S.C. § 842(k)'s reporting requirement also applies to stolen dynamite.

Whether it's lost or stolen, however, the law requires more than just a call to the ATF saying, "I can't find my dynamite." Under 27 C.F.R. § 555.30(c)(5), the dynamite owner is required to report the length and diameter of the lost explosives, if known. (See Fig. 8-7.) Those who wish to comply with the law should probably make it a practice to regularly measure their explosives. Failing to do so poses a serious risk of exaggeration in both length and diameter if the owner is reporting size strictly from memory. And remember: lying to the government about how big your stick is might even expose you to additional criminal penalties under 18 U.S.C. § 1001 for making a material misrepresentation to the government.

OTHER CRIMES INVOLVING EXPLOSIVES

The Safe Explosives Act and its implementing regulations address more than lost explosives. There are dozens of criminal offenses set forth in 18 U.S.C. § 842 and Title 27, Part 555, of the C.F.R., involving the storage, manufacture, and sale of explosives. Some of them are punishable by life in prison or even death. Others carry less severe penalties but are no less federal crimes.

In addition to the Safe Explosives Act, other federal statutes and regulations also contain criminal provisions involving explosives, including those governing hunting, air travel, the mail, and federal properties.

Bomb Making

18 U.S.C. § 842(a)(1) makes it a crime for anyone to "engage in the business of" manufacturing explosives without a license. But don't make the rookie mistake of assuming that the statute actually means what it says. Although the law's text would have you believe it requires a person to "engage in the *business* of" making explosives, federal courts have held that a person is "engaged in the business of" making explosives even if just for personal use. Thus, the law doesn't require any "business" at all.[2]

Stolen Explosives as Collateral for a Loan

Congress and federal regulators have long faced criticism for being too soft on certain lending practices like payday loans and reverse mortgages. To their credit, though, federal lawmakers have taken a hard line on bomb-backed lending. Pledging or accepting stolen explosives as security for a loan are expressly prohibited by 18 U.S.C. § 842(h).

Hunting and Fishing with Bombs

Recall that Chapter 2 discussed the federal prohibition on using explosives to hunt Canada geese and Chapter 5 noted the ban on fishing with explosives in national parks. Other federal properties, like national forests and wildlife refuges, have similar bans. Plus, where state law prohibits hunting a bird with a bomb (for example, in Kentucky), the Federal Migratory Bird Treaty Act makes it a *federal* crime to bring the dead bird to another state.

Prohibited People

Another key feature of the Safe Explosives Act is its helpful list of people who can't legally be sold or given explosives. Examples include felons, fugitives, drug addicts, people committed to mental institutions, and anyone who has renounced their U.S. citizenship. If you find yourself bringing dynamite to a mental institution and weren't planning on committing a federal crime—stop. 18 U.S.C. § 842(d) is pretty strict about it.

Fig. 8-9.

Welding in Your Dynamite Room

True to its name, the Safe Explosives Act, as implemented by 27 C.F.R. § 555.216, prohibits making repairs inside an explosives storage magazine while explosives are still inside.

The law doesn't distinguish between repairs that are likely to cause an explosion and those that aren't, although welding around dynamite is sure to get the neighbors' attention.

Try to Make it Rain with Lasers Without Telling the Government First

When Daniel Ellsberg leaked the Pentagon Papers in 1971, a lone reference to a government program called "Operation Popeye" sat buried within the volumes of top-secret material. The *Washington Post* and the *New York Times* later uncovered that Operation Popeye was a secret weather modification program conducted by the United States government using "cloud seeding techniques" to cause heavy rainfall over strategic sites in Vietnam.

Although the federal government spent roughly $7 million on weather modification efforts in fiscal year 1966 alone, for many Americans the Operation Popeye revelations were the first confirmation that weather modification was anything more than a science fiction fantasy.[3] The *New York Times* called it "meteorological warfare." And in 1977 the U.S. signed an international treaty pledging never to weaponize weather again.

The same year that Operation Popeye was leaked to the public, Congress enacted 15 U.S.C. § 330a, which provides that "no person may engage, or attempt to engage, in any weather modification activity in the United States" without notifying the secretary of commerce on the appropriate forms. Section 330d makes violations a federal crime, punishable by a fine of up to $10,000 upon conviction.

In other words, conducting your own Operation Popeye here in the United States is a federal crime—unless, of course, you fill out the right paperwork.

CHOOSING A WEATHER MODIFICATION ACTIVITY

Not all attempts to change the weather can result in criminal charges under Section 330a. Would-be weather criminals have to engage in one of the eight weather modification activities for which reporting is required by law. Under 15 C.F.R. § 908.3(a), those activities are:

1. seeding or dispersing of any substance into clouds or fog to alter drop-size distribution, produce ice crystals or coagulation of droplets, alter the development of hail or lightning, or influence in any way the natural development cycle of clouds or their environment;

2. using fires or heat sources to influence convective circulation or to evaporate fog;

3. modifying the solar radiation exchange of the earth or clouds through the release of gases, dusts, liquids, or aerosols into the atmosphere;

4. modifying the characteristics of land or water surfaces by dusting or treating with powders, liquid sprays, dyes, or other materials;

5. releasing electrically charged or radioactive particles, or ions, into the atmosphere;

6. applying shock waves, sonic energy sources, or other explosive or acoustic sources to the atmosphere;

7. using aircraft propeller downwash, jet wash, or other sources of artificial wind generation; or

8. using lasers or other sources of electromagnetic radiation.

Now, if there's one important thing to be learned from this list, it's that the government has reason to believe weather lasers are an actual thing. In fact, a 2010 scientific paper entitled "Laser-Induced Water Condensation in Air" explained that short pulses from a 3.5-terawatt laser really can accelerate condensation in the atmosphere and create tiny clouds, thus opening up the possibility of a fully operational rainmaking cloud laser.[4] For those who lived through the 1980s and are naturally wondering, 3.5 terawatts is 3,500 gigawatts.

Other scientists are skeptical, though. A more recent paper published by researchers at the National Center for Atmospheric Research dismissed the cloud laser, calling it a technique that "could not conceivably be useful to any weather modification application."[5] Nonetheless, the fact that something is implausible has never stopped the federal government from banning it.

COST CONSIDERATIONS

True, a 3,500-gigawatt laser isn't exactly cheap. Neither are the C-130 cargo planes that were used in Operation Popeye. Thus, it might seem that a weather modification conviction is financially out of reach for most. But if history is any lesson, lower-cost options—like explosive kites and balloons—may be just as effective and every bit as prohibited under 15 C.F.R. § 908.3(a)(6).

In fact, long before Operation Popeye, Congress appropriated what was then a huge amount of money for "research" into these very techniques. It was the late 1800s, and Civil War soldiers had just spent years in the mud and rain with constant gunfire and cannon blasts. This led some soldiers to believe that artillery blasts might actually cause rain. Included among them was Daniel Ruggles, a Confederate brigadier general who patented his "Method of Precipitating Rain Falls," which consisted of "a balloon carrying dynamite torpedoes at a high elevation in the atmosphere or within the cloud-realm."[6]

Congress was intrigued as well. In February of 1891, the secretary of agriculture appointed another Civil War general, Robert Dyrenforth, to the esteemed position of "special agent of the Department of Agriculture for making experiments in the production of rainfall." His job was to see if blowing stuff up might cause rain. Sure, Dyrenforth wasn't a scientist, but he also wasn't afraid to send floating explosives into the sky. That's just what Congress was looking for, so they gave him $9,000 and sent him off to go try to make it rain.

After about a year of blowing things up in the desert, Dyrenforth prepared a voluminous report for Congress describing his methods for trying to make it rain.[7] He admitted that he had no idea what he was doing at first, but like any good government contractor he made it up as he went along, spent all of the taxpayer money he'd been given, and got no meaningful results. But that's not to say we can't learn from his work.

THE DYRENFORTH METHOD

Early in Dyrenforth's testing, he detonated several balloons full of hydrogen high over the outskirts of Washington, D.C. He bragged that the explosions were heard across the District. He even received letters from locals begging him to stop. Not long after his experiments over the capital city, however, he packed up and moved his operation to a ranch near Midland, Texas, where he resumed his explosive balloon tests.

Dyrenforth's methods, while innovative for 1891, would certainly violate the current-day prohibition on "applying shock waves, sonic energy sources, or other explosive or acoustic sources to the atmosphere." In addition to his signature ten-foot-diameter balloons full of hydrogen, Dyrenforth employed bomb kites in his explosive repertoire. His design was simple: sticks of dynamite strapped to kites.

By all accounts, Dyrenforth's experiments were a total failure. When the explosive balloons and dynamite kites failed to cause rain, Dyrenforth started setting off explosives on the ground, on top of rocks, and for some reason in prairie dog and badger holes.

Fig. 8-10. Explosive Balloons.

In his final report to Congress, he acknowledged that any rain that did occur may well have happened with or without his explosions.

Importantly, though, today's law doesn't require a weather modification activity to be successful to be a crime. The crime occurs when the offender fails to file the right paperwork before engaging in weather modification. Even failed attempts to induce rain with explosive kites can be a federal crime if they aren't properly documented.

PROHIBITED KITE AND BALLOON ALTITUDE

Before you ready balloons packed with explosives, keep in mind that Dyrenforth's experiments were not only sanctioned by Congress, they were also conducted in 1891. Today, even if one were to obtain permission from the secretary of commerce to try to change the weather with explosive kites and balloons, other federal agencies might have something to say about it.

The Federal Aviation Administration has a whole host of regulations specifically concerning kites and balloons. Title 14, Section 101.13, of the C.F.R., for example, prohibits flying a kite or balloon:

1. less than 500 feet from the base of any cloud;
2. more than 500 feet above the surface of the earth;
3. from an area where the ground visibility is less than three miles; or
4. within five miles of the boundary of any airport.

Abiding by these regulations will foreclose any hope of getting a bomb kite into what General Ruggles called "the cloud-realm." Even boring kites with no explosives strapped to them are banned from getting too close to a cloud. (See Fig. 8-11.)

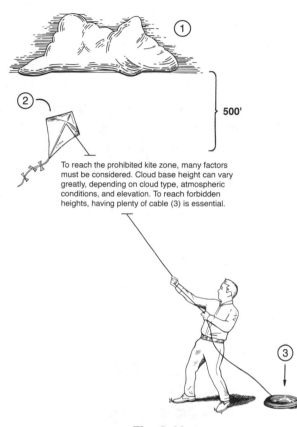

To reach the prohibited kite zone, many factors must be considered. Cloud base height can vary greatly, depending on cloud type, atmospheric conditions, and elevation. To reach forbidden heights, having plenty of cable (3) is essential.

Fig. 8-11.

Sell a Kidney

In the early 1980s, a Virginia doctor named H. Barry Jacobs founded a company called the International Kidney Exchange. His idea was a simple one: his company would broker deals between healthy people who wanted to sell one of their kidneys and those who needed to buy one—all, of course, for a fee.

According to Dr. Jacobs, informed, consenting adults should be free to do as they please with their bodies—and body parts.

The monetary incentive, he thought, would also help increase the desperately needed supply of organs available for transplants.

The whole thing made Congress uneasy. It wasn't necessarily Dr. Jacobs's mail fraud conviction or the fact that he had once had his medical license revoked that worried them. No, Congress knows how to look past that kind of thing. It was their fear that a for-profit organ-buying program might tempt people to sell organs they'd really prefer to keep. Also, Dr. Jacobs probably didn't help his pitch when he proposed flying people in from Third World countries to buy and remove one of their kidneys, then send them back home about a quarter-pound lighter.

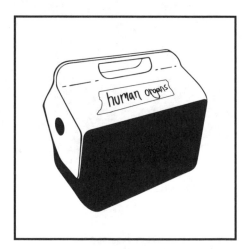

Fig. 8-12. Not Lunch.

When he testified before a congressional subcommittee in 1983, Dr. Jacobs had a chance to address these concerns with federal lawmakers.[8] Among those present was then-representative Al Gore, who wanted to know if people flown in from poor countries in exchange for one of their kidneys "might be willing to give [Jacobs] a cut-rate price just for the chance to see the Statue

Fig. 8-13. Removing an Organ

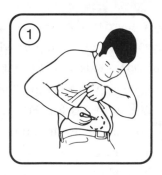

PLAN AHEAD

With a general idea of where the organ is located, the offender first uses a marker to sketch out the cut he'll be making. He may also wish to consult the internet for guidance on exactly where the target organ is located.

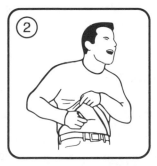

MAKE THE INCISION

Using a sterilized scalpel, a pretty clean steak knife, or a letter opener or something, he makes an incision along the path sketched out in step 1. This step might pinch a little.

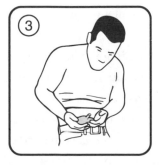

REMOVE THE ORGAN

Once the incision is made, the offender fishes out the organ before he passes out. He'll need to get the organ on ice quickly and, at some point, stitch himself back up. He's now ready to sell his organ.

of Liberty or the Capitol or something." Or, he wondered, if poor donors might pledge their organs as collateral for a car loan or even as payment for medical bills.

Jacobs responded: "I have no idea. You are the lawyer, I am a doctor." In fact, Gore wasn't a lawyer. He also wasn't impressed with Dr. Jacobs's proposal. And so, in 1984, the National Organ Transplant Act was passed into law, making it a federal crime "for any person to knowingly acquire, receive, or otherwise transfer any human organ for valuable consideration for use in human transplantation if the transfer affects interstate commerce."

Because of that, today's criminal kidney seller isn't likely to get help from a licensed surgeon and might be forced to take a more "DIY" approach to organ removal. (See Fig. 8-13.)

Whistle on a CB Radio

47 U.S.C. § 502 makes it a federal crime to violate any rule or regulation issued by the Federal Communications Commission concerning wire or radio communications. That includes using a citizens-band (CB) radio to make certain kinds of prohibited transmissions. You know, egregious stuff—like whistling or making sound effects.

To be a crime, the prohibited transmission must be made knowingly and willfully, and even then the maximum punishment is only a $500 fine for every day the offense occurs. While a low-level CB radio offense won't send you to prison, it could get expensive if you make a habit of it. Still, after sentencing, convicted CB whistlers get to go home to their family (read: parents' basement).

Under 47 C.F.R. § 95.933, doing any one or a combination of the following things by CB radio constitutes a prohibited transmission and can be criminally prosecuted:

- whistling;
- making sound effects;
- talking with people in other countries (except Canada);
- selling something;
- campaigning; and/or
- trying to entertain or amuse people.

Fig. 8-14. Whistling on a CB Radio

(1)

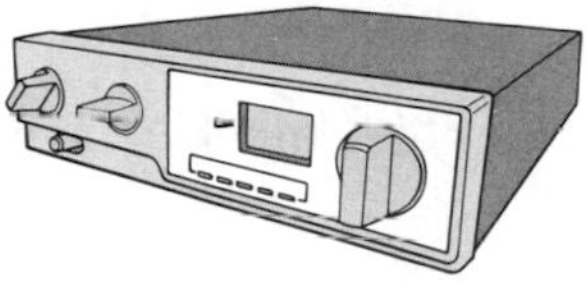

GET A CB RADIO

Any CB radio transmitter, with or without an incorporated antenna or receiver, that is certified by the FCC to transmit on the Citizens Band Radio Service (CBRS) can be used.

(2)

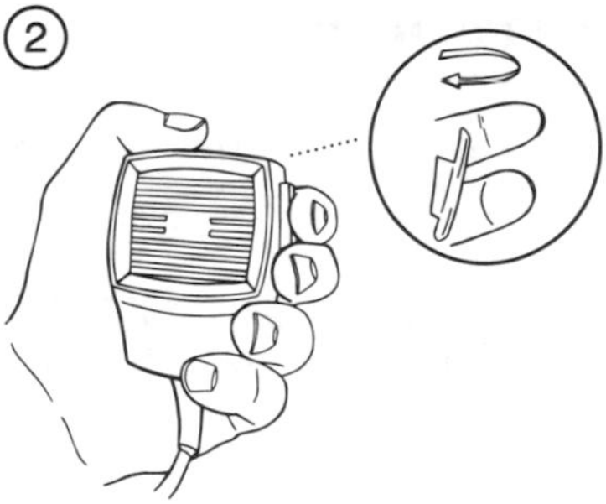

BEGIN TRANSMITTING

Once the CB radio is set up, the offender need only:

1. *Choose a channel.* Ensure that at least one of the six people who still use CB radios hears the transmission.

2. *Press and hold the transmit button.* The radio must be transmitting when the offender unleashes a prohibited transmission.

(3)

GO WILD

This is the part where things can get really crazy. Whistling, performing sound effects, or making any other prohibited transmission are not only great ways to pass the time on the highway, but each is enough for a CB radio conviction.

Until 2017 the regulations also prohibited lying and using pro-
fanity in a CB radio transmission, but the FCC decided those rules
were no longer necessary. When it came to the whistling ban,
however, the feds simply weren't ready to part with it.

The FCC's CB radio regulations also prohibit other things like
long-windedness. Under 47 C.F.R. § 95.957, CB radio operators
must limit their conversations to five minutes. Aside from being
a great reason to have all conversations with your mother by CB
radio, the five-minute limit has one important exception: it's okay
to talk longer if you're assisting a traveler or participating in emergency communications.

Shockingly, however, saying things like "niner" remains completely legal.

Pretend to Be a Member of the 4-H Club

After reading Chapter 1, you may have decided that dressing up
like a mailman isn't your thing. Maybe you don't have the confidence to pull off a set of formfitting postal shorts. But that doesn't
mean you don't like playing pretend. Rest assured, you still have
options.

Consider 18 U.S.C. § 916. That section is one of several "false
personation" statutes found in Title 18, Chapter 43, of the U.S.
Code. It calls for a sentence of up to six months for anyone who
"pretends himself to be a member of, associated with, or an agent
or representative for the 4–H clubs . . ."

Few clubs can claim such elite status. As far as federal law is
concerned, you can pretend to be a Boy Scout, a Freemason, or
even a vegan pretty much all you want. In fact, 4-H is the benefi-
ciary of not one but *two* criminal statutes: 18 U.S.C. § 916 prohibits
the act of pretending to be a 4-H member itself, and 18 U.S.C. § 707

prohibits wearing or displaying the 4-H logo to convince others that you are a member of the club.

Practically speaking, it may be possible to earn a conviction for pretending to be a 4-H member without ever displaying the 4-H emblem. According to its national website, the 4-H club has no official uniform and none is required. Still, few things scream

Fig. 8-15. Playing Pretend

(1) DRESS THE PART

Although the 4-H uniform isn't mandatory for participation in 4-H events, it might be enough to convince other club members that they're dealing with an authentic member.

For liability under 18 U.S.C. § 707, however, a kerchief and soda jerk costume won't be enough. To violate that statute, the offender must display the official 4-H emblem, "consisting of a green four-leaf clover with stem, and the letter H in white or gold on each leaflet."

(2) TRY TO BLEND IN

Like a ridiculously wholesome agricultural biker gang, 4-H members can smell outsiders. Effective interlopers in the society of head, hands, heart, and health must assimilate quickly and undetectably.

Seasoned offenders may even befriend some livestock at the first opportunity in order to blend in.

"I'm a 4-H member" quite like that classic green kerchief and all white ensemble, capped off—of course—with a 4-H hat bearing the official 4-H emblem.

INTENT REQUIRED

Unlike many of the other crimes discussed in this book, intent to defraud is required before 4-H cosplay will land an offender in federal prison. This requires the offender to have a scheme to obtain something of value by pretending to be a 4-H member. It also assumes that there are actually perks out there that only 4-H members can access.

Contrary to what your mom may have told you about 4-H, however, the "friendships" are not a thing of value. To be guilty, fake 4-H members must generally set their sights on money or property.

The good news for countless young Americans out there is that it remains completely legal to pretend you *aren't* a member of 4-H.

Use the Character "Woodsy Owl" or His Slogan "█████ █ █████, █████ ██████"

By the early 1970s, Americans trusted only one cartoon character to make them feel guilty about the environment, and that was Smokey Bear. Despite the fact that Smokey was often depicted as if he'd just been caught in the act of burying a park ranger whose uniform he'd stolen, Smokey had been well-known and -liked in households across the country for nearly thirty years.

In 1971, however, a new woodland character emerged on the national scene, this time to talk about pollution. His name was Woodsy Owl, and according to the United States Department of Agriculture Forest Service, he was "a whimsical fellow" with "his heart set on motivating kids to form healthy, lasting relationships with nature." By statute—yes, *by statute*—Woodsy is an owl who "wears slacks (forest green when colored), a belt (brown when colored), and a Robin Hood style hat (forest green when colored) with a feather (red when colored), and who furthers the slogan, '█████ ██ █████, ████ ████████.' "9

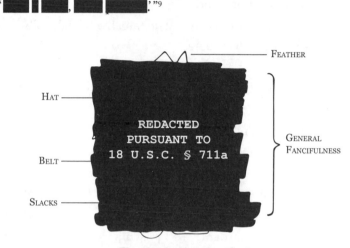

Fig. 8-16. Woodsy Owl.

If you're unfamiliar with Woodsy Owl, that's okay. Today, his work is largely done by Leonardo DiCaprio anyway. In fact, there was even a time when much of Congress itself had never heard of Woodsy—that is, until a bill was introduced to make it a federal crime for anyone to use Woodsy's likeness without permission.

Like any criminal legislation, Congress took the Woodsy Owl Act very seriously. After all, it would be creating a new federal law that could deprive a person of their liberty. So, in September 1972, when the Woodsy Owl bill was up for a vote in the Senate, Senator Hugh Scott (R-PA) made clear that he was prepared to ask the important questions before allowing it to become law. On the Senate floor, Scott asked: "Mr. President, reserving the right to object—and I will not object—what is a 'Woodsy Owl'?"

Senator Mike Mansfield (D-MT), who had obviously spent some time studying the bill carefully, responded: "I think it has something to do with the Forest Service and a campaign to bring about protection of the environment."

After that robust discussion and debate, the bill officially had bipartisan support in the Senate:

MR. SCOTT: If it is for the ecology or for motherhood or for the flag, I have no objection.

MR. MANSFIELD: Or for the Republican Party.

MR. SCOTT: Or for the Republican Party.

But things heated up a bit in the House of Representatives. When the Woodsy Owl bill came to the floor there two years later, Representative Gene Snyder (R-KY) posed an even harder question than Senator Scott before him.[10] He asked:

> *Am I in error that if this bill becomes law and if I say,* "█████ ██, ████ ████" *I can go to jail for 6 months unless I get the Secretary of Agriculture to approve my saying it?*

Snyder was mostly right, but the proposed law required more: use of Woodsy's image or his slogan had to be done "knowingly *and for profit*" (emphasis added) to be a crime. The Speaker of the House was quick to remind Snyder that he could only be imprisoned if someone paid him to use Woodsy's catchphrase. Even then, the Speaker noted, a prison sentence for doing so was possible but "highly unrealistic."

Unsatisfied, Representative Snyder replied:

A great many unrealistic things are running around loose in this country. Angela Davis is loose. The Chicago Seven are loose. Ellsberg is loose after giving away the secrets of the country, and so on. Now we want to send somebody to jail for saying, "███ ██ ████, ████ █ ██████."

Apparently, Congress had some other pressing matters before it that Snyder thought were more deserving of attention than the Woodsy Owl bill—things like the then-impending impeachment of President Richard Nixon. In fact, Snyder thought the Woodsy Owl bill was representative of a much deeper dysfunction on the Hill. He continued:

Mr. Speaker, I suppose it is no wonder that our country is in the turmoil and stress that it is in. Under this legislation to "use" the character "Woodsy Owl" or the associated slogan "███ ██ ████, ████ █ ██████" for profit without the authorization of the Secretary of Agriculture can cause one to be sent to jail for 6 months, fined $250, or both; all this while Angela Davis, the Chicago Seven, and Daniel Ellsberg are free.

While the Judiciary Committee is busy reporting out "all American" legislation like this "Woodsy Owl" bill, the committee lets languish antibusing legislation, the antibusing constitutional amendment, the antiabortion constitutional amendment, and delays on its impeachment proceedings.

Well, Mr. Speaker, I suppose the "All American" vote is "aye" and I will go along but the Congress should shoulder its responsibility and face the important issues that are before our Nation. The country is in distress.

The President blames the Congress.

The Congress blames the President.
They both blame the courts.
The American people can rightfully blame all three.

Despite these concerns, other members of Congress felt that the preceding three decades of success with the Smokey Bear campaign more than adequately justified the new Woodsy Owl law and that the criminal penalties were nothing to worry about. Charles Wiggins (R-CA) dismissed the risk of "indiscriminate use of the criminal penalty" in connection with either Woodsy Owl or Smokey Bear. He noted that the statutes provided for both civil and criminal penalties. In his view, federal prosecutors could be trusted to select the right remedy.

Ultimately, Congress kept prison on the table for Woodsy Owl offenders just as it had in the Smokey Bear Act. The Woodsy Owl bill became law in 1974. Today, 18 U.S.C. § 711a technically still makes using Woodsy's likeness a viable option for becoming a federal criminal, though there has never been a conviction.

DEATH OF A GOVERNMENT CARTOON CHARACTER

If you aren't quite ready to become a federal criminal but still have your heart set on exploiting government cartoon characters for financial gain, don't lose hope. Sure, Woodsy Owl and Smokey Bear are protected by criminal statutes *now*, but government characters have lost their statutory protection in the past.

One government cartoon character who was stripped of his statutory protection in heartbreaking fashion is Johnny Horizon—the ruggedly handsome face of a national anti-litter campaign that began in 1968. Back then, the Bureau of Land Management (BLM) was trying to capture some of the same Smokey

Bear magic the Forest Service had been milking for decades. So Johnny Horizon was born.

Johnny had it all. As the law would later make clear, he was tall and lean, he was "the symbolic outdoorsman," and he represented "the thoughtful visitor to the public lands."

In 1969, however, BLM faced questions after it asked Congress to approve a $100,000 budget to fund the nascent Johnny Horizon program. The Senate Appropriations Committee chairman, Alan Bible (D-NV), admitted to the BLM: "I am familiar with 'Smokey the Bear,' but I don't know about Johnny Horizon." And that was Johnny's problem. Congress wanted to know exactly how this unknown cartoon cowboy, who hadn't yet made a dime for the government, was going to start pulling his weight like the shirtless bear before him.

The BLM's assistant director of administration explained to the committee that Johnny Horizon just needed a statute protecting his likeness the way the Smokey Bear Act of 1952 had done for Smokey. With a similar statute, BLM could start licensing Johnny's likeness for revenue and prosecutors could start throwing people in prison for misusing Johnny's image. In Washington, that's what's known as a classic win-win.

In fact, BLM had big plans to sell things like Johnny Horizon litter bags, hats, shirts, boots, and other Johnny merch. Johnny even released a record with folk singer Burl Ives. The record's jacket claimed that "Johnny Horizon wears no badge or uniform and enforces no law," although that wasn't entirely true. He did have a law. In 1970, Congress passed Public Law 91-419, codified as 18 U.S.C. § 714, which made it a federal crime to knowingly use the character "Johnny Horizon," or his name, in a way that was likely to "cause confusion, or to cause mistake, or to deceive." So maybe he didn't wear a badge, but he could totally get you arrested.

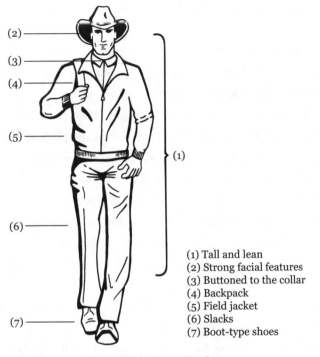

(1) Tall and lean
(2) Strong facial features
(3) Buttoned to the collar
(4) Backpack
(5) Field jacket
(6) Slacks
(7) Boot-type shoes

Fig. 8-17. Johnny Horizon.

The new law described Johnny as "a tall, lean man, with strong facial features, who wears slacks and sport shirt buttoned to the collar (both green, when colored), no tie, a field jacket (red, when colored), boot-type shoes (brown, when colored) and who carries a backpack."

By the mid-seventies things were looking up for Johnny. He had his statute, he had celebrity friends, and he was "fully endorsed" by the Country Music Association. On September 19, 1974, Gerald Ford even issued a presidential proclamation naming the month in honor of Johnny Horizon for his anti-littering work.

As he became more famous, though, Johnny needed more cash. Year after year, BLM came to Congress asking for more and more money to feed the Johnny Horizon machine. The bureau requested $200,000 for the 1972 fiscal year, $220,000 for 1974, and, for 1976, its ask exploded to $302,000. Again Congress wanted answers.

In the House Appropriations Committee hearings, Representative K. Gunn McKay (D-UT) asked the BLM if it had conducted any internal analysis to determine if the Johnny Horizon program had been successful in cleaning up America. A bureau representative responded:

We have not conducted any internal analysis specifically devoted toward the effectiveness of the program. However, it was Secretary Morton's feeling that the program has been very effective.

Outside the beltway, that's roughly translated as "No."

Things got even worse for the 1977 fiscal year. Johnny told Congress he needed $373,000. He wanted a shiny new logo and he had a new slogan: "Let's Make America a Better Place to Be." Sure, the new slogan was catchy. Heck, it was borderline presidential. But during the Senate hearings in February of 1976, lawmakers wanted to know if there was any proof the program was even worthwhile. This time the bureau told Congress they were looking into it.

Then came the really bad news. Effective September 30, 1976, Johnny was fired. BLM had scrapped the Johnny Horizon program. A few years later Congress unceremoniously repealed Johnny's statute. In a single line, Public Law 97-258 revised him out of the U.S. Code as follows: "Strike out section 714." There was no reference to "Johnny" or "Mr. Horizon." There was no "Goodbye and thank you for your service." Congress was done with the flattery of his height and strong features. He was just "section 714" now, and his place in the U.S. Code was gone.

All at once, Horizon was out of work and an act of Congress had deemed him less worthy of protection than an owl dressed like Robin Hood or the very bear whose shadow Johnny had lived in his whole life. Of course, the "official" explanation is that Johnny's program had "fulfilled its purpose." Yet even the BLM itself has noted the curious timing of Johnny Horizon's demise, suggesting that Ruth Bader Ginsburg may actually be the one responsible.[11]

Yes, *that* Ruth Bader Ginsburg.

In April 1977, Ginsburg coauthored a report for the U.S. Commission on Civil Rights entitled "Sex Bias in the U.S. Code."[12] In it, Ginsburg went through the federal statutes section by section to identify examples of bias against women. For example, Ginsburg took issue with 18 U.S.C. § 3056, which extended Secret Service protection to the "wife" of a former president, and she recommended that the law be changed to protect a former president's "spouse" in anticipation of a female president. Ginsburg won that battle, and the statute was later revised to say "spouse."

Ginsburg also proposed a number of other changes in the code, such as replacing instances of the word "man" with "human," "man-made" with "artificial," and even "manpower" with "workforce."

But the future Supreme Court justice also took particular aim at Johnny's statute, section 714. According to the report:

A further unwarranted male reference appears in 18 U.S.C. § 714, which regulates use of the "Johnny Horizon" anti-litter symbol. According to the congressional reports, this tall, lean figure with sports clothes, hiking boots, and a field jacket is "a representative of a rugged outdoorsman who loves our for-

ests, deserts, mountains, lakes, streams and terrain." This sex stereotype of the outdoorsperson and protector of the environment should be supplemented with a female figure promoting the same values. The two figures should be depicted as persons of equal strength of character, displaying equal familiarity and concern with the terrain of our country.

True, Johnny technically got the axe from BLM in the fall of 1976, but the real death blow to his legacy wasn't dealt until Congress wrote him out of existence in 1982, just a few short years after Ginsburg's report.

This all raises questions that may never be answered. Questions like: Was Johnny really the victim of his own overly expensive rock-star lifestyle? Was he fired because of bureaucratic infighting at the BLM? Or was Johnny Horizon actually a casualty of Ruth Bader Ginsburg? And is it fair to end a book about silly-sounding federal crimes by asking questions that sort of imply a Supreme Court justice may have killed a cartoon character?

America may never know.

Acknowledgments

This book isn't the product of my work alone; it comes from the countless investments that others generously have made in me.

I am deeply grateful to those who follow the @CrimeADay Twitter account and interact with it daily. This includes the artists, dogged journalists, formerly incarcerated people, judges, lawyers, insufferable D.C. policy nerds, and even some of the same lawmakers and federal regulators I like to make fun of as often as possible. You've helped make the CrimeADay project what it is. I can't express how lucky I feel to be part of an important conversation with people I respect and admire, and others who anonymously say such incredibly vile things to me that I'm not even mad. On a more serious note: it's been an honor to be a touch of comic relief amidst all those who are fighting for a more equitable justice system.

My editor, Matthew Benjamin, and all the great people at Atria, brought their unrivaled vision and expertise to this project. My literary agent, Leah Spiro, believed in this project from the first time she saw it (though she has excellent taste otherwise), and she expertly guided me through the process of bringing this book to print.

Two lawyers who made me the lawyer I am today, Jim Bergenn and Ross Garber, are simultaneously excellent humans and attorneys—a feat that completely defies science.

And of course, I could have done none of this without my friends and family. My parents contributed literally 100 percent of my DNA. My wife, Sarah, somehow never questioned the value of an illustrated book of silly-sounding crimes. My son, Luke, helped by routinely reminding me that there are more important things to focus on than being a lawyer, or writing a book, or certainly tweeting silly crimes every day. Finally, as a lawyer, I'd be remiss if I didn't expressly reserve the right to have other children in the future to whom my gratitude shall, without limitation, apply retroactively.

Notes

INTRODUCTION

1 Overview of Federal Criminal Cases, Fiscal Year 2017, United States Sentencing Commission, June 2018, https://www.ussc.gov/sites /default/files/pdf/research-and-publications/research-publications /2018/FY17_Overview_Federal_Criminal_Cases.pdf.

BY MAIL

1 Danny Lewis, "A Brief History of Children Sent Through the Mail," Smithsonian.com, June 14, 2016, https://www.smithsonianmag.com /smart-news/brief-history-children-sent-through-mail-180959372/ (citing "Parcel Post Won't Accept Children," *Los Angeles Times*, June 14, 1920).

2 *United States v. Wilson*, 32 U.S. 150 (1833).

3 *United States v. Lloyd*, No. CRIM.A. 95-0403-01, 1995 WL 672516, at *3 (E.D. Pa. Nov. 9, 1995).

4 H.R. 10773, To Amend Section 1730 of Title 18, United States Code: Hearings before Subcommittee No. 2 of the Judiciary Committee, House of Representatives, August 9, 1967 (Testimony of Adam G. Wenchel).

5 United States Postal Service Office of the Inspector General, Delivery Vehicle Fleet Replacement, Report No. DR-MA-14-005-DR, June 10, 2014, https://www.uspsoig.gov/sites/default/files/dr-ma-14 -005-dr.pdf.

6 Indictment, *United States v. Douglas Hughes*, 15-cr-00063 (D.D.C. 2015).

7 *United States v. Powell*, 423 U.S. 87 (1975).

8 Hearing Before the Committee on the Judiciary, Senate, S. Hrg. 99-672 (October 16, 1985).

9 Drug paraphernalia and youth: Hearing Before the Subcommittee on Criminal Justice of the Committee on the Judiciary, United States Senate, 96th Congress, second session, November 16, 1979.

10 Hearing Before a Subcommittee of the Committee on Interstate and Foreign Commerce, House of Representatives, 77th Congress, second session, H.R. 5674, February 3 and 4, 1942.

11 *United States v. Johnson*, 149 F.2d 53 (7th Cir. 1945).

WITH ANIMALS

1 16 U.S.C. § 1331.

2 *United States v. FMC Corp.*, 572 F.2d 902, 905 (2d Cir. 1978).

3 50 C.F.R. § 21.29(f)(9)(i).

4 *United States v. Drake*, 655 F.2d 1025, 1028 (10th Cir. 1981).

5 Marine Mammal Protection Act of 1971, House Report No. 92-707, December 4, 1971.

6 H.R. Rep. Conf. No. 92-1488, 92d Cong. 2d Sess. 24 (1972).

7 "Can a Canine Detect Polar Bear Pregnancy?" CincinnatiZoo.org, November 4, 2013, http://cincinnatizoo.org/blog/2013/11/04/can-a-canine-detect-polar-bear-pregnancy/.

WITH MONEY

1 Eighteen pence. To counterfeit is death. Burlington in New Jersey: Printed by Isaac Collins. Photograph. Retrieved from the Library of Congress, www.loc.gov/item/2002723321/.

2 "President Obama Grants Nine Pardons," https://obamawhitehouse.archives.gov/the-press-office/2010/12/03/president-obama-grants-nine-pardons; "Obama pardons ex-Marine convicted of cutting pennies in 1963," *Los Angeles Times*, http://articles.latimes.com/2010/dec/05/nation/la-na-coin-pardon-20101205.

3 *United States v. Sheiner*, 273 F. Supp. 977, 980 (S.D.N.Y. 1967), aff'd, 410 F.2d 337 (2d Cir. 1969).

4 "If She's Right, Bill's a Criminal," PolitiFact, December 19, 2007, http://www.politifact.com/truth-o-meter/statements/2007/dec/19/hillary-clinton/if-shes-right-bills-a-criminal.

5 Fitness Guidelines for Federal Reserve Notes, Federal Reserve Services, December 8, 2017, https://www.frbservices.org/assets/financial-services/cash/federal-reserve-fitness-guidelines.pdf.

6 *United States v. Brown*, 938 F.2d 1482, 1484 (1st Cir. 1991).

7 *United States v. Van Auken*, 96 U.S. 366 (1877).

8 *United States v. von NotHaus*, No. 5:09CR27-RLV, 2014 WL 5817559, at *2 (W.D.N.C. Nov. 10, 2014).

WITH FOOD

1 21 C.F.R. § 152.126(a)(3).

2 21 C.F.R. § 150.140(b)(2).

3 9 C.F.R. § 319.309.

4 9 C.F.R. § 317.8(b)(5)(ii).

5 9 C.F.R. § 590.560(h).

6 7 C.F.R. § 58.649.

7 Warning Letter, CMS# 532236, Food and Drug Administration, September 22, 2017, https://www.fda.gov/ICECI/EnforcementActions/WarningLetters/2017/ucm577393.htm.

8 Deena Shanker, "The FDA Has Decided That Vegan Just Mayo Is Actually Mayo After All," Quartz, December 17, 2015, https://qz.com/576679/the-fda-decides-that-vegan-just-mayo-is-actually-mayo-after-all/.

9 FDA at a Glance, Food and Drug Administration, August 2018, https://www.fda.gov/downloads/AboutFDA/Transparency/Basics/UCM617928.pdf.

10 *Investigations Operations Manual*, Food and Drug Administration, 2017, https://www.fda.gov/downloads/ICECI/Inspections/IOM/ucm127390.pdf.

11 *United States v. Eaton*, 144 U.S. 677 (1892).

12 *In re Kollock*, 165 U.S. 526 (1897).

13 *Collins v. State of New Hampshire*, 171 U.S. 30 (1898).

14 "Square Oleo Pats Draws Law's Arm," *Hartford Courant*, April 9, 1952; see also "The Great Butter Battle. Regulation of the Manufacture and Sale of Oleomargarine," Connecticut State Library, July 15, 2014, https://ctstatelibrary.org/the-great-butter-battle-regulation -of-the-manufacture-and-sale-of-oleomargarine/.

15 *Defect Levels Handbook*, Food and Drug Administration, https://www .fda.gov/Food/GuidanceRegulation/GuidanceDocumentsRegulato ryInformation/SanitationTransportation/ucm056174.htm.

16 Per capita consumption of selected cheese varieties (Annual), United States Department of Agriculture Economic Research Service, 2017, https://www.ers.usda.gov/data-products/dairy-data/.

17 United States Standards for Grades of Swiss Cheese, Emmentaler Cheese, United States Department of Agriculture. 2001. https:// www.ams.usda.gov/sites/default/files/media/Swiss_Cheese%2C_Emmentaler_Cheese_Standard%5B1%5D.pdf.

18 Upton Sinclair, *The Jungle* (New York: Doubleday, Page & Co., 1906).

19 9 C.F.R. § 424.23.

20 9 C.F.R. § 381.171.

21 Font-i-Furnols, Maria, "Consumer studies on sensory acceptability of boar taint: A review," *Meat Science*, 2012, (citing earlier studies).

22 International Pasta Organization, 2013 Survey on World Pasta Industry, 2013, http://www.internationalpasta.org/resources/World %20Pasta%20Industry%20Survey/IPOstatreport2014low.pdf.

WITH ALCOHOL

1 Homer Simpson, "Homer vs. the Eighteenth Amendment," *The Simpsons*, Season 8, Episode 18 (1997).

2 Internal-revenue Manual, Compiled by Direction of the Commissioner of Internal Revenue from the Laws and Regulations Now in Force, for the Information and Guidance of Internal-Revenue Agents and Officers, United States, Office of Internal Revenue, August 1, 1879.

3 *United States v. Carter*, 516 F.2d 431 (5th Cir. 1975).

4 "Smoke Screen Used to Aid Bootlegger's Flight," *Popular Mechanics* 44 (1925), 740.

5 Hearings Before the House Committee on the District of Columbia, 68th Congress (1924).

6 *Boston Globe*, AP, May 2, 1929.

7 S.C. Code Ann. § 56-5-5030.

8 Vt. Stat. tit. 23, § 1093; N.C. Gen. Stat. § 20-136; Va. Code § 46.2-1086; Va. Code § 46.2-109.

9 "Interstate Transportation Discourages Pursuit," *FBI Law Enforcement Bulletin* 29, no. 2 (December 1960).

10 *Rubin v. Coors Brewing Co.*, 514 U.S. 476 (1995).

11 *United States v. Best*, No. 5:11-CR-00414 HRL, 2012 WL 3027544, at *1 (N.D. Cal. July 24, 2012).

ON FEDERAL PROPERTY

1 Based on data made available by the U.S. Geologic Survey; see also "Managing Natural Resources," Government Accountability Office, https://www.gao.gov/key_issues/managing_natural_resources/issue_summary.

2 Brian C. Kalt, "The Perfect Crime" (2005), MSU Legal Studies Research Paper No. 02-14, https://ssrn.com/abstract=691642.

3 *Federal Register* 48, no. 127 (1983), 30252.

4 Romana Lefevre, *Rude Hand Gestures of the World*, (San Francisco: Chronicle Books, 2011).

5 Desmond Morris, *The Naked Man*, (New York: Thomas Dunne Books, 2009).

6 *United States v. Poocha*, 259 F.3d 1077 (9th Cir. 2001); *United States v. Lanen*, 716 F. Supp. 208, 209 (D. Md. 1989); *United States v. Chung Lee*, No. CRIM. A. 91-226, 1991 WL 193422, at *1 (E.D. Pa. Sept. 20, 1991).

7 *United States v. Lanning*, No. 1:10CR47, 2012 WL 1986780, at *1 (W.D.N.C. June 4, 2012); *United States v. Lanning*, 723 F.3d 476, 484 (4th Cir. 2013).

8 "Handkerchief Pool," National Park Service, https://www.nps.gov/features/yell/ofvec/exhibits/treasures/thermals/hotspring/handkerchief.htm.

9 George D. Marler, *Inventory of Thermal Features of the Firehole River Geyser Basins and Other Selected Areas of Yellowstone National Park*, Geyser Observation and Study Association, 2004 (PDF); Scott T.

Bryan, *The Geysers of Yellowstone*, (Louisville, CO: University Press of Colorado, 2018, 5th ed.).

10 "Yellowstone Geyser Spews Trash from the 1930s," CBS News, October 6, 2018, https://www.cbsnews.com/news/yellowstone-geyser-erupts-spews-decades-old-trash-2018-10-06/.

11 *United States v. Cortez*, 449 U.S. 411, 417 (1981).

12 *United States v. Arnold*, No. 6:10-CR-0009-MJS, 2010 WL 4630262, at *5 (E.D. Cal. Nov. 8, 2010).

13 *Hesterberg v. United States*, 71 F. Supp. 3d 1018, 1025 (N.D. Cal. 2014).

14 *United States v. Worthington*, 531 F. Supp. 2d 672, 673 (E.D.N.C. 2008).

15 36 C.F.R. § 2.10(b)(3).

16 Sydney Gottlieb, *Alfred Hitchcock: Interviews*, (Jackson: University Press of Mississippi, 2011).

17 Todd David Epp, "Alfred Hitchcock's 'Expedient Exaggerations' and the Filming of *North by Northwest* at Mount Rushmore," originally published in *South Dakota History* 23, no. 3 (Fall 1993), 181–96, reprinted as "*North by Northwest*," *American Experience*, https://www.pbs.org/wgbh/americanexperience/features/rushmore-north-northwest/.

18 Unsourced claim. Cats are the worst, though.

19 Truman C. Everts, "Thirty-Seven Days of Peril," *Scribner's Monthly Magazine*, vol. III (November 1871).

20 "About the Region," National Park Service, https://www.nps.gov/locations/alaska/about-the-region.htm.

21 36 C.F.R. § 13.1.

22 *United States v. Henderson*, 243 F.3d 1168, 1173 (9th Cir. 2001).

23 *Senate Congressional Record*, April 19, 1876, at 2580-81.

24 United States v. Weissberger, 951 F.2d 392, 394 (D.C. Cir. 1991).

25 Laurel Wamsley, "DOJ Drops Case Against Woman Who Laughed During Sessions Hearing," NPR, November 8, 2017, https://www.npr.org/sections/thetwo-way/2017/11/08/562823691/charges-dropped-against-woman-who-laughed-during-sessions-hearing.

26 Jacki Petito, "The Big Cheese: Presidential Gifts of Mammoth Proportions," Smithsonian, January 7, 2017, http://npg.si.edu/blog/big-cheese-presidential-gifts-mammoth-proportions.

ON THE HIGH SEAS

1 *United States v. Howard*, 26 F. Cas. 390 (C.C.D. Pa. 1818).

2 Hearing on the Bill (H.R. 383) to Prohibit Shanghaiing and Peonage in the United States, February 2, 1906.

3 *United States v. Domingos*, 193 F. 263, 264 (C.C.N.D. Fla. 1911).

4 Herbert Asbury, *The Barbary Coast: An Informal History of the San Francisco Underworld*, (New York: A. A. Knopf, 1933).

5 *United States v. Anderson*, 24 F. Cas. 812, 812 (C.C.S.D.N.Y. 1872).

6 *United States v. Sullivan*, 43 F. 602, 602 (C.C.D. Or. 1890).

7 *United States v. Greenpeace, Inc.*, 314 F. Supp. 2d 1252, 1255 (S.D. Fla. 2004).

8 *Jordan v. Williams*, 13 F. Cas. 1115, 1117 (C.C.D. Mass. 1851).

9 *Magee v. Oregon Ry. & Nav. Co.*, 46 F. 734, 736 (C.C.D. Wash. 1891); *Turbett v. Dunlevy*, Case No. 14,241 (F.D. Pa. 1848).

10 KoriRumoreandJonathonBerlin,"SerialStowaway:20AirportIncidents Involving Marilyn Hartman," *Chicago Tribune*, March 30, 2018, http://www.chicagotribune.com/news/data/ct-serial-stowaway-timeline-of-incidents-htmlstory.html.

IN OTHER WAYS

1 *United States v. 2000 Plastic Tubular Cases, More or Less, Toothbrushes*, 352 F.2d 344 (3d Cir. 1965).

2 *United States v. Belmont*, No. 8:14CR375, 2015 WL 13101997, at *3 (D. Neb. June 15, 2015), *aff'd*, 831 F.3d 1098 (8th Cir. 2016); *United States v. Graham*, 305 F.3d 1094 (10th Cir. 2002).

3 "Weather Modification and Control, a Report Prepared at the Request of Hon. Warren G. Magnuson, Chairman for the Use of the Committee on Commerce," 89th Congress, 2nd session, Report No. 1139. April 27, 1966.

4 Philipp Rohwetter, Jérôme Kasparian, Kamil Stelmaszczyk, Zuoqiang Hao, Stefano Henin et al., "Laser-Induced Water Condensation in Air," *Nature Photonics* (2010).

5 Duncan Axisa and Tom P. DeFelice, "Modern and Prospective Tech-

nologies for Weather Modification Activities: A Look at Integrating Unmanned Aircraft Systems," *Atmospheric Research* (2016).

6 United States patent no. 230067A.

7 Letter from the secretary of agriculture in response to Senate resolution of February 23, 1892, transmitting the report of the agent of the Department of Agriculture for making experiments in the production of rainfall. Ex. Doc. No. 45. 52nd Congress, first session; Timothy Egan, *The Worst Hard Time*, (New York: Houghton Mifflin, 2006).

8 Hearings before the Subcommittee on Health and the Environment of the Committee on Energy and Commerce, House of Representatives, 98th Congress, first session, on H.R. bill 4080. Serial No. 98-70, 1984.

9 16 U.S.C. § 580p.

10 120 Cong. Rec. 9308 (1974).

11 Michael Campbell, *Meet Johnny Horizon,* Northwest Passage, Summer 2009, https://www.blm.gov/sites/blm.gov/files/documents/files/Northwest_Passage_Issue5.pdf.

12 United States Commission on Civil Rights, *Sex Bias in the U.S. Code: A Report of the U.S. Commission on Civil Rights,* U.S. Govt. Printing Office (1977).

About the Author

By day, Mike Chase is a criminal defense lawyer. By night, he's the legal humorist behind the @CrimeADay Twitter feed, where he offers a daily dose of his extensive research into the curious, intriguing, and often amusing history of America's expansive criminal laws. Mike's work has made him the go-to commentator on the countless weird and esoteric federal criminal laws buried deep in the books.